FREUD
Conflict and Culture

FREUD
Conflict and Culture

Edited by Michael S. Roth

IN ASSOCIATION WITH
THE LIBRARY OF CONGRESS

ALFRED A. KNOPF　*New York*　1998

Owing to limitations of space, all acknowledgments for
permission to reprint previously published material may be
found on page 273.

Library of Congress Cataloging-in-Publication Data
Freud : conflict and culture / edited by Michael S. Roth. — 1st ed.
p.   cm.
"In association with the Library of Congress."
Includes bibliographical references and index.
ISBN 0-679-45116-1 (alk. paper)
1. Psychoanalysis.   2. Psychoanalysis—History.   3. Freud, Sigmund, 1856–1939.
I. Roth, Michael S., [date].   II. Library of Congress.
BF173.F896   1998
150.19'52'092—dc21   98-12373
CIP

Photographic reproduction is by permission of A. W. Freud et al.,
by arrangement with Mark Paterson & Associates.

This publication and the exhibition *Sigmund Freud: Conflict and Culture*
were made possible by the generous support of:

Discovery Communications, Inc.
Department of Cultural Affairs,
City of Vienna
Austrian Cultural Institute, New York
Alfred A. Knopf, Inc.
James Madison Council of the Library
of Congress
Mary S. Sigourney Award Trust,
New York
Dr. and Mrs. Kenneth Altshuler
Dana Foundation, New York

Ministry of Science and Transport,
Austria
Lotte Köhler Foundation
American Psychoanalytic
Foundation
Austrian Airlines
Österreichische Lotterien
Hoffmann–La Roche Inc.
New-Land Foundation, New York
O. S. Wyatt Jr., Houston
Peter Sobolak, Vienna

and
the generosity of private contributors

For Jeremy, Max, and Sophie

CONTENTS

PART III *Absorption and Diffusion*

PART IV *Contested Legacies*

FOREWORD

James H. Billington, The Librarian of Congress

CONTROVERSY STILL ABOUNDS in medical, literary, and academic circles over Sigmund Freud and his work. Yet few would disagree that his chief legacy—the psychoanalytic movement—has had an enormous impact on Western culture in the twentieth century. In the more than fifty years since receiving the first Freud materials, the Library of Congress has assembled an unparalleled collection of Freud materials, a selection of which is featured in the exhibition *Sigmund Freud: Conflict and Culture*.

The Library's resources, which now total more than 112 million items in diverse formats, include sizable holdings useful in researching the history of the psychoanalytic movement. The Sigmund Freud Collection began in 1942 when the noted analyst David Baumgardt made a small gift of Freud materials. The collection expanded considerably after the Library reached an agreement in 1951 with the Sigmund Freud Archives, Inc., in New York City. The Archives—then headed by Dr. Kurt R. Eissler, now headed by Dr. Harold P. Blum—began to transmit letters and other manuscripts, transcripts, photocopies, oral history, interviews, photographs, and printed materials to the Library. By late 1984, they totaled more than 30,000 items.

The other major donor to the Freud Collection was the psychoanalyst's daughter, the late Anna Freud, who in 1970 decided to convey her father's and her own personal papers, mostly correspondence and family materials, to the Library. Freud had wished his personal papers to be destroyed, but neither his widow, Martha, nor his daughter felt she could comply with his request. At Anna's death in 1982, a wealth of important material began coming to the Library. She once told our curators: "I gave [the papers] to the Library of Congress because yours is the greatest library in the world and I knew they would be safe there."

The Library's curators, on their own initiative, also began to collect Freud materials, as well as other related materials that expanded our psychoanalytic archive, gradually organizing this growing array of materials by format. Today, the Rare Book and Special Collections Division holds early, very scarce publications by Freud as well as books from his personal library. The many photographs of Freud acquired over the years are in the Prints and Photographs Division. Some 350 original tapes of interviews by Dr. Eissler with people who knew Freud are in the Motion Picture, Broadcasting, and Recorded Sound Division, along with "home movies" of Freud, his colleagues, and his family made during the 1920s and 1930s.

The majority of the Freud materials—some 50,000 items—rests in the Manuscript Division. It includes Freud's correspondence, notably a long series of early letters to his boyhood friend Eduard Silberstein, beginning in 1871; some 1,500 letters exchanged with his fiancée Martha Bernays; his now famous letters to Wilhelm Fliess during the development of psychoanalysis; some of his diaries; and much else. During the 1980s, the Library obtained many more materials on the psychoanalytic movement, including the papers of such notable figures as Alfred Adler and Princess Marie Bonaparte. Some of the items came with restrictions on access, but by the year 2000 most of the Sigmund Freud Collection will be open to researchers.

This volume is an important supplement to the exhibition *Sigmund Freud: Conflict and Culture*. Here, Michael S. Roth, the exhibition's curator, and eighteen other essayists explore Freud's life, his work, and his legacy, as well as the climate of opinion surrounding them. The essays in this collection thus function as a type of extended commentary or narrative, elaborating on the content of the exhibit. I hope that this volume will not only add to the current scholarship (and illuminate the intense debate) surrounding Freud's work but also serve to motivate a new generation of researchers to mine the Library's Freud Collection for the continuing study of the impact psychoanalysis and Freud's thinking more generally have had on our society.

FREUD

Conflict and Culture

INTRODUCTION

Michael S. Roth

THE OCCASION for this volume is the exhibition *Sigmund Freud: Conflict and Culture*, mounted by the Library of Congress. Examining the decisive impact of Freud's work on twentieth-century culture, the exhibition is composed of three main parts: "Formative Years," "The Individual," and "From the Individual to Society." It begins with Freud's formative years in late-nineteenth-century Vienna, emphasizing points of contact between his intellectual development and important political and cultural events. In Section II, we are introduced to the fundamental concepts in psychoanalytic theory, and are shown how Freud used those concepts in the treatment of some of his most important patients. The search for concealed desires, in conflict with one another and with reality, is emphasized as a key facet of psychoanalytic inquiry that has become part of our common culture. The "talking cure" is a model for the modern investment in coming to terms with one's past. Section III shows how Freud applied his ideas concerning individual human psychology to the task of understanding the dynamic, conflicted functioning of society and culture. His theories of the violent origin of civilization and his understanding of the function of religion, art, and science in contemporary society are explored. The third section also shows us the diffusion of Freud's ideas through the formation of professional psychoanalysis, and their application in a variety of cultural arenas from the arts to the sciences. The exhibition articulates Freud's contested legacies, providing viewers with a sense of how issues he explored remain vital to us, even as his findings and methodology have come under intense critical pressure. Our notions of identity, memory, sexuality, and, most generally, of meaning have been shaped in relation to—and often in opposition to—Freud's work. Neither the exhibit nor this volume tries to construct a case for this influence being positive or negative; rather, they attempt to explicate his approach to finding meaning by exploring concealed and conflicting desires. Throughout the exhibit we are offered a sense of the pervasiveness of psychoanalytic ideas, even as we come to see that these ideas have been subject to deep criticism from Freud's time until our own.

At the end of his life Freud faced some of the most intense crises of the twentieth century, crises that were sweeping Europe toward the violence of World War II. From the psychoanalytic perspective, they could be understood as explosions of repressed impulses, of conflicts long concealed by the constructions of civilization. More than fifty years later, sexuality and aggression have remained at the center of our concerns on both the individual and the societal levels. Freud did not offer prescriptions for coping with their awesome power, but by turning our attention to the role they play in our private and public lives he provided us with a language for addressing some of our most compelling concerns.

This introduction outlines the themes of the three principal sections of the exhibition. Many of these themes are taken up by the essays of this volume, which are grouped into four parts. The biographical and historical essays of Part I pursue connections between Freud's life, work, and historical context. The essays in Part II take on some of the thorniest issues in his thinking, those having to do with who we are as political, moral, and intellectual beings. Part III looks at some of the paths down which psychoanalytic ideas have traveled, and some of the interesting collaborators and critics who have joined forces with, or marshaled their energies against, ideas that had become doctrines and institutions. Part IV focuses on some of the key controversies surrounding psychoanalysis as theory and as therapy. Although Freud's ideas are pervasive in contemporary culture, there is no consensus about any of his important concepts or their application.

Section I: Formative Years

The exhibition begins with the introduction of Freud's family history, his early years in the small Moravian town of Freiberg (now part of the Czech Republic), and his formative period in Vienna. Rather than presenting a detailed chronology of Freud's early years, this section instead emphasizes some of the crucial turns in his personal and professional life, establishing a sense of Freud as a young man in Vienna trying to build a family and a professional reputation. We see how his scientific training in neurology brought him to study with Jean Martin Charcot of the Salpêtrière in Paris, where he began his decisive work with hysteria and hypnotism. With these subjects Freud moved further away from his neurological training (discussed in Oliver Sacks's essay) toward an interpretive psychology, trying to decipher the meanings of hysterical symptoms and other human actions (such as dreams and slips of the tongue) that seemed beyond conscious, rational control. Despite this lack of control, Freud was committed to the idea that these occurrences were meaningful, and he concentrated his efforts on developing techniques for determining what they meant. The exhibition also inquires to what extent Freud remained indebted to his particular scientific training in a rapidly changing field, and how closely his methods of interpretation were tied to his immediate context in fin-de-siècle Vienna.

Section II: The Individual

A. Therapy

Following the journey from hypnosis to psychoanalysis, we see how Freud haltingly stepped from commanding his patients (with hypnotic suggestion) to stop having symptoms to creating conditions in which they could grasp the significance of these symptoms. Through the case of Bertha Pappenheim (alias Anna O., the famous patient of Freud's colleague Josef Breuer) one can see the movement from hypnosis to *free association*, the latter becoming a crucial tenet of the psychoanalytic approach to clinical treatment. Anna O. named her own treatment the "talking cure" because it was by describing her traumatic experiences and feelings to the physician that she seemed to experience some relief.

Although Anna O.'s treatment was not nearly as successful as Breuer and Freud claimed it to have been, the real Bertha Pappenheim did eventually overcome her disabling psychological difficulties to become one of the founders of social work and of the Jewish women's movement in Germany. If the case of Anna O. marked the transition from hypnosis to the talking cure, we are still left with the question of what role suggestion continued to play in either the preservation or the alleviation of symptoms. In other words, did the psychoanalyst still make use of the suggestive powers of the hypnotist even as he moved away from overt commands to the patient? If suggestion is used in subtle forms to steer the patient toward imitating a "healthy" personality, is this the sign of a cure or of the depth of the illness? The problem of suggestion is still relevant to various forms of psychotherapy today, insofar as they remain committed to the notion that the patient is responsible for changes in his or her personality. In this collection, John Forrester, Harold P. Blum, Hannah S. Decker, and Adolf Grünbaum are all concerned with the issue of suggestion, although their diverse ways of dealing with it may be taken as a sign of the complexity of a problem in clinical work that also cuts to the heart of our values about what it means to be a free, responsible individual.

After this background to the development of Freud's clinical practice, the exhibition presents selections from two of Freud's most developed case studies: "the Rat Man" and "the Wolf Man." The former was the story of a young lawyer, Ernst Lanzer, plagued by powerful obsessions concerning rats, torture, and punishment. His obsessions were traced to his deep ambivalences about sexuality and about his father. Obsessional acts and thoughts expressed this ambivalence even as they obscured it. Sergei Pankejeff, who actually became famous during his lifetime as "the Wolf Man," suffered from debilitating compulsions and fears, which Freud understood as resulting from his sexual development having gone awry at a very early age. The techniques of *interpretation* are emphasized in this section of the exhibit to show how Freud tried to find meaning in the bizarre symptoms and associations of his analysands. Lanzer died in World War I, and Pankejeff's psychological problems persisted throughout his life. The Wolf Man remained an object of fascination for analysts interested in Freud's techniques; interpretations varied, but none, it seemed, led to a cure. We see in this section how Freud worked his clinical notes into the published version of the case, trying to use the therapeutic work to substantiate the development of his theories. How did Freud and his patients come to believe that his interpretations were on the mark, and how can we judge them in retrospect?

The last patients included in the "Therapy" section are Dora (Ida Bauer) and H.D. (Hilda Doolittle). These cases effectively bookend Freud's psychoanalytic career, with Dora at the beginning of the century and H.D. at the end of Freud's life. The cases are good illustrations of the ideas of *transference* and *countertransference*, ideas that are explored in Decker's essay. Freud meant to interpret Dora's "hysterical" symptoms objectively, but instead ended up insisting that they must have the significance that his theory of the sexual roots of hysteria required. The result was, as he admitted, a botched case in which the doctor tried to convince a young woman that she really did desire the attentions of an older man who was trying to seduce her. As feminist scholars have emphasized, Freud saw conflict in Dora's psyche but failed to recognize the psychic costs of conflict between men and women in society. Dora refused Freud's attempt to make sense of her experience and feelings and abruptly left the analysis.

Near the end of his life, Freud treated the poet Hilda Doolittle, who shared with him a passion for antiquities and for investigating the depths of the personality. If Dora's case ended acrimoniously, the H.D. sessions evinced powerful positive feelings between analyst and patient, as the latter made clear in her book *A Tribute to Freud*. Both cases illustrate how important the emotional investments of analyst and analysand are for their interactions. These investments can derail treatment or allow it to overcome enormous difficulties. But here the exhibition leaves the visitor with an open problem: how to know whether any interpretation in therapy is accurate, given the fact that it might be accepted or rejected only on the basis of the emotional investments of the doctor and patient. This is the problem of suggestion that was already apparent in hypnotic therapy, and it continues to haunt all attempts to understand what happens between analyst and analysand, and, perhaps, between any two people engaged in some form of sustained communication.

B. Theory

The "Theory" section begins with the theory of *dreams*, "the royal road to a knowledge of the unconscious," as Freud called it. We see how the interpreter aims to find the meaning of the dream by uncovering its hidden, motivating desire: "Behind every dream lies a wish." Freud's method of interpreting dreams as well as jokes, slips of the tongue, and symptoms was to show that they were signs of concealed, conflicting desires. This view was and has remained controversial. For Freud, powerful desires always give rise to conflict, and the theory of dream formation tries to account for how this conflict finds some form of release in bizarre nocturnal expression. Dreams require interpretation because their powerful, motivating wishes are disguised, obscured by the manner of their expression. What force keeps these desires concealed?

This question leads into the concepts of *repression* and the *unconscious*. "Repression" is the force that keeps us from being aware of conflicting desires, of impulses that would undermine our sense of ourselves and our place in the world. These unruly desires are made inaccessible to our thinking; the "unconscious" is the name Freud gave to that realm of inaccessibility. Our repressed desires appear to us, according to psychoanalysis, only in the disguises of dreams, symptoms, and other incoherent, seemingly uncontrolled actions. The exhibition presents some of Freud's various attempts to map these different features of the mind in spatial terms. This proposed structure of the mind gives rise to the question: What kinds of desires are so powerful and disruptive that they have to be forced away from our conscious lives?

The answer lies in the powerful forces of human *sexuality* and *aggression*. Freud's theory of the sexual development of the individual cuts to the core of his conception of human life as driven by conflict. Sexual drives conflict with one another, with social conventions, and, most fundamentally, with reality. The sexual drives remain powerful and unsatisfied and are expressed indirectly in a variety of covert signs and symptoms. We desire what we cannot have or feel we have lost, and the unsatisfied desires find outlets in the most surprising ways. After World War I, Freud paid increasing attention to the phenomenon of aggression, and in *Beyond the Pleasure Principle* (1921) he speculated that a death instinct was as important as the sexual instinct in our psychic constitution. He saw the fundamental conflict in our lives as that between eros and thanatos—love and death—a perpetually unresolved conflict that finds various outlets in both our daily lives and in the world's major events.

In this section we see some of Freud's most important manuscripts on the subjects of sexuality and aggression, as well as representations of Oedipus and related figures. Freudian psychoanalysis became famous (or infamous) for its insistence on the oedipal myth as the model for the conflict at the heart of our individual and group lives. Freud thought he had found a universal paradigm for understanding how conflicting desires form an individual life. In this volume, the essays of Ilse Grubrich-Simitis and José Brunner examine how he used this myth as a vehicle for thinking about the fundamental strata of social life. Yet even as he was developing this model, questions arose regarding its evidential base, its relevance for women, and its connection to the particular biographical/historical origins of psychoanalysis.

C. Office/Study Area

This section of the exhibition displays artifacts from Freud's office and study, giving viewers some sense of the spaces in which he treated patients and crafted his ideas in writing. Models of the iconic psychoanalytic couch and the desk at which Freud worked have special prominence. As Patrick J. Mahony's essay in this volume explains, Freud's devotion to work was deep and consistent all through the years of his long career. He regarded work as an expression of psychic conflict, but an expression that reduced the pain of that conflict to tolerable levels. Helping patients achieve or rediscover the capacity to love and work was the basic Freudian idea of a cure for psychopathology. Love and work did not eliminate conflict, but they were signs that it could be productive, even pleasurable. This installation in the exhibit gives us a sense of some of the spaces in which love and work intersected in Freud's psychoanalytic practice.

SECTION III: FROM THE INDIVIDUAL TO SOCIETY

The next major section of the exhibition moves from the individual to society. First, we look at the expansion of psychoanalysis and the critical reaction to that expansion. Next, we examine the growth in Freud's own areas of inquiry, from theories of the individual psyche to theories of civilization, progressing from the archaeology of the past to an examination of the surfaces of contemporary social life. This section of the exhibit, "From the Individual to Society," is made up of three parts: "Expansion and Criticism," "Theories of Society," and "Crises."

A. Expansion and Criticism

This section is concerned with the development of psychoanalysis as a profession and with the movement of Freud's ideas into a variety of cultural realms. As Freud's sphere of inquiry expanded to include the basic questions of moral and political life, his followers applied his theories about conflict, desire, and the unconscious in new areas. For many intellectuals and artists these ideas seemed to offer new possibilities in understanding both the achievements and the failures of modern society. Although there have been enthusiasts who have seen psychoanalysis as a means of fulfilling the ancient commandment "Know thyself," there have also been critics who viewed the new enterprise as yet another fall into deception or illusion. In this section, the exhibition traces the growth of psychoanalysis as an inspiration to new modes of thought and its development as a professional institution from the early days of Freud's Wednesday Society in Vienna to the growth of the International Psychoanalytic Association and Freud's pivotal trip to the United States in 1909. The essays of Edith Kurzweil and Robert Coles in this volume are concerned with the different routes of dissemination of Freud's ideas in America.

The exhibit also emphasizes how, throughout the evolution of psychoanalysis, Freud's ideas have been hotly contested, and that as he sought to consolidate his theories in institutions and theoretical orthodoxy, he labeled prominent thinkers (e.g., Alfred Adler and Carl Jung) dissidents or even heretics. As psychoanalysis expanded and diffused into the realms of medicine (especially in the United States), art, and popular culture, the criticism of Freud's ideas and his practices also accelerated. In the face of this criticism, Freud was mindful of creating and controlling his intellectual legacy. He attempted to do this through his writings about the origins of his own ideas and of the movement he founded. In the decades following his death, many of Freud's basic assumptions were challenged by neurobiological research and clinical psychology and psychiatry, as his own reasoning and use of evidence have been challenged by philosophers, historians, and literary critics. If Freud's work continues to provoke constructive engagement in the sciences, arts, and humanities, it seldom does so without a critical dimension. There are two principal aspects of the critique of Freudian psychoanalysis: biographical/historical skepticism regarding

Freud's accounts of his cases and his interpretations, and philosophi-
cal/scientific argument against the logic and structure of his theories.
These two dimensions form the major axes of the "Contested Legacies" section of this volume.

Despite the criticism of some of its basic concepts and modes of
explanation, the psychoanalytic model of culture as an expression of
unconscious conflict became a potent force for popular and scholarly
understanding in the twentieth century. Freud's ideas animated
research from medicine to the humanities, from psychology to the
social sciences. His theories would often be greatly modified, but the
challenge of reading the signs of repression and desire remained a
powerful impetus to research, speculation, and creativity. Freud's ideas
are still at the heart of some of our most important debates: from
repressed memory and child abuse to the status of interpretation in the
sciences, from the place of sex and violence in our culture to the relation of the mind to the body.

B. Theories of Society

The first part of "Theories of Society" is devoted to Freud's speculations on the origins of human social organization. He theorized that
our societies have created mechanisms—analogous to psychological
mechanisms that inhibit the satisfactions of our basic desires—to
ensure forms of social regulation and repression. At the root of organized human life in common is the prohibition against incest, and
Freud speculates that this taboo had its genesis in the guilt stemming
from the murder of a powerful patriarch. After the tyrannical father is
killed, the sons continue to follow his dictates. Guilt, competition, and
fear ensure obedience even when the father is not there to enforce his
laws. In the psychoanalytic model, violent revolution does not resolve
conflict, it just displaces it onto different levels. The exhibit here displays the key Freud manuscripts dealing with these issues, as well as
those sources in anthropology and neo-Darwinian thought on which
he drew. Some of the objects from his collection of prehistoric artifacts
are also shown. The archaic for Freud is not something one outgrows
at either the individual or social level but something that remains a
vital, and often disruptive, part of existence at any level of development. The emphasis on the archaic as active, on a history that is alive

in us, is as important in the psychoanalytic approach to social life as it was in its approach to the individual. How is this active past made manifest at the social level? Given his understanding of symptoms as expressions of conflict and his speculations on the violent origins of society in male sexual competition, how did Freud view the development of the elaborate cultural constructions that societies would eventually produce?

This question marks the transition to the next part of this section on theories of society, "The Problem of Culture," which tries to make clear how Freud understood cultural products as expressions of basic psychological conflicts, as social analogues for individual dreams and symptoms. Religion, art, and science are, from the psychoanalytic perspective, products of impulses that are denied a more directly sexual or aggressive satisfaction. This view is manifest in Freud's dismissive critique of the infantilism of religion, his interpretation of artworks as indirect (sublimated) attempts at satisfaction, and his nuanced confidence in the scientific effort to arrive at a reasonable accommodation of desire in the world. Later on, psychoanalysts would often write with more appreciation of the "compromise" satisfactions of these cultural constructions, emphasizing their positive contributions to what they imagined to be a balanced individual or social life. Freud's notion of an essential conflict at the core of culture, however, informed all his writings in this field, and was the basis of his general pessimism about the negative effects of powerful, unsatisfied desires. If religion, art, and science fail to alleviate the conflicts at the heart of the human condition, then what are the consequences of this failure? If our forms of social life fail to meet our basic psychological needs, then what happens to the unfulfilled desires within society? These are the vital questions about the relation between our civilization and our deepest impulses, and those who wrote in Freud's wake turned to general forms of cultural study in an attempt to address them.

C. Crises

One of the reasons why psychoanalytic perspectives have seemed particularly relevant to a variety of thinkers throughout the twentieth century is that apparent progress has been punctuated by bizarre, disturbing, and powerful archaic forces. If social life originates in an unresolved, and unresolvable, conflict, then the seeds of fundamental disruptions in our civilization are always present. This Freudian view of crises is the subject of the last part of the exhibition.

In emphasizing the radical nature of sexuality, Freud inspired some thinkers and activists who found hope in the possibilities of feminist reform and the utopian emancipation of eros. Others believed the psychoanalytic goal to be the elimination of repression in the service of both individual and social liberation. For Freud, however, liberation also meant the unleashing of aggression. From World War I until his death in 1939, Freud saw increasingly violent and irrational "symptoms" of the conflicts all around him. Seemingly senseless wars, escalating anti-Semitism, and the threat of Nazi domination were the crises that surrounded Freud in his later years, and he tried to interpret them in terms of his model of psychological conflict. This part of the exhibit illustrates how Freud's life and work intersected with these crises, from the beginning of World War I until the ascendant Third Reich forced the aged Freud to flee Vienna for the safety of London. Images from this period, from shell-shocked soldiers to Nazi book burning, to Freud's own emigration, as well as his written reactions to these events, offer a powerful testimony of how this thinker, formed in the nineteenth century, tried to grapple with the enormities of the twentieth. Psychoanalysis indeed was a victim of these crises even as it offered ways to explain them. Now we may wonder whether this context of violence illuminated or distorted the psychoanalytic view of the human condition.

Epilogue

The biographical elements in this last part of the exhibit illustrate the links between Freud's life and work that were also present in the opening section. His theories were formulated in the wake of Marxism and Darwinism, both of which placed strong emphasis on struggle as the engine of change, and which developed in a century when broad historical conflicts had reached extraordinary dimensions. Although the conflicts that Freud concentrated on were internal—people at war with themselves, and with the cultural authorities they had internalized—he thought that the way we managed (or failed to manage) those conflicts had everything to do with the explosions of violence that had so scarred the modern world. As the specific events that influenced Freud's thinking recede into history, the concern with the violent power of sexuality and aggression has only intensified. Freud did not provide any solutions as to how we might escape this violence, nor did he propose ways of weakening its devastating force. However, he developed a powerful account of the connection between culture and conflict, and thus incisively identified a fundamental problem of the twentieth century—a problem that shows no sign of disappearing as we move into the twenty-first.

PART I

Freud Writing and Working

T HE COUCH AND THE DESK: twin icons of Freud's career. For almost all of his professional life, he combined clinical work with writing, bridging the scientific and the literary. It was during his therapeutic work with patients that associations were gathered, observations made, and resistances encountered. And it was in the course of his writing that ideas were explored, tested, elaborated, or dropped. The couch and the desk, of course, can be situated in relation to different contexts. The cultural ferment and political crises of fin-de-siècle Vienna were part of Freud's daily existence, sometimes intruding dramatically on his personal and professional life while at other times forming a loose urban forum for the slow expansion of the psychoanalytic circle. The conservative establishment in Vienna and the cultural politics that struggled against it produced the hothouse in which would grow the modern movements in art, philosophy, and science. Psychoanalysis was surely part of these rebellions against the conventions of the turn of the century. However, if much of Freud's work was done in Vienna, his concerns and approach to problems drew on intellectual traditions that went far beyond that immediate context. As Ilse Grubrich-Simitis and Michael Molnar note in their essays, Freud drew upon bodies of thought (some with little scientific credibility in his own time) far afield from medicine or neurology in an effort to address perplexing individual and societal issues. The founding myths of the Western tradition, and its classic texts, from those of the ancient Greeks to those of Shakespeare, remained deep resources for his thinking throughout his professional life. This is evident in his informal notes, as he took stabs at making sense of signs he could not yet read, to decipher codes for which he had not (yet) found a key. These notes were often the beginning of writing projects which would lead Freud into uncharted waters: areas of inquiry that would require far more interpretation and speculation than attention to empirical evidence. He kept at it: trying to solve these riddles that had more than a medical dimension, that concerned the human condition most generally. As Patrick J. Mahony emphasizes in his essay, Freud was driven to work and driven by it, from listening to himself and those around him to looking at texts and pictures, and writing, always writing. Was anything not grist for this mill? It needed to turn. John Forrester emphasizes how it turned in a way that would implicate both reader and writer, inviting us—or daring us—to turn to our dreams and our wishes and learn to see them as expressive of a latent content we had hitherto ignored. This latent content could never be exhausted: it held countless traces of who we were, what we wanted, and who we desired to be.

"Nothing About the Totem Meal!"

ON FREUD'S NOTES

Ilse Grubrich-Simitis

T HE BEAUTY of his prose is perhaps Freud's only achievement that has not yet been contested. However, although his brilliance as a writer has often been analyzed, for decades his manuscripts have remained disregarded. During the last few years, in the course of preliminary work toward a historical-critical edition of his writings, I focused my attention on these documents, which today are kept in the Library of Congress; samples of these precious handwritten pages are being displayed for the first time in the exhibition *Sigmund Freud: Conflict and Culture*. To my surprise, my study of the manuscripts yielded profound insights into the fascinating microcosm of Freud's scientific and literary creativity.[1]

BEFORE EXAMINING the specific holograph category of the notes, I would like to comment on Freud's writing habits as I have been able to reconstruct them from my study of the manuscripts. During his lifetime but especially after his death, a legend arose among his pupils and followers concerning the alleged effortlessness with which he wrote his books and essays. It was thought that he usually began with the writing down of a work at a relatively late phase, i.e., only when it had matured within him—even to the subtleties of the final wording—so that he only needed, as it were, to copy it from a textual image stored in his mind's eye. Sándor Radó, for example, in an interview as late as the 1960s, mentioned the manuscripts: how breathtaking it had been—

Freud had simply written them down without any previous notes or drafts, practically without any need to make corrections.[2] However, the documents tell us otherwise. They show that Freud's writings were produced, as a rule, in an exhausting process of hard work, and were usually drafted in several written stages. Freud himself, by the way, made no secret of the drudgery involved, describing it often enough in his letters.

From his correspondence we can furthermore deduce two basic conditions upon which the success of Freud's thinking and writing process depended. The first was an intermediary state between passivity and activity in which he entrusted himself to the dark rhythm of preconscious and unconscious forces. Scenting an idea, as it were, he waited over and again—often for a long time—until he was seized by a mood of impetuosity in which sporadically emerging associations and premonitions no longer withdrew behind the threshold of consciousness but finally, in quick thrusts, organized themselves into incisive *Gestalten.* These are described, especially in the letters to Wilhelm Fliess, almost as if they were living creatures with their own dynamics of growing and moving, as if he only needed to serve as a container for them. To characterize the final stage of the creative process, Freud himself used the birth metaphor and spoke of "frightful labour pains."[3]

However, even the preliminary stages of this process were not phases of uninterrupted well-being. In order to set them in motion—and this is the second basic condition—the tension generated by a moderate state of psychic and/or physical pain, a "modicum of misery,"[4] as Freud described it, was necessary. This subtle unhappiness remained the spur to Freud's creativity throughout his life. It was perhaps a derivative of mostly unconscious anxieties of being lost, of starvation and of death, anxieties from which he tried to free himself from one work to the next, but which he could only allay temporarily.

What part did the motor activity of writing itself play? Judging from the holographs, it would seem that, almost from the beginning, the act of writing was an intrinsic part of the creative process, accompanying and sustaining it. The confrontation with his own thoughts in their written form first presented Freud with a concrete surface for his work of self-criticism. Absolutely necessary for the materialization of a work, however, was the process of writing itself: jotting down notes and sketching drafts, he felt his way into a new work, safeguarding it for a while almost as if it were a piece of himself, an intimate possession, before gradually relinquishing it while working out the fair copy.

As a rule, Freud's writing proceeded in three stages. The *notes* served as a first informal record of spontaneous observations, associations, and ideas. The *drafts* embody the second stage of this characteristic progression. These are detailed preliminary manuscripts, although written in the form of key words—in a sense, they are similar to an X-ray picture in which the bare bones of the argument are faithfully represented. In composing the *fair copy*, the third and final step, Freud filled in the linguistic tissue, as it were, meticulously reworking the prose and effecting the transition from the private to the public wording. It was only in this last phase of the writing process that his artistry produced that unequivocal individuality, that compelling presence characteristic of almost all his texts.

To TURN NOW to the earliest phase of the writing process: the notes. In 1941, when the editors of the *Gesammelte Werke*, among them Anna Freud, published a volume of posthumous works, they included two pages of Freud's notes under the heading "Findings, Ideas, Problems. London June." These entries obviously date from 1938, the period of exile. In their preface the editors state that this was the only surviving sheet of such notes. This statement, made in 1940 during the war, shortly after Freud's death, was certainly consistent with the impression the editors had of his literary bequest at that time. However, in the course of research in the Manuscript Division of the Library of Congress, I discovered that an abundance of notes had been preserved—that there indeed exists an unknown opus of notes which has remained virtually unexplored.

Many of these notes are dated with the day and the month; some include the year. This information, as well as variations in the handwriting, indicate that they derive from very different periods of creation. As far as their individual length is concerned, they range from one-word notes to relatively detailed texts, almost like drafts, interspersed with those having the form of scientific aphorisms. In studying these quasi-aphorisms, readers familiar with Freud's oeuvre can easily recognize the information stored in their succinct sentences or sentence fragments which, like the genes of a germ cell, determined the growth of works originating at the same time.

It is not easy to convey the distinctiveness of the notes, their delicate pointillistic structure. And this is not simply because of their thematic disparity: they are reticent texts, private texts, neither polished nor refined, unadorned grammalogues of an ongoing scientific soliloquy. They were clearly intended solely for Freud's own use. This means that one will look in vain for the courtesy with which Freud, in his published texts, paid heed to and furthered his readers' understanding. He wished as a rule to spare them effort, and his published works so impress us with their natural elegance that one might think that their contents had been easily come by. The notes, by contrast, show us the struggling researcher, dispirited at times, faced with the daunting complexity of the human mind.

In what follows I will examine a few selected themes that preoccupied Freud throughout his life: notes relating to his work with patients, to linguistic phenomena, to dreams, to civilization, and finally the key words to one of his major works: *Totem and Taboo*.

A CONSIDERABLE number of sheets are devoted to *notes about what happened during sessions*, to the immeasurably rich material produced by Freud's daily therapeutic interaction with his patients. In fact, it is through these handwritten traces that we may be able to fully appreciate that the revolution in the traditional doctor-patient relationship— i.e., to get the patient to talk, to listen to him, to talk to him, indeed to be imbued with the belief that the patient has something to say about his sufferings—was a brilliant stroke not only of therapeutic technique but of research strategy as well. The notes demonstrate clearly that Freud's most important allies in the process of making his discoveries were his analysands.

In his "Recommendations to Physicians Practising Psycho-Analysis" he wrote: "As regards instances, I write them down from memory in the evening after work is over."[5] With the help of such note-taking, in brief and very brief vignettes, he seems to have collected material related to currently emerging theoretical ideas, or even to have been led toward abstract conclusions through this assiduous collecting of details.

The patients are often identified only by their first names, and occasionally we may think we recognize them as figures familiar from the published works. Some statements of patients are recorded verbatim, for example: "The attack is an extract from the history, says patient." In a list of ten points documenting the theoretical results of his research into hysteria, also preserved among the notes, we find an echo of this remark: "The hysterical attack corresponds to a memory from the patient's life; it consists of the return of the scene experienced [. . .] and the associated expression of the emotion." Here, as with the other nine points, those familiar with the published writings on hysteria by Breuer and Freud can make links to the preliminary communication "On the Psychical Mechanism of Hysterical Phenomena" of 1893,[6] and finally to the *Studies on Hysteria* of 1895.[7]

The daily grind of clinical work is also documented in untiring observations on the many and varied forms in which obsessional neurosis can be expressed, on compulsive ideas and acts, as well as on their underlying logic. Many of these notes bear witness to Freud's caution in erecting hypotheses. An example is his vigilance in his research into the etiology of neurosis, in watching for the smallest hints from his patients that would help him to judge the relative weight to be given to real traumatic experiences on the one hand and pathogenic fantasies on the other. This fundamental question occupied Freud throughout his life. Contrary to the distorting assertions of the popular contemporary anti-Freud polemic, he never dismissed the possible pathological influence of external reality, of factual traumatic events and experiences or the memories of them and their subsequent psychic elaboration.

For today's reader, for whom all this constitutes basic common psychological knowledge and who can scarcely imagine a world without it, these notes made nearly a century ago convey with great immediacy the exertion that went into the revolutionary discovery of the ubiquity and depth of transference processes and of the development of the first elements of a psychoanalytic technique. At that time Freud still found it necessary to admonish himself in the notes: "I still too readily forget that everything unclear is transference." The first note under the heading "Transference & impediment" contains a renewed call for self-discipline and meticulousness: "This must be taken more sharply." At the end he sums up: "After all ΨA [psychoanalysis] is at a disadvantage compared with suggestive therapy, because it makes the tr[ansference] negative early on [and] provokes conflicts, but through overcoming these it has a curative effect."

Many notes written during this pioneering phase bear witness to the fact that Freud's pressing search for a completely new way of relating to his patients and what they told him also dominated his thinking beyond the consulting room, for example, in his private reading. Especially in devising the instruments through which he could finally gain access to the unconscious inner world, he fashioned for his own use countless hints from others, using analogies and borrowing metaphors. This is illustrated by the following undated entry, found under the heading "Quotations & analogies": "For the proper attitude to the work of interpretation: Burckhardt. Hist[ory of] Greek Civilization p. 5, intense effort is actually least likely to secure the desired result here; quietly attentive listening with steady diligence takes one further."

This not only reminds us of the frame of mind that Freud adopted when writing—that intermediary state between passivity and activity mentioned earlier—it also contains the germ of the idea of "evenly suspended attention," i.e., the technical concept he later elaborated, which describes the analyst's characteristic attitude toward the patient's communications, that is, *not* to focus or strain the attention because of the concomitant danger of discovering nothing but that which one already knows and expects to find. In a letter to Wilhelm Fliess on January 30, 1899, Freud mentioned this inspiring reading matter: "For relaxation I am reading Burckhardt's *History of Greek Civilization*, which is providing me with unexpected parallels."[8] Indeed, if one examines the introduction to Burckhardt's book, in which the expression "quietly attentive listening" is to be found, one comes across an abundance of further analogies to attitudes and ideas typical of Freud. Among these are Burckhardt's uncompromising criticism of academic practice in his field, his demand for radically new methods, and his avowal that the most important facts in need of research were not external events but "the interior of bygone mankind [*das Innere der vergangenen Menschheit*]"; research into the history of civilization lives from that "which sources and monuments unintentionally [. . .], yes [. . .] *unconsciously*[9] communicate." Thus, through this note on Burckhardt, a hitherto hidden genealogy of psychoanalytic thought is suddenly documented.

MANY OF THE notes give evidence of Freud's *fascination with language* and his linguistic genius. They strike us as remnants of a continuous, multidimensional work of translation—from symptom to unconscious conflict, from manifest to latent dream content, from transference constellation to childhood scene, from primal fantasy to real events in prehistory.

In one set of notes with the title "How hy[steria] approaches the roots of language" we read:

> Actually psychoneurosis. One of my pat[ients], who had fallen ill after a quarrel with his brother Richard, from then on showed a pathological aversion to everything that reminded him of his brother[.] He did not even want to think of getting rich because his brother's name was Richard. He himself thought this compulsion a ridiculous detail due to the similarity in sound of the word & of the initial letter. But now L. Geiger ([in] Origin of Language) shows that the word "rich" comes from the same root as the similar syllables in the names Heinrich, Friedrich, Richard, and the Latin Rex.

One could list any number of examples recorded in the notes of such "syllabic chemistry," as Freud, in *The Interpretation of Dreams*,[10] once called this process of setting verbal elements free and recombining them. They are eloquent illustrations of the gradual revelation of the significance of semantic and syntactic aspects of language in the workings of unconscious psychic processes.

IT IS WELL KNOWN that Freud pursued his semiotic studies especially with *dream* material. He was above all fascinated by the phenomenon of dream symbolism, even long after the publication of his *Interpretation of Dreams* at the turn of the century. In fact, most of the supplements to the later editions of this great book pertain to the theme of symbolism. He explicitly emphasized that although he had from the beginning recognized the existence of symbolism in dreams, only gradually did he reach an adequate appreciation of its extent and significance. Among many other traces of this ongoing research process, we find in the notes a lengthy list in which symbols and what they invariably represent are correspondingly reported, often embedded in the specific dream texts, specific dream interpretations from which Freud had obtained them.

The original manuscript of *The Interpretation of Dreams* has been lost. According to his own account, Freud threw it into the wastepaper basket as soon as he received the first printed copy. However, it will be possible in the future, by studying the many notes on the theme of dreams, to reconstruct—more accurately than the mere comparison of the subsequent editions allows—the successive stages of revision to which the author subjected his magnum opus in the course of three decades.

From the notes we learn, for example, that in the first ten years after the book's publication, Freud was preoccupied with, among other topics, supplementing the section in the fifth chapter on so-called "typical dreams." These typical dreams are closely related to the theme of dream symbolism in that Freud assumed that their stereotyped scenarios had the same meaning for each dreamer and that their basic features could be interpreted without the individual dreamer's specific associations. In addition, through their invariability, he hoped for hints toward an understanding of the supraindividual, perhaps phylogenetic sources of the dream language.

A somewhat lengthier and undated script seems also to belong to this research context. It has the heading "My individual characterization of dreams," and one can assume that Freud is exploring his memory for his *own* typical dreams. The entry begins as follows: "I should like to distinguish between dreams with sensations & others. The first group include: flying, falling, swimming, paralysis, the second is well known. [I.e.] Death of relatives, examination, nakedness, Oedipus dream, perhaps also money dream, travel dream, going through a flight of rooms."

I will quote only one passage from this note script—the entry concerning the death of relatives:

> I can remember only a single example of the dream death of living relatives. Shortly after the birth of my youngest girl, I

dreamt, without an affect of anxiety, that her little predecessor was lying dead but rosy-cheeked in the cradle. In analysing [this dream] I remembered that, as an 8 y[ear-old] [?] boy I had crept along after the birth of the last sister [. . .] to the cradle of her predecessor, who was then 1 y[ear] old and sleeping rosy-cheeked[,] & thought as I did so: now you are no longer the youngest.

Freud had five younger sisters—in this respect he had been tested by adversity.

Finally an example of how a dream, interpreted in the course of self-analysis, is briefly sketched as a reminder, to be fully developed in the published text in a manner that enables the reader to follow the train of thought without difficulty. In the note manuscript we read:

I dr[eamt] in Klobenstein: The Pope has died. No explanation. In the morning Martha asked: Did you hear the dreadful noise of the bells early today? I hadn't. Pope was ill at the time. Revenge on Tyrolese.

In *The Interpretation of Dreams* we find:

In another dream I [. . .] succeeded in warding off a threatened interruption of my sleep which came this time from a sensory stimulus. In this case it was only by chance, however, that I was able to discover the link between the dream and its accidental stimulus and thus to understand the dream. One morning at the height of summer, while I was staying at a mountain resort in the Tyrol, I woke up knowing I had had a dream that *the Pope was dead.* I failed to interpret this dream— a non-visual one—and only remembered as part of its basis that I had read in a newspaper a short time before that his Holiness was suffering from a slight indisposition. In the course of the morning, however, my wife asked me if I had heard the frightful noise made by the pealing of bells that morning. I had been quite unaware of them, but I now understood my dream. It had been a reaction on the part of my need for sleep to the noise with which the pious Tyrolese had been trying to wake me. I had taken my revenge on them by drawing the inference which formed the content of the dream, and I had then continued my sleep without paying any more attention to the noise.[11]

All these records of dreams and their interpretations preserved in the notes demonstrate anew how Freud, throughout his life, ardently anticipated further insight through the untiring study of dream material. He literally hoarded it. These documents, mute until now, unmistakably show that having once found his *via regia*, his royal road to a knowledge of the unconscious, he indeed never deviated from it for the rest of his life.

NOT ONLY HIS research into dreams but the entire cosmos of Freud's thinking is to be found in the notes. Occasionally, some aphorisms connected with his writings on *civilization and religion* catch one's eye, for example:

> Men cannot tolerate being bereft of parents[,] & so they create a new parental couple from God and nature [God the Father and Mother Nature]: foundation, ultimate foundation of religion [is] man's infantile helplessness.

Or a group-psychological consideration:

> If something for which a people reproaches itself from its past later recurs ucs. [unconsciously], then [it is] as a reproach to another [people]. [. . .] Exact analogy with the situation in individual psychology, paranoia, which is in a similar position with just such reproaches[.] Persecution mania. Self-reproaches projected onto others.

And as an illustration of such projective processes, there is a note under the heading "A source of antisemitism":

> The fact that antis[emitism] is generated in the nursery is clear. Irma has a physical horror of any Jew. When she was a child they said (in Ofen [i.e., the western part of Budapest])[,] if there was any trace of incontinentia alvi on a child's vest: the Jew has wiped his mouth on it again.

YET ANOTHER category of notes are those in which Freud's thinking seems to be *approaching a particular subsequently published work*, as though he were approximating it through note-taking. The notes to *Totem and Taboo*, which are especially extensive, demonstrate this. From the preparatory phase of this work, Freud's first great contribution to the theory of civilization, these papers surprisingly record countless moments in his reflections, especially with respect to the famous fourth essay, "The Return of Totemism in Childhood." This closing essay constitutes the climax of the book; comprising as it does the so-called "phylogenetic construction," i.e., the hypothesis of the murder of the primal father in the prehistoric family as the origin of the sense of guilt and of cultural institutions. The text thus provides a theory of the genesis of civilization and is at the same time a fundamental statement about human aggression.

A large portion of the notes consists of jottings Freud made while reading, including records of the author and the title of the book with which he was preoccupied. In the left-hand margin he noted the page reference to those passages that seemed to be significant to his own research and jotted down the relevant context in key words. He underlined certain passages or selected quotations and further recorded bibliographical details concerning additional sources. In what appears to have been a passionate reading expedition probably lasting several months, he followed up the bibliographic references with the relevant literature, working his way from author to author and from book to book.

In order to illustrate the character of these reading notes, I will use a short passage written while Freud was studying Wilhelm Wundt's *Elements of Folk Psychology*. Here he records:

[p.] 228 Ancestor cult: declares it secondary
         otherwise does not fit theory.
[p.] 231. Animal ancestor went before, but how
   p 233 With family—ancestor cult—dissol[ution] of totemism

And then, underlined and with an exclamation mark:

Nothing about the totem meal!

This exclamation mark betrays Freud's disappointment, a disappointment that can only be understood when we call to mind one of the main objectives he was following in the fourth essay of *Totem and Taboo.*

As I have already indicated in describing the notes on dreams, Freud, in analyzing his own dreams and those of his analysands, had come across certain stereotyped elements that he thought belonged to a supraindividual, inherited part of the dream vocabulary originating from a phylogenetic source. The so-called "primal fantasies" that Freud encountered over and again in his clinical work—fantasies of parental intercourse, castration, patricide, and incest with the mother—had a similar immutable quality. These are the few typical, apparently autonomous phantasmal patterns that shape the human mind independently of personal experience. They seem to generate conflict and produce illness, but to follow a different line of causation than individual experience, which is equally influential although incomparably more variable. Freud was convinced that the individual was compelled to remember prehistoric experience in the form of primal fantasies.

Furthermore, he was always impressed by the power and the terror of the primal fantasies, by their pervading quality of reality. It was as if he, who had grown up with nineteenth-century physicalism and evolutionism, imagined that something so concrete and so oppressive, exerting such an undiminished effect on each generation, must in the last resort be grounded in *real events in the material external world* and—analogous to animal instincts—be handed down in the soma. It is well known that he obstinately held Lamarckian evolutionary mechanisms to be responsible for this transmission, although even then these were regarded as untenable by experts in the field. However that may be, in his speculative inquiry concerning which concrete dramatic and traumatic events might be present, as an archaic heritage, in the mind of modern man, and even today give rise to inner turmoil, the totem meal seems to have occupied a special place. There are two reasons why this ritual might have interested him so strongly: first, because each totem meal was preceded by a factual sacrificial killing; and second, because the communal devouring of the slaughtered object represents a physical form of internalization, concretely paving the way for identification with the lost object and thus for superego development.

It is therefore not surprising that Freud should have recorded the few available references to the totem meal with special care. The page of notes on the book *Cultes, mythes et religions* by Salomon Reinach, the French archaeologist and theorist of religion, is headed: "Reinach essential for references to totem meal. [. . .]" In fact, it was Reinach's work that had alerted Freud to W. Robertson Smith's lectures on the religion of the Semites, which finally set the longed-for totem meal before him. In contrast to other experts, Robertson Smith held the view that the totem meal as a sacrificial ritual had, from the beginning, been part of the totemic system. Freud allied this hypothesis, which he unaffectedly celebrates in *Totem and Taboo*, with the psychoanalytic deduction that the totem animal is a father substitute, and established thereby, as he himself remarks, "an unsuspected correlation between groups of phenomena that have hitherto been disconnected."[12] And here we may recall that it was originally the animal phobias of childhood, understood as a displacement of anxiety relating to the father, that had led Freud to his intensive preoccupation with totemism.

The phylogenetic construction, with the totem meal at its core, cannot be discussed here in more detail. Certainly, modern ethnology has shown this strange theory to be untenable. Nevertheless, it is necessary to stress that these ideas were not simply flights of fancy but rather a desperate makeshift construction designed to yield answers to serious questions that even today defy scientific investigation—questions that Freud wanted at the very least to preserve in the form of quasi-mythological images. Above all, these questions concern inherited dispositions and the somatic basis for specific transculturally recurring mental contents.

IN CONCLUSION, a few summarizing comments on the function of Freud's note-taking. Undoubtedly, especially in his pioneering phase in the 1890s, these notes were finger exercises for an entirely new way of depicting the inner world of man. However, the principal function of the notes remained, throughout Freud's life, the gathering of details. On the one hand, he used this mass of material to curb his tendency to speculate fancifully, to hastily construct "series" and "formulae," to systematize too early. In a letter to Sándor Ferenczi in the summer of 1915, shortly after he sent Ferenczi the draft of his twelfth metapsychological essay, which was indeed highly speculative and which he rejected soon afterward, he wrote, calling himself to order, as it were: "I maintain that one should not make theories—they must fall into one's house as uninvited guests while one is occupied with the investigation of details."[13] The notes constantly reminded and cautioned him to return to this investigation of details. On the other hand, they served the immediate purpose of preserving the material from which later hypotheses and theories could emerge, to a certain extent due to an incremental effect. As he described it in "The Disposition to Obsessional Neurosis":

> This is the starting-point of the small new fragment of theory which I have formulated. It is of course only in appearance that it is based on this one observation; actually it brings together a large number of earlier impressions, though an understanding of them was only made possible by this last experience.[14]

Leafing through the manuscripts of the notes today, one gains the impression that from the very beginning of his working life Freud preserved these preliminary stages of his published writings. From time to time—and not only in 1938 during his preparations for emigration—he seems to have gone through them and sorted them out. Those which he had not yet made use of in his published works, but which he either held to be worth keeping or which he still intended to follow up, were extracted or cut out. He apparently threw the rest away. In reading these sheets, one might suppose that this procedure of inspection and selection assumed at times for Freud the nature of a critical inventory, a personal historiography of his ideas.

The manuscripts of the notes are so valuable for our knowledge of Freud because they contain elements of the raw material of the oeuvre and offer a uniquely firsthand glimpse of the investigator of the unconscious *at work*—utterly private and very human, and occasionally at that joyful creative moment in which an observation, an association, and the first tentative formulation of an hypothesis interlock.

Translated by Veronica Mächtlinger

Freud's World of Work

Patrick J. Mahony

In the words of King Macbeth, let us die in harness.

A ND HE WORKED and he worked and he worked. And miles to go before he slept. He peered into his dreams and discovered he worked there, too, and then proclaimed that we all do dream-work. And he listened to jokes, only to trace their origin to joke-work. And he wrote about his infantile self, a mere nineteen months, self-enlisted into child labor—mourning the death of his still younger brother Julius—and he wrote that we all do mourning-work not only at death but also at the high noon of life. And he wrote another Genesis valid for tomorrow as well as for yesterday. In the beginning there was work: a drive is "a measure of the demand made upon the mind for work in consequence of its connection with the body."[1] And then there was wish: "Nothing but a wish can set our mental apparatus to work."[2] And it came to pass that as Freud chose psychoanalysis over hypnosis, he was favoring a treatment that meant much more work for the patient—working, working over and through.

One of Freud's unforgettable insights could serve as a motto for his own lifetime commitment to work. The value he placed on the therapeutic function of work can hardly be overestimated: "No other technique for the conduct of life attaches the individual so firmly to reality as laying emphasis on work; for his work at least gives him a secure place in a portion of reality, in the human community."[3] Still in all, a qualitative factor entered into Freud's evaluation of work—it should be a *Leistung*, which in German means "efficient work," "achievement," or "performance." Strachey's misleading translation presents Freud as stating that the doctor merely aims to restore "some degree of capacity for work and enjoyment."[4] More than has been generally appreciated, throughout his own psychoanalytic career Freud attempted to carry out to the letter his ideal of *Leistung*, or achievement in a broad range of activities. Detailed, comprehensive studies have yet to be done on Freud's day-to-day clinical work; his years of lecturing at the university, congresses, and in numerous societies; his writing; his editorial tasks with psychoanalytic journals; his tireless role as founder and organizer of his own psychoanalytic association; and his time-consuming editorial negotiations with presses over the years.

Historians have not fully realized how much the concept of work as *published* achievement figured in Freud's early personal relations and how much it informed his critical judgments of others. For example, Freud confided that his relations with his generous mentor Josef Breuer came to grief over publication: "I believe he has never forgiven me for having lured him into writing the *Studies* with me and so committed him to something definite."[5] A more revelatory case involves Wilhelm Fliess, Freud's internist colleague and the most intimate male friend he ever had. It is widely recognized that the pair fell out over theoretical disagreements as well as over an increasing number of personal conflicts. There was, however, another factor of decisive importance: the effective work of publication. During the years 1887 to 1900, the period of their relatively positive friendship, we are able to trace Freud's disillusionment with his friend not only because of theoretical issues but also because of the latter's failure to publish, which for Freud was a sign of inability or ineffectiveness. Freud's psychological writings apart, his neurological texts for that period surpass Fliess's in quantity by an astonishing degree.

In that critical year, 1897, Freud's last work on neurology appeared, as did a volume by Fliess, which was finished in the year preceding. He had never been able to keep up with the rhythmic fury of Freud's productivity, but from 1897 to 1900 Fliess was left far behind and managed to write only a short article. Although their shared ideal of productivity was rapidly becoming material for a desperate dream, Freud continued to importune his friend for testimony of scriptive performance. Let us cut open the envelopes containing four of Freud's letters from that time:

June 1897: [I hope] that instead of a short article you will within a year present to us a small book which solves the organic secrets.[6]

February 1899: You can write [in letters] of nothing but the tremendously huge work which is all too hard for the powers of a human being.[7]

June 1899: The announcement that you are engaged in research perhaps may mean, [that] instead of writing? And [thus the] postponement of the date on which I can read something of yours?[8]

August 1899: Your work has apparently changed into a pupa for me: will I be able to catch it as a butterfly, or will it fly too high for me?[9]

Obviously, Fliess's continued failure to produce effective work and publish it provoked in Freud not only impatience but also barely controlled scorn. We know that Freud had a surprising amount of energy. Vacations tended to be a time not of physical rest but of tireless activity. Colleagues much younger than he observed during their walking or mountaineering trips how he excelled them in vigor. Intellectual tasks proved even more stimulating to him. In the best of times, Freud was driven to spend the greatest part of the day in intellectual work; in the worst of times, he relied on it to combat depression. When, for example, the death of his favorite grandson caused him great suffering, Freud wrote to Ernest Jones, describing it as "a loss not to be forgotten" and then adding, "But let us put it aside for the moment, life and work must go on, as long as we last."[10] On the same occasion he wrote to his friend Oskar Pfister with a similar message about stoic commitment to work: "I do as much work as I can, and am grateful for the distraction. The loss of a child seems to be a grave blow to one's narcissism; as for mourning, that will no doubt come later."[11] Only the most disabling sickness at the end of his life drove him away from fulfilling his need for creative stimulation. In an early letter to Pfister we read perhaps Freud's finest depiction of his single-minded dedication to work, "a free play of the imagination" that he would like to enjoy up to the very moment of death:

I cannot face with comfort the idea of life without work; work and the free play of the imagination are for me the same thing, I take no pleasure in anything else. That would be a recipe for happiness but for the appalling thought that productivity is entirely dependent on a sensitive disposition. . . . I have one quite secret prayer: that I may be spared any wasting away and crippling of my ability to work because of physical deterioration. In the words of King Macbeth, let us die in harness.[12]

Freud wanted to die in harness, and he realized the preponderant part of that wish not in dream but in reality.

We must give full credence to Freud's assertion that courage was a preeminently enabling factor in his commitment to work. As he wrote to his fiancée, Martha: "My whole capacity for work probably springs from my character. . . . [My colleague Josef Breuer] told me that he had discovered that hidden under the surface of timidity there lay in me an extremely daring and fearless human being."[13] Far from being a narcissistic banality, Freud's self-reflection came from his depths and would have won the ready assent of Nietzsche.[14]

It was courage, in fact, that helped Freud announce theories that would disturb the sleep of the world; it was courage that helped him to continue working while braving social isolation, if not ridicule; and it was courage that enabled him to endure the turmoil that grew within the very psychoanalytic organization he had founded. For that organization, like others, is not a privileged sanctuary free from the undesirable characteristics that Freud discovered in the dynamics of group psychology:

We have an impression of a state in which an individual's private emotional impulses and intellectual acts are too weak to come to anything by themselves and are entirely dependent for this on being reinforced by being repeated in a similar way in the other members of the group. We are reminded of how many of these phenomena of dependence are part of the normal constitution of human society, of how *little originality and personal courage* [emphasis added] are found in it, of how much every individual is ruled by those attitudes of the group mind.[15]

35

In this regard, we should not forget that a courageous commitment to his beliefs drove Freud until the end of his life. Old age, cancer, and over twenty operations in his last years did not publicly prevent him from either mitigating his previous therapeutic positions (1937) or from railing against anti-Semitism.

The furious pace of Freud's work was spurred on by a sublimated erotic motivation. We cannot exaggerate the importance of Freud's avowal that an essay entitled "Nature" influenced his professional decision to switch from philosophy to medicine. Mythopoetic descriptions of Nature, such as the following, rang in Freud's ears: "She dwells in none but children; and the mother, where is she? She is the sole artist. . . . She has analyzed herself in order to enjoy herself. . . . She has set me within. She will also lead me without. I commit myself to her."[16] As if extending the essay into his own life, Freud committed himself to the study of this "goddess," noting that his hero Leonardo da Vinci repeatedly advocated "a return to Mother Nature."[17]

When working on a text, Freud had the habit of talking about his preoccupation as a serious liaison. He took the French expression about marrying ideas, *épouser les idées*,[18] as something more than just a figure of speech. *The Interpretation of Dreams* is the most revelatory manifestation of this underlying libidinal meaning, as it is of so many other aspects of Freud's work. As an expository device of his Dreambook, Freud used a narrative setting in which he accompanies the reader on an exploration of an impressive landscape. Since Freud himself believed landscape to be a maternal symbol, the journey he depicts is more than an artistic device; in fact, he has wedded his epistemological exposition to a retrogressive investigation of the maternal body, first oedipal and then pre-oedipal.[19] One might even say that all his subsequent works were an extended Dreambook recording his grappling with a symbolized Nature/Mother.

Physical stimulus played a major role among the factors determining Freud's mode of work. If Freud missed out on discovering the anesthetic qualities of cocaine, he did not overlook its impact on one's energy. The story of his experience with cocaine began in the early spring of 1884. By June of the same year an ecstatic Freud proudly wrote up his conclusions: "One senses an increase of self-control and feels more vigorous and more capable of work; on the other hand, one misses that heightening of the mental powers which alcohol, tea, or coffee induce. . . . I have tested this effect of coca, which wards off hunger, sleep, and fatigue and steels one to intellectual effort, some dozen times on myself."[20] A well-meaning recommendation that a seriously ill friend accept injections of cocaine led to an addictive tragedy and had, along with some subsequent unfortunate events, the side effect of dampening Freud's enthusiastic use of the drug as a means of improving his work.

Another story about physical stimulants was also tragic, though not immediately so. The etymology of Freud's first name (Sigmund: "victory-mouth") is an ironical gloss on the fact that his cigar smoking became a fatal addiction; however beneficial to his creative process, it accelerated if not caused the oral cancer that eventually killed him. Freud's daily consumption of cigars approximated twenty,[21] and as his considerable, as yet unpublished correspondence with Max Eitingon repeatedly tells us, he rebelled at the thought of abstaining from his *Arbeitsmittel* (work medicine): "The sum of my various infirmities raises the question as to how much longer I shall be able to continue my professional work, especially since giving up the beloved habit of smoking has brought about a great reduction of my intellectual interests."[22] And yet, although Freud's smoking became a necessity in his creative theorizing, he realized that his "work medicine" prevented him from resolving certain psychological problems.[23]

Freud's self-destructive addiction to nicotine raises the general question of his reliance on pain. An aphorism located near the end of the *Project for a Scientific Psychology* sheds light on his intense self-dedication to work: "Unpleasure remains the sole means of education."[24] Certainly Freud would have harbored some reservation about the lament of Shakespeare's Rosalind: "O how full of briers is this working-day world!" (*As You Like It*, act 1, scene 3, line 12). Accordingly, it is somewhat of a stretch to believe that Freud had to work too hard for a living, and that if he had had fewer financial obligations, he would have exploited his creative gifts that much more. Abundant evidence points to the contrary: to various friends he acknowledged that he needed some measure of physical or psychic pain in order to create. His greatest period of creativity, in fact, was attended by serious, prolonged discomfort. A month before the appearance of *Studies on Hysteria*, Freud described his tyrannical desideratum this way: "A man like me cannot live without a hobby-horse, without a consuming passion, without—in Schiller's words—a tyrant. I have found one. In its service I know no limits."[25] Perhaps Freud flinched before the regressive pull of complete well-being and thus depended on some measure of irritation to drive his creativity. Irritation, it would follow, was Freud's requirement not just for working but for *Leistung*, working well, achieving.

A current misconception about creativity in general, and about Freud's creativity in particular, needs to be addressed. Workers in the ever-burgeoning field of creativity research have done much to dispel the false notion that renowned scientists, functioning in a state of continual inspiration, create fully finished products. For example, in his widely acclaimed study, Howard Gruber[26] demonstrated that Charles Darwin gradually achieved his insights through sustained assiduity, not through a burst of creative illumination. Freud's extraordinarily inspirational month of October 1897 is an exception that proves the rule. The mass of his private and public writings testifies to his nonlinear development; the close reader regularly observes how key ideas were foreshadowed, forgotten, rejected, and repeatedly modified before reaching their final form.

Attention to Freud's written work allows us to discover, as no other consideration can, important insights into the origins of psychoanalysis, the peculiar nature of his genius, and the distinctiveness of his Dreambook, the greatest work in the history of psychoanalysis. The composition of that book constituted an organizing experience in Freud's life and had a profound and lasting influence. In fact, there are many reasons for one to claim that the rest of Freud's works were but an extension of *The Interpretation of Dreams* and his self-analysis.

The following findings, which correct Didier Anzieu's acclaimed account,[27] highlight Freud's modality of working in his self-analysis.[28]

> 1) In May 1897 Freud sat down to compose his *Interpretation of Dreams* but quickly fell into a writing block, which then precipitated a systematic self-analysis starting in June 1897.
>
> 2) The most tortuous, as well as the most exalted, part of Freud's writing career was his systematic self-analysis, which concentrated on dreams and was carried out in writing. His self-analytic experience was guided by the tenet that dreams are recoverable as psychic transcriptions par excellence by their externalized transcription and interpretation; in every sense his self analysis was a rite of passage.

3) The impulsive, as well as the symbolic, nature of the writing in *The Interpretation of Dreams* shows that dreaming and writing were not so much collateral as coinvolved activities for Freud.

4) Freud's self-therapy was not just a writing cure but also a publishing cure.

5) Because his writing was a "writing out" in every sense of the term, his self-cure was only partial.

6) Pertinently, during his own writing cure Freud did not bring about even one "talking cure."

After the 1890s, Freud's written self-analysis continued in various ways throughout his career. His daughter even adopted the practice, as we read in an unpublished letter to her father: "Now finally I also believe your idea that if one is alone, one can analyze dreams only by means of writing."[29]

As time passed, Freud looked upon writing as a necessary relief from clinical work. As he avowed to Karl Abraham, "I have to recuperate from psychoanalysis by working, otherwise I should not be able to stand it."[30] But there was a deeper level of meaning to Freud's writing; more than just a working medium, it was for him a personally, as well as professionally, organizing and creative experience. He would have agreed with St. Augustine, who said: "Admittedly, therefore, I try to count myself among those who write as they progress and who progress as they write."[31] Along this line we might remember that Freud often divided his literary work into two types: the commissioned (which he disliked) and the spontaneous. In the latter type, Freud fashioned an instrument that stimulated both his own and his readers' associative and critical processes.[32] His daring enterprise displayed, in part, his way of contending with the Kafkaesque awareness that his scientific language, by its nature, was metaphorical and distorting, and yet that it was *only* by virtue of such distortion that he could perceive psychical processes.[33] It is quite to the point that Freud's famous case histories, much more than his general cultural treatises, stand out as sterling specimens of impulse-driven composition.[34]

A crucial message in Freud's writings is that he expects his readers to work in order to understand him; in other words, he summons us to "reading-work." Permeating his writing is the implied understanding that any subject, and especially psychoanalysis itself, is apt to be misread; his exposition of psychoanalysis, furthermore, bears the implicit plea for a self-applied psychoanalysis. Thus, more than anyone else, Freud tells us best how to read him, in the sense that all his writings on psychopathology are also reflexive insights on understanding and misunderstanding the text. In any one of his texts, Freud adopts a strategy to get his readership to read in a certain way; the alert reader will focus on both the content and the communicative strategy. In sum, an informed reading of Freud involves examining the tension between his overall advice on how to read his work and the particular strategies contained in any one text.[35]

Not only was Freud a great writer, he wrote prodigiously. Writing was essential to both his professional and his personal identity, and Freud wrote constantly—including finished preanalytic and psychoanalytic treatises, drafts, travel journals, visitors' books, diaries, copious notes, chronological records, translations, and a mountainous correspondence. Although he destroyed large quantities of his manuscripts at least three times in his life (in 1885, 1907, and 1938), what remains of his literary production is impressive. If we take the estimated 14,000 extant letters out of the some 20,000 that Freud wrote and if each were edited to occupy an average of a page and a half in print, we would have an edition of 21,000 pages, or more than three times the length of *The Standard Edition of the Complete Psychological Works of Sigmund Freud*. A dream awaiting tomorrow's tomorrow, the complete publication of Freud's extant work would easily comprise some 150 volumes.

Let us close at the end of Freud's life of driven work. We might imagine him, in tired silence, reading these words in Emerson's essay "The Method of Nature": "When Nature has work to be done, she creates a genius to do it." Better yet, we might imagine Freud intoning with Ovid the lofty cry:

> *Iamque opus exegi quod nec Iovis ira nec ignis*
> *nec poterit ferrum nec edax abolere vetustas*

> And now I have accomplished my work that neither
> Jove's ire nor iron weapon nor consuming age will
> be able to destroy.

> (Ovid, *Metamorphoses*, book 15, lines 871–72; my translation)

Sigmund Freud's
Notes on Faces and Men

NATIONAL PORTRAIT GALLERY, SEPTEMBER 13, 1908

Michael Molnar

Freud's notes, translated by Michael Molnar[1]

13 SEPT 08
NOTES ON FACES AND MEN
NATIONAL PORTRAIT GALLERY

Shakespeare looks completely exceptional, completely unenglish —Jacques-Pierre.

In general people's appearance does not show that they are anything, even less what they are.

Most of all kings and nobles look somewhat similar, but their finery may have much to do with that. It plays a much smaller part in old portraits, one was not ashamed at that time of one's characteristic ugliness. Of course one has to take the painter into consideration. In some pictures easy to see how he spoils a face.

The great heroes often have children's faces, like Nelson and Wolfe. The truly heroic expressions in the tradition of the Zeus of Phidias belong to artists, Lord Leighton, Tennyson, Bulwer. Actors somehow lack independence. Least of all can be seen in the faces of great doctors and natural scientists, only Darwin has a gloriously idiosyncratic physiognomy, but not that of a research scientist. Philosophers are mostly emaciated, the abstract is visible. Locke, even Newton.

Only in one face Sydney Smith does humour form the content both of the features as also of the life and the work. Matros [?] Fox has an unbelievably mean physiognomy. Pitt a real king's face, more like a king than the Georges, something like Emperor Josef—

Castlereagh the great resemblance to the young Bonaparte.

William III clever and perverse like Walter Fürst. Conspicuous the beauty of some generals: Marlborough. Nobles have the best faces.

It is natural that people's appearance only shows the degree of their gross sublimation: philosophers, clergy, not doctors and scholars who may gain gross satisfaction from their work.

Face is race, family and constitutional predisposition, of which only the last factor is interesting, actually mostly raw material, there is too little in it of experience, least of all of choice of career.

Seems that hero and conqueror natures must frequently content themselves with becoming writers and artists because they find no way open.

Born writers seem to be those who remained childish: Goldsmith, Shelley.—Mill & Pope animated clergymen's faces—asexual—

Famous women plain on principle.—The European types obviously recur everywhere. Lord Leighton—very similar to Krafft-Ebing.

—Only humour betrays itself in the features, seems constitutional. Scholars and scientists so frequently completely insignificant.

Shakespeare is a typical head like Homer—Gomperz—Em. Loewy—Hartel—Socrates.

Some people look completely original, only like themselves.

Nicholas Bacon is a brutally jovial acromegalic.

Byron obviously took care dressing himself up.

Background to the "Notes on Faces and Men"

London is so vast a subject of study, that any unaided attempt to explore its intricate thoroughfares, and visit the many objects of interest, occasions considerable expense and a great loss of time.[2]

"If you take a walk through the streets of London," Freud wrote, "you will find, in front of one of the great railway termini, a richly carved Gothic column—Charing Cross." This sounds like the beginning of a guidebook, but the sentence comes from the first Clark University lecture of 1909 and the subject was memory. Freud went on to compare Charing Cross and "the Monument" in the City to memory's symbols. The hysteric, he added, is like a Londoner who still weeps on seeing these representations of past disasters, for "*hysterical patients suffer from reminiscences.*"[3]

Every city is haunted by past traumas commemorated by monuments, though their architecture is no more static than the memories themselves. The original Charing Cross was, in fact, destroyed in 1647, and an inexact replica erected in 1863: in the inscription on the Monument, a section blaming the great fire of 1666 on a "Popish faction" was erased in 1830. Londoners pay little attention to these relics. It is the tourist with a guidebook and no other business to distract his attention from history, and especially the solitary tourist, who is the nearest equivalent to the exemplary hysteric.

In September 1908 Freud visited London for the first time. He spent a week there, walking its streets and parks, visiting museums, and writing letters home in which he described the city and its inhabitants, detailed his expenses and his travel plans, and repeatedly complained about his solitude. But London was not to blame, he added, for the fact that the only person he might have visited there was not there at the time. He did not name that person, but a previous letter from Manchester noted he would not be seeing his nephew John, who was away on a journey. Perhaps John had moved to London: at any rate, Freud's Manchester letter is the last mention of his name.[4]

The mystery of John's disappearance from his uncle's life—and, it seems, from the face of the earth—is a curious footnote to Freud's relationship with England, or even with other people in general. For John was a key figure in the infantile memories Freud examined in his self-analysis during the 1890s: he was the first playmate and rival, a precursor of Freud's future need for both a close friend and an enemy.[5]

John's absence (or whoever else's it might have been) left Freud alone with memories, the city's and his own. The two cannot always be distinguished, even though this was his first visit. A place is a culture, and Freud had been in contact with the idea of England ever since his family's diaspora. The first documentation of that contact, and his first known piece of writing, is a letter of around 1863, written when he was seven, to Manchester, and it is a reply to a (lost) letter from John. He was glad to receive that letter, Freud wrote, but unfortunately he did not understand any of it. (Probably his former playmate/rival was again demonstrating his superiority, by writing in English.) The reply was addressed not to John but to his father, Emanuel. Freud thus surmounted his ignorance by transferring his attention and affections from the son to the father, an act of *Aufhebung*, or abrogation, equivalent to sublimation.[6]

In early September 1908 Freud had spent a week with Emanuel, who was twenty-three years older than he—a benevolent half-brother, half-father. After this stay in the north of England where he had all the comfort and company he could wish for, the solitude of London was a shock, and on September 12 he suffered a bad attack of homesickness. However, the following day he had recovered and enjoyed a long walk through Hyde Park. His account in a letter home indiscriminately blends past and present, real lives and monuments: it mentions the fairy-tale beauty of the English babies and the equally fabulous ugliness of their nurses, and describes the Albert Memorial with its petrified symbols of the arts and sciences. Freud also noted the nearby obelisk honoring John Hanning Speke, the discoverer of the source of the Nile. Had he not once, in "The Aetiology of Hysteria," referred to his own "discovery of a *caput Nili* [Nile source] in neuropathology," namely, the pathological effect of infant sexual experience?[7]

The letter of September 13, with this lighthearted guide to Hyde Park, may have been written around midday, before the visit to the National Portrait Gallery. Like the Albert Memorial that morning, the gallery was another sort of "memory theatre," in this instance, a specifically British one. Freud's only record of his visit consists of the one and a half pages of jotted notes, translated above; their chief aim seems to be to fit the features of particular portraits into generic groups or types.

Then, as today, the National Portrait Gallery was divided into historical periods and occupations. Thus military leaders or rulers or men of letters each have their separate rooms; this may well have given Freud the idea of identifying common factors in their appearance. The gallery was intended to depict the evolution of a nation, and when it was founded in 1856 (the year of Freud's birth), it was planned as a visual archive of British history. Artistic excellence was not a criterion in the selection, and as Freud remarks: "In certain pictures it is easy to see how he [the artist] spoils a face." But this was not the main hindrance to his classificatory purposes. Even if one otherwise disregards, as Freud did, the artistic conventions that necessarily intervene between object and viewer, any attempt to relate dynamic psychology to a static portrait goes against the grain. Consequently, his observations blend psychoanalytic categories with biological generic classification.

Sublimation and character typology are two clear themes that give structure to the apparently haphazard notes. This raises the question of why they were never to be used or further elaborated. Among several probabilities, one is that those themes fed into other work of that period, most notably " 'Civilized' Sexual Morality and Modern Nervous Illness," but also "Jensen's *Gradiva*," "Leonardo da Vinci," and "Character and Anal Eroticism," or, conversely, that they were derived from previous work, such as *Three Essays on the Theory of Sexuality*. Another likely reason is that the notes are too specific to the gallery. Moreover, they would have been hard to write up without further reference to the portraits, and it was to be another thirty years before Freud returned to London. A third reason, already indicated, is that any potential narrative linking static appearance and a developmental view of character involves a clash of classification systems. Added to the unresolved conceptual structure, there is the possible complication of unresolved transference to the portraits.

This final conjecture can best be illustrated by reference to two extraordinary faces that caught Freud's attention, in part because neither seemed to fit its type. The first was the Chandos portrait of Shakespeare (catalogue no. 1 in the collection's listing), which is the subject of Freud's first note: "Shakespeare looks completely exceptional, completely unenglish—Jacques-Pierre." This is also the opening note of a theme that later involved Freud more deeply, namely, the identity of "the Stratford man." But at this point, in 1908, the question is primarily one of typology—Shakespeare looks "unenglish." "Jacques-Pierre" refers to a conjecture that the name had a French origin, thus recuperating Shakespeare for mainland Europe.[8]

Despite his Anglophilia and his naturalized relatives, Freud still regarded the English as foreigners, and consequently in some respect inaccessible. In Hyde Park that Sunday morning, he had been, very sympathetically, observing them and their habits; his attentiveness to national traits, or their absence, continued in the portrait gallery that afternoon. Because Shakespeare was so much a part of his culture, like Goethe or Heine, one can understand this effort to recuperate him for

Europe. A subsequent note refers to the "European type" in implicit contradistinction to an English or Celtic one. This racial physiology can be seen in a later note on Shakespeare, in which he is typecast among ancient Greeks, a Jewish archaeologist, an Austrian minister of education, and a Greek scholar, thus bringing him squarely into the European fold: "Shakespeare is a typical head like Homer—Gomperz—Em. Loewy—Hartel—Socrates." Since "head" (*Kopf*) also denotes a thinker and these are intellectuals, here cranial form is, apparently, linked to a character configuration or predisposition.[9]

This Europeanized Shakespeare foreshadows the figure who was eventually to become Freud's favorite candidate for the Bard's title: Edward de Vere, seventeenth earl of Oxford. As a courtier and scion of the old Anglo-Norman nobility, de Vere seemed a far more cultured, cosmopolitan, and, above all, accessible figure than the enigmatic Stratford burgher. Here one should note the similarity of this maneuver of cultural recuperation with that performed upon Moses. In place of a primitive and tribal original, Freud was to substitute a cultured aristocrat. The motive for the substitution in both instances appears similar—the intellect, which is to be granted primacy, must be represented by a cultured individual who has sublimated his drives.

During his walks round London, Freud, like most good tourists, visited Westminster Abbey. There, at the tomb of Elizabeth I, he was led to consider a Shakespearean problem—the psychological inconsistencies in *Macbeth* which he thought connected both Macbeth and his wife to their common historical prototype, Queen Elizabeth. Part of this question was debated in "Those Wrecked by Success" (*Some Character-Types Met with in Psychological Work*, 1916). Another part had biographical implications—how would the Stratford commoner have had any contact with, or knowledge of, the queen's character? A book he read in the 1920s, J. Thomas Looney's *"Shakespeare" Identified in Edward de Vere, the Seventeenth Earl of Oxford*, seemed to provide the answer. But, Freud conceded, in the end ". . . we stand in the same relation to people of past times as we do to dreams to which we have been given no associations."[10]

The other extraordinary face was Charles Darwin's: "Least of all can be observed in the faces of great doctors and natural scientists, only Darwin has a gloriously individual physiognomy, but not that of a research scientist [*Forscher*]." A subsequent note attempts to indicate why, in general, doctors and scientists are so nondescript: "It is natural that people's appearance shows nothing except the degree of their gross sublimation: philosophers, clergy, not doctors and scholars who may gain gross satisfaction from their work." One corollary of this note appeared in the *Three Essays on the Theory of Sexuality:*

> What we describe as a person's "character" is built up to a considerable extent from the material of sexual excitations and is composed of instincts that have been fixed since childhood, of constructions achieved by means of sublimation, and of other constructions, employed for effectively holding in check perverse impulses which have been recognized as being unutilizable.[11]

The implication of Freud's gallery note may be that religion and philosophy offer no practical outlet for instinctual energy; hence the continual effort of sublimation leaves the greatest physical trace. On the other hand, since the activity of doctors and scientists or scholars allows part of the instinctual energy to attach itself to an object in the world, their less laborious sublimation leaves little visible trace. All of this raises the incidental question of how sublimation relates to repression and whether repression, too, is physically represented, for the notes refer only to sublimation as the factor that forms individual features.

Also, sublimation works within the confines of a genetically and racially determined conformation: "Face is race, family and constitutional predisposition, of which only the last factor is of interest, actually chiefly as raw material, there is too little in it of experience, least of all of the choice of career." This comment, coming more than halfway through the jottings, seems to be the result of viewing several rooms of the gallery (maybe all of it, if the notes were jotted down afterward) without arriving at any general connection between face and occupation.

The notes interweave different lines of thought. For example, kings and nobles are similar ("but their finery may be to blame for that"), and this reemerges later as "Nobles have the best faces." Or some early comments on childishness and heroic faces are taken up again in a remark on the conspicuous beauty of some military leaders, like Marlborough. The themes of beauty, heroism, and childishness are a sort of secondary, conceptual revision of the morning's walk in Hyde Park, with its heroic monuments and its fairy-tale babies and nurses. However, and more importantly, they reflect aspects of sublimation. Some of the most marked occupational genotypes are those where sublimation appears to be a concomitant of severe repression. The emaciation of abstract thought marks Locke and Newton: Mill and Pope have asexual, "priestly" expressions. But beauty and childishness may be products of a career that stems directly from infantile fantasies, as in the case of poets (Shelley and Goldsmith) or military leaders (Nelson and Wolfe). For the fulfillment of infantile fantasies means happiness, and that entails less distortion of the constitutional predisposition than more convoluted combinations of sublimation and repression. It is also interesting that writers and heroes merge in three heroic faces: Lord Leighton, Tennyson, and Bulwer-Lytton. Here for once the influence of artistic convention is invoked, for the three are compared to Phidias's Zeus; Freud does not, however, mention that the portraits cited are all by G. F. Watts and were executed in the Victorian pseudoclassical manner.[12]

The sharp contrast between the childish or heroic poets and the nondescript doctors and scientists has undertones of an early conflict in Freud's life over his choice of career. It was during his first stay in England in 1875, when he was a young student, that he reconsidered his previous ideal of pure research. On September 9, 1875, a letter to his friend Eduard Silberstein documented the change:

> Who knows, dear friend, but that after I have completed my studies a favorable wind might not blow me across to England for practical work. Let me confess to you: I now have more than one ideal, a practical one having been added to the theoretical one of earlier years. Had I been asked last year what was my dearest wish, I would have replied: a laboratory and free time, or a ship on the ocean with all the instruments a scientist needs; now I waver about whether I should not rather say: a large hospital and plenty of money in order to reduce or wipe out some of the ills that afflict our body. [. . .] A respected man, supported by the press and the rich, could do wonders in alleviating physical ills, if only he were enough of an explorer to strike out on new therapeutic paths.[13]

Perhaps Freud was influenced by the impressions of his relatives who had "made good" in England. Even his ambivalent description of his nephew John as "an Englishman in every respect, with a knowledge of languages and technical matters well beyond the usual business education," is tinged with approval, and in general letters show that he respected the practical lives of the Manchester Freuds. Meanwhile, he himself still had nothing but his fantasies.

Above all, though, it was probably admiration for the British scientific tradition that had inclined him away from pure research in favor of a more socially useful career. The philosophy he was reading that year under Franz Brentano's guidance reinforced this inclination, for his letter to Silberstein comments: "I am more suspicious than ever of philosophy." And the letter listed a British role of honor, of scientists who had become his models—"Tyndall, Huxley, Lyell, Darwin, Thomson [later Lord Kelvin], Lockyer, et al."

When Freud entered the National Portrait Gallery on September 13, 1908, he was walking into this aspect of his own history, as well as that of England's. Many other portraits also featured prominently in his personal pantheon; as a young man he had read Lord Macaulay with pleasure and John Stuart Mill with respect. During his engagement to Martha Bernays, he wrote of his love for Milton's *Paradise Lost* and spoke of the Puritan revolution as the period of world history that most interested him, and he was later to express his admiration for Cromwell by naming his second son Oliver.[14] All these faces, and those of other eminent literary and scientific figures, made the gallery Freud wandered through in September 1908 into a particularly evocative memory theater. Past ambitions or distant dreams of adventure may be revived by the sight of previous heroes. Such memories might underlie the implicit question in these notes about the nature of literature and science: the childishness and heroism of poets contrasts sharply with the nondescript quality of the doctors and scientists. The portraits represent epistemologies.

Freud's great precursor Darwin, alone among the faceless scientists, is "idiosyncratic," and there is nothing childish about Shakespeare, "the great psychologist."[15] Separately, their portraits represent an unresolved conflict between the narratives of memory and the laws of science; together, their presence in these notes forms a sort of hybrid image or condensation of those two problematical fundamentals.

A face is always an interface or conjunction of mind and body. "Face is race, family and constitutional predisposition . . .": this note brings genetic factors to the fore, leaving little room in the picture for mental activity. If "constitution" is the mind's biological base, "predisposition" is that part of it affected by life's experiences: the term "constitutional predisposition" thus encapsulates an uneasy blend of biology and psychology.

Insofar as they attempt to bridge the gap between appearance and experience, these notes seem like a theoretical throwback. Once psychoanalysis had adopted narrative strategies, the dynamic complexity of recounted memory and experience progressively reduced the relevance of static physical typologies. Thus the notes remained marginal and unpublished, another abandoned project. However, certain themes they sketched, such as the physical traces of sublimation, persisted. In London again, thirty years later and just after completing his curious "historical novel" *Moses and Monotheism*, Freud supposedly remarked to Salvador Dalí, "Moses is flesh of sublimation."[16] But the phrase is cryptic, the authority for it doubtful, and the question of its significance must remain hanging, like the notes and their portraits.

Portrait of a Dream Reader[1]

John Forrester

THE INTERPRETATIONS OF DREAMS, Freud wrote in 1931, "contains the most valuable of all the discoveries it has been my good fortune to make. Insight such as this falls to one's lot but once in a lifetime."[2] Critics and admirers agree.[3] What are the ingredients of *The Interpretation of Dreams* that convince everyone of its importance?

The Interpretation of Dreams is many things: a scholarly treatise, an ingenious yet lucid set of rules for interpreting dreams, a bold scientific theory of dreams upon which is built a revolutionary psychology of the unconscious. But it is also a window on the inner life of its author and an intimate diary of the life and work of a cultured Jewish physician living in fin-de-siècle Vienna, who records with irony and humor the private lives of his cultivated and witty patients as well as his own. In an imperfectly though deliberately disguised manner, it charts an adventure, a quest in search of a scientific Holy Grail that will make its discoverer rich, honored, and famous forever. And finally, in prose of immense distinction, with its asides and reflections on the foibles, failings, and deep motivations of all human beings, it belongs to the tradition of moralist essays. *The Interpretation of Dreams* is all these things, yet it is also something more: it is the founding document of a new scientific movement much as, forty years before, Darwin's *Origin of Species* was.

Freud recognized these many facets and the tensions between them:

For this book has a further subjective significance for me personally—a significance which I only grasped after I had completed it. It was, I found, a portion of my own self-analysis, my reaction to my father's death—that is to say, to the most important event, the most poignant loss, of a man's life. Having discovered that this was so, I felt unable to obliterate the traces of the experience. To my readers, however, it will be a matter of indifference upon what material they learn to value and interpret dreams.[4]

However autobiographical it may be, Freud claims, the book is still a work of science: the attendant personal dimension of the dreams and their analyses can be discounted by Freud's readers without loss of substance.

"How," Jacques Derrida astutely asks, "can an autobiographical writing, in the abyss of an unterminated self-analysis, give birth to a world-wide institution?"[5] In complete contrast to the posture of indifference toward the author that Freud recommends a reader should adopt, there is an opposed view, which recognizes that precisely because the book is "a portion of my own self-analysis," it is exemplary and originary of psychoanalysis itself: the first self-analysis in history, and the epitome of all analyses.[6] The dream book functions for the reader in much the same way as do all first-order scientific achievements, as described by Thomas Kuhn: as a paradigm or, better, as an exemplar of method, theory, and even of the inner life.[7]

If, as many analysts claim, true self-analysis is impossible, then who was Freud's analyst? The two most obvious candidates are Wilhelm Fliess and Freud's patients (a collective analyst). Most have assumed that Freud's analysis was achieved through his intense friendship with Fliess, conducted primarily in Freud's letters to his "sole audience" in Berlin and supplemented by their occasional meetings. Freud's analysis was, as he himself described it in *The Interpretation of Dreams*, published at the end of 1899, based in part upon the methodical transcription of his dreams, which was meant for Fliess's eyes only.[8] All through 1897, the letters to Fliess are brimming with advances in clinical and theoretical ideas, confessions of his dreams and his childhood, complaints about his body, and stories of his family. Then, in December of that year, Freud starts to write to Fliess in a new genre: "the Dr[eckology] [Shitology], in which I now deposit my novelties."[9] Included in the "Dreckology" were dreams, which Freud asked Fliess to return so that they could be inserted, probably with little emendation, in the dream book.

In this way, the hypothesis that Fliess was Freud's analyst inexorably leads one to posit that every reader slips into Fliess's reading chair and becomes Freud's analyst. To be this analyst is to be the object of a transference, whose traces can be detected in the manner in which the writer invokes and calls upon Fliess's shade—the reader. The most telling pointer is the concept and function of the censor. The idea of the censor, so central to Freud's theory of the dream, developed hand in hand with Fliess's interventions qua censor in the composition of Freud's first draft in the spring of 1898. The first hint of the idea of censorship is the graphic and textual "Russian censorship" of foreign newspapers as they crossed the border in December 1897: "Words, whole clauses and sentences are blacked out so that the rest becomes unintelligible."[10] By May 1898 Freud was writing at high speed, sending two chapters to Fliess in less than three weeks, with Fliess now firmly in place as the author's, if not yet the dreamer's, omnipotent censor:

> I shall change whatever you want and gratefully accept contributions. I am so immensely glad that you are giving me the gift of the Other, a critic and reader—and one of your quality at that. I cannot write entirely without an audience, but do not at all mind writing only for you.[11]

At the congress Freud and Fliess held in early June, Fliess decisively exerted his influence by censoring from the manuscript of the dream book the one completely analyzed dream of Freud's, which brought the latter's writing to a standstill; he was still "mourning the lost dream"[12] in October 1898. By December 1898 Freud had decided to brave the dream literature; in May 1899 he was still dithering, but later that month he suddenly set to with eagerness and renewed confidence. A substantially revised structure of the book emerged, and from then on Freud wrote fluently and with great confidence; he sent the first section to the printer at the end of June. Throughout the summer, he sent chapter after chapter in manuscript, and then in proof, alternately to the printer and to the censor, confessing that Fliess's wielding of the red pen was necessary because he had "lost the feeling of shame required of an author"[13] and had thus lost control of the dialectic of revealing and concealing that formed one of the principal axes of the dream book's plot. This dialectic had initially been played out with Fliess first as object of reverence and of sustenance—and later, implicitly, of criticism and contempt—and then as censor of Freud's excessive self-revelations.

Why was it necessary for Freud to reveal himself to his readers? Because his patients' dreams were, he somewhat unconvincingly claimed, marred by the presence of neurotic features.

> But if I was to report my own dreams, it inevitably followed that I should have to reveal to the public gaze more of the intimacies of my mental life than I liked, or than is normally necessary for any writer who is a man of science and not a poet. Such was the painful but unavoidable necessity; and I have submitted to it rather than totally abandon the possibility of giving the evidence for my psychological findings. Naturally, however, I have been unable to resist the temptation of taking the edge off some of my indiscretions by omissions and substitutions.[14]

In this way, the book opens with the dialectic of the dreamer reluctantly revealing himself despite himself, with the reader consequentially invited to be curious and critical, prurient and censorious, all at once. The indiscreet dreamer (Freud) and the censorious critic (Fliess) are immediately brought onstage as the principal actors in the book itself.

At the opening of chapter 2 of the book—the crucial moment prefacing Freud's emergence as the main protagonist of his own book—the plea concerning his unwilling entry into the spotlight and the necessity of entrusting himself to the discretion of the reader is restated, this time more forcefully:

> There is some natural hesitation about revealing so many intimate facts about one's mental life; nor can there be any guarantee against misinterpretation by strangers.[15]

And the powerful theatrical effect that will, finally, justify this self-exposure is now revealed:

> And now I must ask the reader to make my interests his own
> for quite a while, and to plunge, along with me, into the minut-
> est details of my life; for a transference of this kind is peremp-
> torily demanded by our interest in the hidden meaning of
> dreams.[16]

Here, finally, is the bait—and the hook—by which the reader becomes
interested in, fascinated by, engaged with Freud's book: he[17] is
requested to *transfer* onto the dreamer portrayed in the book. The
structure of Freud's sentence acknowledges that the reader must give
up something—his own interests—in order to then take on something
else—Freud's interests. Freud makes it clear that the reader will be led
not only to the *general* problems of dreams but also to *specific* ones—
through his own dreams. The reader will thus, by passing relatively
rapidly through the stage of curiosity over Freud's indiscretions,
become a Freudian—someone who reads his own dreams like Freud
did his.[18]

Like that other model of skillfully crafted, semiautobiographical
scientific advocacy, Darwin's *Origin of Species*, Freud's first priority was
to elicit and then meet his reader's skeptical responses to a bold theory.
He forestalls the criticisms by voicing them on the reader's behalf. The
censor and the censored keep on changing places. The strategy is quite
deliberate: the entire architecture of the book expresses this principal
thesis. Consider: Having agreed to accompany Freud on his "imaginary walk,"[19] having been led along the "concealed pass" of the specimen dream of chapter 2 (the famous dream of Irma's injection),[20] "all at
once" the reader, together with Freud, contemplates the "finest
prospects" that "open up on every side,"[21] armed with the basic finding
supplied by the dream: "When the work of interpretation has been
completed, we perceive that a dream is the fulfillment of a wish."[22] But
the promised goal recedes; "concealment," not steady candor, "provides the drama of the dream book," as Alexander Welsh notes.[23]
Chapter 3 attempts to confirm that wish fulfillment is the universal
characteristic of dreams using reasonably transparent dreams, including a number from children. These dreams set an engaging tone, as do
the dreams of convenience: the medical student who oversleeps and
dreams he is already in the hospital, the newly married woman who
dreams she is having her period so as to postpone the responsibilities
of motherhood. But Freud knows full well that their charm is not suffi-

cient to establish the thesis or to lull his critic: nor does he wish them to. He *needs* the skeptical critic, his reader, to be vigilant so that he will become embroiled in the next step of the argument.

Thus Freud opens chapter 4, "Distortion in Dreams," with a very different welcome for the reader.

> If I proceed to put forward the assertion that the meaning of *every* dream is the fulfilment of a wish, that is to say that there cannot be any dreams but wishful dreams, I feel certain in advance that I shall meet with the most categorical contradiction.[24]

You, the reader, are *certain* to deny me! There then follows a long paragraph in quotation marks in which the critic voices his categorical contradiction. Even when the "natural" voice of Freud finally emerges from outside the quotation marks, it confesses that "anxiety-dreams make it impossible to assert as a general proposition that dreams are wish-fulfilments; indeed they seem to stamp any such proposition as an absurdity."[25]

Yet Freud has not lost his battle; far from it—he has simply opened up the terrain on which he will win over the skeptical critic. All he has to do is to make a distinction, here for the first time in the book, between the *manifest* and the *latent* content of the dream; the reader's critical objection is left high and dry, tilting at the windmill of the manifest, while Freud can consolidate his discoveries by bringing to light the mysteries of the latent content. With the distinction between latent and manifest, he repeats the founding act of splitting in the writing of his dream book, between dream and interpretation, between writer and censor, between discretion and exposure. With the idea of "latency," Freud both specifies the object of interpretation—the interpreter is seeking what is latent, not what is manifest—and firmly establishes the sense of ever-present secrecy which is such a seductive feature of the reader's progress through the book. Like Sigmund Freud, who dreamed of erecting a plaque at Bellevue, "where the secret of dreams revealed itself"[26] to him, each reader will go in search of the secret not only of the dream but also, through the "transference peremptorily demanded" of him, of Sigmund Freud and, beyond him, of his own inner dream life.

The idea of the latent is then explored through the analysis of another of Freud's dreams, a dream whose fundamental feature was the dreamer's struggle to conceal from *himself* his contemptuous judgment of a friend as a simpleton. Disguise in dreams—the very principle of latency—amounts to a defensive distortion, entirely analogous to the dissimulation practiced in everyday social life by a person in the presence of someone with power over him. Freud drives the point home: "When I interpret my dreams for my readers I am obliged to adopt similar distortions,"[27] indicating how he, too, adopts a disguise in the face of the all-powerful and censorious reader. Here we come upon that fundamental posture of the Freudian in relation to the world so aptly described by Paul Ricoeur: "As a man of desires I go forth in disguise."[28] But the very act of disguise and dissimulation itself is two-sided: I dissimulate for the *others*, but I find a way of making the secret available for *your* eyes only. "The stricter the censorship, the more far-reaching will be the disguise and the more ingenious too may be the means employed for putting the reader on the scent of the true meaning."[29] The reader switches, from paragraph to paragraph, from being the censor from whom the truth must be hidden to being Freud's complicit partner in seeking, and then hiding, the secret truths of the adept. What is bad news for one party to the power struggle, for instance, a censoring governmental agency, will be good news for the insurrectionists plotting in disguise. In this way, the anxiety dream of those in power is identical with the wish fulfillment of those under their thumb.[30]

Throughout the book, Freud plays a game of hide-and-seek with the reader, revealing his innermost secrets and then arbitrarily, though with apparent reluctance, closing the door. The whole strategy of dream analysis is an implementation of techniques of circumventing censorship. This dialectic of the secret wish striving for expression and the censorship ensuring its suppression is played out between dreamer and every reader, who is invited to follow in Fliess's footsteps:

> The first reader and critic of this book—and his successors are likely to follow his example—protested that "the dreamer seems to be too ingenious and amusing." This is quite true so long as it refers only to the dreamer; it would only be an objection if it were to be extended to the dream-interpreter. In waking reality I have little claim to be regarded as a wit. If my dreams seem amusing, that is not on my account, but on

account of the peculiar psychological conditions under which dreams are constructed; and the fact is intimately connected with the theory of the jokes and the comic. Dreams become ingenious and amusing because the direct and easiest pathway to the expression of their thoughts is barred: they are forced into being so. The reader can convince himself that my patients' dreams seem at least as full of jokes and puns as my own, or even fuller.[31]

Such passages, preempting the reader's response, link him in a chain with the first reader and invite him to inspect his own dreams: "Actual experience would teach them better," Freud remarks later in the book.[32] We know with what determination Freud rose to the challenge of Fliess the skeptical censor; he wrote a whole book, *Jokes and Their Relation to the Unconscious*, to "refute," or at least lay to rest, the implicit charge of the overingenuity of the dream interpreter.

However, the true skeptic, immune to the pleasures of collusive complicity, is still waiting for a reply. It is to silence this skeptic that Freud introduces a third party—the clever, wily, and skeptical patient who, in the course of Freud's psychoanalytic interpretations, subjects him to "a remorseless criticism, certainly no less severe than I have to expect from the members of my own profession. And my patients invariably contradict my assertion that all dreams are fulfilments of wishes."[33] So, for the first time in the dream book, the patient occupies center stage. He—or rather she, since Freud's most sympathetically, and thus critically, intelligent patients were women—does so as principal critic, insistently asking: "How do you fit that in with your theory?"[34] The "cleverest of all my dreamers"[35] dreamed of spending her holiday near her hated mother-in-law:

The dream showed that I was wrong [about the nature of dreams]. *Thus it was her wish that I might be wrong, and her dream showed that wish fulfilled.* But her wish that I might be wrong related in fact to [my inference that] at a particular period of her life something must have occurred that was of importance in determining her illness. She had disputed this, since she had no recollection of it; but soon afterwards it had turned out that I was right. Thus her wish that I might be wrong, which was transformed into her dream of spending her holidays with her mother-in-law, corresponded to a well-justified wish that the events of which she was then becoming aware for the first time might never have occurred.[36]

This is the model for Freud's answer to his critic's categorical contradiction: every such contradiction is not only a refutation of his theory but embodies the *wish* that he might be wrong. In this way, every possible criticism of the theory is undercut.[37]

In 1909 and then in 1911, Freud supplemented his account of these dreams by calling them "counter-wish dreams" (*Gegenwünschträume*), dreams elicited by a person's first contact with psychoanalysis—we might also call them *GegenFreudträume*.

> I can count almost certainly on provoking one of them after I have explained my theory that dreams are fulfilments of wishes to a patient for the first time or to people who have heard me lecturing. Indeed, it is to be expected that the same thing will happen to some of the readers of the present book; they will be quite ready to have one of their wishes frustrated in a dream if only their wish that I may be wrong can be fulfilled.[38]

What is so important about this strategic argument of Freud's is that it finally places the reader in the position of the *patient*, dreaming refutations of Freud's theory. The patient—and now the reader—is always (in resistance) a counter-wisher. On one side of this staged confrontation between interpreter and skeptic there is the reader, easily provoked into a bloody-minded refusal of Freud's arguments and interpretations.[39]

> The layman asks: "Where is the wish-fulfilment?" And instantly, having heard that dreams are supposed to be wish-fulfilments, and in the very act of asking the question, he answers it with a rejection.[40]

On the other side, fully prepared, there is not only the wily interpreter but also the wily dreamer, Freud dreaming dreams and their solutions to order as he wrote the book. The willfulness of Freud, the theoretician of the dream whose dreams become nothing but theory, is thus the match of the willful reader, whose first impulse on reading Freud's book, on hearing him speak, will be to dream a refutation of him. They make a right pair, it would seem. Indeed, that is the strategy of Freud's writing: they *are* a right pair.

There are two diametrically opposed ways of characterizing this process of identification and transference between Freud and his reader, between desirer and censor. The first sees the *autobiographical* dreamer and writer as the central protagonist of the dream book, and thus views the reader's involvement with "Freud" as a form of personal and intimate seduction in which the reader and author perform Freud's perfectly choreographed dance of disclosure and withdrawal. The second way of characterizing the reader's involvement with the dream book is as a process of confirming, or being convinced of, the *scientific*, as opposed to the autobiographical, truth of the theories advanced in the book. Freud's scientific strategy in this respect is resolutely universalistic: the propositions he advances are only important insofar as they have the form "All X's are Y's"—all dreams are wish fulfillments.

Freud's was never a statistical sensibility, despite the rise of statistical thinking in the late nineteenth and early twentieth centuries, particularly in the burgeoning human sciences.[41] A statistical law would not be serious science for Freud. He took it as an axiom that if one could find meaning in *one* dream, then it was methodologically justified to treat *all* dreams as meaningful. Even more boldly, he assumed that if one could discover the truths of the unconscious in one subject, for example, the "author" of this book, those truths would hold for all humans. Freud assumed that one dreamer stood for all dreamers, just as contemporary physicists might assume that one substance subject to gravity may stand for all substances, or biologists might assume that one sample of hemoglobin may stand for all samples, unlike those biometricians or statisticians whose object of study was the very diversity of characteristics in a field of phenomena.

The psychoanalytic axiom is: "Understanding of myself is both necessary and sufficient to understanding someone, anyone. And you, dear reader, do likewise, by understanding me." We can gauge his own sense of the actual reader of *The Interpretation of Dreams* from the preface to the second edition of 1909,[42] which asserted that *The Interpretation of Dreams* had not been, and by implication would never be, read and understood by "the professional circles to whom my original preface was addressed"—"my psychiatric colleagues," "the professional philosophers," and the "reviewers." Nor do Freud's "gallant supporters" count as the target readership. So who did count as the readership of his dream book? Only the common readers, "a wider circle of educated and curious-minded readers," constitute the appreciative and approved readership of his book. Only the dreamers, the potential patients, the potential autoanalysts, the potential Freudians count.

> The interpretation of dreams is in fact the royal road to a knowledge of the unconscious; it is the securest foundation of psycho-analysis and the field in which every worker must acquire his convictions and seek his training. If I am asked how one can become a psycho-analyst, I reply: "By studying one's own dreams."

So wrote Freud in 1909, addressing the first grand public of psychoanalysis, in Worcester, Massachusetts. He always retained his sympathy for mavericks, self-taught analysts, the lone dream analyst:[43] his ideal reader may be entirely at odds with the institutions of psychoanalysis, but as long as he plants himself firmly on the privileged terrain of self-analysis, i.e., dreams, he will very likely turn out a better Freudian than otherwise. The true Freudians, the backbone of the psychoanalytic movement, are Freud's readers, not the psychoanalysts. Freud has consistently been one of the best-selling mass paperback authors of nonfiction throughout the Western world in this century, and is still so today. Reading Freud is an obligatory passage point for entry into psychoanalysis.[44] It is this requirement of reading him that differentiates psychoanalysis from other international scientific, cultural, or political movements. Psychoanalysis is a scene of writing—as Derrida in 1965 acutely dubbed the psychoanalytic space of theory[45]—and, above all, of reading.

PART II

Interpretation, Suggestion, and Agency

FREUD SAW INTERPRETATION as a process of making sense of a person's present by exploring the disguised significance of the past, and especially by uncovering the conflicts arising out of that past. Psychoanalytic interpretation does not eliminate or even defuse conflict, but it does aim to make meaning out of a person's history, enabling him or her to better cope with the present. Interpretation begins with a sign or symptom, and makes sense of that sign by constructing its genealogy, hoping, by so doing, to bring meaning and direction to the present. This meaning and direction are at the core of Freud's understanding of freedom, a freedom that does not promise happiness but that does insist we acknowledge our powerful and conflicting desires. John E. Toews examines how Freud came to emphasize this acknowledgment in regard to the Oedipus complex. How do we come to be moral subjects who desire, and how do our desires both fuel and challenge our capacity as moral subjects? For Freud, as Toews emphasizes, we can achieve a kind of autonomy only within the context of modes of identification with others. Our moral independence is accomplished only through others. José Brunner explores how the Oedipus story works not only for the formation of the individual but also at the level of social relations. Brunner's Freud is a deeply political thinker; his theories address the deep structures and dynamics of power and authority. The family is an arena of power struggles, and psychoanalysis illuminates these struggles by being attuned to the multiplicity of ambivalences that arise from them. However, Brunner, like Toews, notes that Freud relied on a patriarchal understanding of power and autonomy that often reduced gendered complexity to masculinist norms.

Suggestion plays a key role in psychoanalytic thinking about both the achievement of moral autonomy and the dynamics of political struggle. Suggestion is another term for influence, but its connection to the force of hypnosis points to the fact that powerful influences are often unconscious. That's how hypnosis was said to work: under its spell, we cannot fight a suggestion of which we are unaware. As Harold P. Blum emphasizes, Freud moved away from this authoritarian use of suggestion and began to see this influence as something that itself had to be consciously analyzed. But how could any interpretation break out of the circle of suggestion? Wouldn't the analysand's transference of emotions onto the doctor and the analyst's countertransference of desires onto the patient always open new possibilities for suggestion to work in the most subtle ways? Blum sees Freud laboring against this kind of "contamination." Hannah S. Decker's essay on the Dora case shows Freud reflecting retrospectively on his own failure to be aware of how his patient's (and his own) emotions got in the way of understanding. Yet even as Freud acknowledged his mistakes, the psychoanalyst's reliance on patriarchal norms was never more clear than in this case study. As Decker's essay points out, Freud's "Dora" shows his increasing awareness of suggestion and transference in therapy, but it also displays his efforts to turn a failed therapeutic intervention into a successful case study. How, we might ask, is suggestion working from this text on us, its readers?

Having and Being

THE EVOLUTION OF FREUD'S OEDIPUS THEORY AS A MORAL FABLE

John E. Toews

ON OCTOBER 15, 1897, in the midst of a crisis of personal, professional, and cultural identity which had undermined Freud's previous theoretical assumptions and had turned him into his own most interesting patient, he wrote to his Berlin colleague and intimate confidant Wilhelm Fliess:

> Being totally honest with oneself is a good exercise. A single idea of general value dawned on me. I have found, in my case too, [the phenomenon of] being in love with my mother and jealous of my father, and I now consider it a universal event in early childhood. . . . If this is so, we can understand the gripping power of *Oedipus Rex*, in spite of all the objections that reason raises against the presupposition of fate; and we can understand why the later "drama of fate" was bound to fail so miserably. Our feelings arise against any arbitrary individual compulsion . . . but the Greek legend seizes upon a compulsion which everyone recognizes because he senses its existence within himself. Everyone in the audience was once a budding Oedipus in fantasy and each recoils in horror from the dream fulfillment here transplanted into reality, with the full quantity of repression which separates his infantile state from his present one.[1]

Almost a decade would pass before a fully developed theory of the Oedipus complex as the "nuclear complex" of the neuroses would appear in Freud's published work, and it was not until 1913 that he would venture the general claim that "the beginning of religion, morals, society and art all converge on the Oedipus complex."[2] Nevertheless, from its inception in the late 1890s, the story of Oedipus in the form of its Sophoclean dramatization provided the narrative, mythic frame for the distinctive psychoanalytic perspective on the impersonal, universal "fate" governing human existence.

According to a report of Freud's disciple and biographer Ernest Jones, Freud had identified himself in fantasy with the heroic Oedipus—who had divined the riddle of the Sphinx and saved the people of Thebes—at a time when he first began to imagine his life in terms of the calling of scientific research—the unriddling of the secrets of nature—during the early 1870s. In 1906 his first circle of disciples presented him with a birthday medallion portraying a bust of Freud confronting the Sphinx and inscribed with the words from *Oedipus Rex:* "Who knew the famous riddles and was a man most mighty." Freud had been overwhelmed by this uncanny return of his earlier fantasy, this mirroring back of the secrets of his vaulting ambition.[3] In the self-recognition of 1897, however, the earlier identification with the heroic Oedipus gained a new dimension. In the story of Oedipus Freud found a concrete narrative representation of the content of the riddle as well as an exemplar of the role of the riddle solver.

In the first published account of the psychoanalytic meaning of Oedipus, in *The Interpretation of Dreams*, both dimensions of this identification were displayed. Freud repeated the claims of the Fliess letter: the Oedipus story was so universally compelling because it presented us with a concrete representation of what we really were, of the elemental forces shaping our primal fate.

> His destiny moves us only because it might have been ours—because the oracle laid the same curse upon us before our birth as upon him. It is the fate of all of us perhaps to direct our first sexual impulse towards our mother and our first hatred and our first murderous wish against our father. Our dreams convince us that this is so. King Oedipus, who slew his father Laïus and married his mother Jocasta, merely shows the fulfillment of our own childhood wishes.[4]

However, this recognition of ourselves in the mirror of Oedipus is not simple or easy. We "shrink back" from it, Freud insists, "with the whole force of the repression by which those wishes have since that time been held down within us." We have forgotten, and remained ignorant of, the fate that has "been forced upon us by Nature" and is so "repugnant" to our moral values. In Sophoclean art, however, the ameliorating reconciliation with our fate through speech and narrative understanding is also articulated. In the symbolic representation of a "process of revealing" that Freud compares "to the work of the psychoanalyst," the poet "unravels the past, brings to light the guilt of Oedipus," thus "compelling us to recognize our inner minds in which these same impulses, though suppressed, are still to be found."[5] The Oedipus story seems to represent both the human moral problem and its possible resolution.

At first reading, Freud's original formulation of the psychoanalytic meaning of the Oedipal story may not seem particularly "moral" or easily definable as a "moral fable." In fact, the moral dimension of the Freudian version of the story seems primarily negative, a disconcerting demystification of moral assumptions by uncovering their all-too-human origins. We are all psychologically guilty of the horrendous crimes we find most abhorrent—incest and murder. Resistance to remembering and recognizing the story as our own is tied to its morally repugnant dimension, to the fact that it reveals to us our uncivilized, primal desires. At the same time, however, recognizing ourselves in Oedipus is something of an ethical achievement, an assumption of guilt and responsibility in the creation of human suffering, including our own. The story of Oedipus is not just a revelation of who we are beneath our moral armor but a story of how we have come into possession of that armor, and a story of how we may become wise in grasping not only our primitive and amoral but also our refined and moral identities.

Freud's moral animus in his accounts of the meaning of Oedipus in 1897 and 1899 seems directed primarily at a form of conventional moralizing exemplified by nineteenth-century bourgeois "fate dramas," in which the fate of the individual was attributed to the impotence of the human will in the face of external circumstance. The moral "solution" within this perspective could only be defined in "theological" or transcendent terms, through obedience to, or propitiation of, the will of the omnipotent "Other." Such dramas, Freud implies, do not correctly frame the moral problem of the relationship between human freedom and our common, and unavoidable, human "fate."

The central question is not so much one of the specific content of moral principles or rules as it is one of their origins, and thus of the grounds on which they are formulated and obeyed. The power of the Oedipus story is that it forces us to recognize the full scope of our ethical dilemma, and consequently of the only authentic or viable paths toward its possible "resolution."

The ethical or moral implications of Freud's "discovery," through self-recognition, of the meaning of the oedipal story emerge more clearly if it is placed in the context of the rather different story of our human fate which preceded it in Freud's intellectual development during the 1890s—the story of "seduction," or traumatic infantile sexual abuse. The Oedipus theory emerged from the abandoned ruins of the seduction theory, which, like the Oedipus theory, was also formulated in terms of a "story." In a lecture delivered to the Vienna Psychiatric and Neurological Association on April 21, 1896, just a year and a half before his announcement of the meaning of the Oedipus story to Fliess, Freud claimed he had uncovered the *caput Nili* (source of the Nile) of psychopathology in traumatic experiences of childhood sexual seduction. Freud claimed that in each of the eighteen cases of hysteria he had subjected to detailed analysis, his persistent, laborious method of memory reconstruction had culminated in the discovery of an originating, repressed, unconscious memory of infantile sexual trauma. Once this memory had been reconstructed, the story of the formation of the pathological symptoms became "self-evident," its inner "logic" coherent.[6] The repressed memory of the trauma could then be consciously integrated into the patient's life history, its pathological emotional charge dissolved. Once the traumatic occurrence—and the guilty party—were remembered and named, the patient could regain the narrative coherence and self-mastery of which she had been robbed.

The full articulation of the seduction theory was the culmination of years of clinical observation and theoretical labor, but just a few months after Freud announced it to his scientific peers, he began to have severe doubts about its validity. He ceased to believe that the evidence provided by his patients was a credible basis for reconstructing the reality of the histories of their suffering. "I no longer believe in my *neurotica*," he wrote to Fliess in September 1897.[7] Like a historical detective reading the evidence as clues pointing to an originating deed (the crime of seduction), Freud had read his patient's verbal and behavioral signs as representations of a reality that could be publicly acknowledged as "objective," a network of associative and causal linkages originating from the nucleus of the sexual trauma. Although the sequences of events that were set in motion by the traumatic experience might be psychic or "internal," they were imagined as occurring like any objective series of events that, in principle, could be reconstructed by a competent, disciplined observer. Although the historical "documents" provided by patients were fragmented, distorted, and full of gaps (resulting from the psychic resistances to conscious remembering of events originally forgotten because of their ego-threatening character), Freud was confident that it was possible to wring a residue of historical truth from the available clues. In the fall of 1897, however, he began to doubt that the dreams, fantasies, and symptoms of his patients referred to or represented, even in distorted form, this kind of historical reality. It was not that new evidence had turned up which contradicted his theory. Rather, Freud simply could not believe the evidence he possessed: he could not recognize himself anymore in these stories that he had worked so hard to reconstruct. Just prior to his revelation that everyone was "a budding Oedipus," he confessed he could not believe that everyone (and again this meant especially himself, his primary "patient") was a victim of acts of childhood seduction. In a retrospective account, Freud simply stated that once he ceased to trust the evidence on which he had grounded his belief in his historical reconstructions, the "floor" or "foundation" (*Boden*) of reality collapsed beneath his feet.[8]

Freud's abandonment of the seduction theory had significant ethical implications. The theory itself was defiantly scandalous; it blamed the sufferings of the younger generation on the secret sexual perversions of their hypocritical elders, on those who held power over their fate and who had betrayed their trust. It traced the source of human suffering to the acts of the powerful and absolved the victims of complicity in their fate. To know oneself and tell one's own story was in some sense an act of absolution. It was this reality that was shaken when Freud lost confidence in the seduction theory of the origin of the neuroses.

The displacement of the seduction theory by the Oedipus theory in 1897 was based not on new clinical evidence or the discovery of mistakes in logical deduction but on a new set of assumptions that informed Freud's reading of the evidence and his constructions of narrative and logical coherence. The shift in Freud's perspective was particularly evident in two areas—the construction of unconscious "psychic reality" as the particular domain or "continent" of psychoanalytic knowledge, and the definition of sexuality as the fundamental energy and agency of this unconscious psychic reality.

Both the existence of unconscious mental life and the priority given to sexuality in the development of that life preceded the oedipal theory. The seduction theory entailed the existence of a sequence of psychic events, repressed and forgotten, which were not directly accessible to the patient's consciousness. The evidence provided by the patient's symptoms, involuntary associations, hypnotic utterances, dreams, and fantasies needed to be read with interpretive ingenuity in order to reconstruct the internal psychic history of the memories that they represented only in distorted, fragmented, and indirect ways. Freud recognized that much of the material provided by his patients was "fictional" long before 1897, but he had remained confident of his ability to distinguish the core of authentic representation from imaginary constructions. When his faith in his ability to make this distinction between "true" and "fictional" representations collapsed in 1897, he turned his "defeat" into a "triumph"[9] by reading the fantasies and fictions as representations of the intentions that produced them, as "objectifications" of unconscious wishes: distorting mirrors of the internal formation of a psychic reality rather than obscured windows on a reality of external events. The evidence now became revelatory of a different kind of truth—the truth of the unconscious subject, the unconscious as intentional agency—rather than as a reservoir of memories of past events. The patient's ability to tell her own story now depended not so much on her recounting the truth about what had happened as on her ability to express who she was as a subject, to make her deepest intentions conscious and articulate without deception or guile. The meaning of the speeches and texts of the patient could now be reconstructed as representations of unconscious agency, or the unconscious "subject" that manifested itself through them. Freud remained true to his previously defined calling as a historian and archaeologist of psychic life. However, the history now at issue was the history of the formation of the unconscious (imagined as an intentional subject or agent despite the continuing use of the model of a mechanical apparatus) through the signs in which it inadvertently revealed its intentions.

Freud never denied that fantasies or dreams might have external reference, that they might in fact function at some level as representations of events external to the subject. Nevertheless, he did insist, with increasing self-confidence, that the "object" of psychoanalytic knowledge was the dynamic processes through which the unconscious assimilated experiences into its own structures of meaning and molded them into the shape of its own intentions and wishes. The consequences of this shift are strikingly displayed in the differences between the case studies published in *Studies on Hysteria* (1895) and "Dora," or "Fragment of an Analysis of a Case of Hysteria" (written in 1901, published in 1905). Whereas the patients of the *Studies* suffer from the consequences of repressed memories of traumatic events, Dora suffers primarily, in Freud's view, from the repression and denial of her own psychosexual desire. She is the agent of her own history, complicit in her own suffering; her cure cannot come from learning the truth of what happened to her, but only from speaking the truth about herself.

Recognition of the significance of sexuality, and especially of infantile sexual experience, in the history of neurotic suffering also preceded the discovery of the Oedipus complex. The scandal of the seduction theory derived precisely from its claim that neurotics suffered from the effects of infantile sexual experiences. But after 1897 Freud's focus shifted to the agency of the child as a sexual subject, to the originating role of infantile psychosexual "desire" in the formation of the human subject and its inner conflicts. The Freudian history of desire, however, is not a completely internal history. Sexual desire is shaped into an identity, constructed as the desire of an individual subject, in the context of the universally inhibiting natural and sociocultural conditions in which it is placed. Although sexuality is redescribed in subjective terms as desire, the satisfaction and recognition of desire remain confined by the limiting structures of the "world." As Freud reworked his individual life stories within the model of Oedipus, the "inner" and "outer" reality issue took an increasingly different form. How did the subject experience the inhibiting impact of its natural and cultural worlds? Were there universally repeated events in all childhoods which structured the inhibition and repression of desire? And if the shaping of individual histories was determined by the limiting structures of "reality" or natural and historical "necessity," how were those structures shaped and institutionalized in the first place?

The transformations of Freud's assumptions in the late 1890s informed the meaning(s) he gave to the Oedipus story. The reality reference in the Freudian version of the Oedipus story is the inner psychic reality of unconscious sexual desire. The events of the story are "objectifications" of wishes, not reflections of "external" events. As a historical "event," the Oedipus complex is a wide-ranging structural transformation, more like the French Revolution than the Battle of Waterloo. The trauma of the Oedipus story is the trauma of the transformation of desire, of a radical, "revolutionary" moment in the transition of desire from one state of being, one form of identity, to another. It marks the entry of the subject of desire into the network of social relations and the symbolic world of cultural values. It is not just one stage, like any other, in the history of desire. It is, rather, an "epochal" moment. As a moment in the formation of psychosexual desire, the Oedipus complex is not about biology, the frustration of instinctual needs, or about submission to the power of "external" social forces. It may be described as a transition from nature to culture, or "socialization," but only in the "immanent" sense of a process of the internalization of meaning within the individual, the acceptance of the self-regulation of law on infinite desire. As Freud noted in his case studies of both "the Rat Man" and "the Wolf Man," the oedipal moment in the history of desire was a sequence of particular subjective events, but it was also universal since the structure within which these subjective "events" were experienced forced the wishes of the desiring subject into a specific shape, regardless of individual differences and idiosyncratic situations. "The uniformity of the content of the sexual life of children, together with the unvarying character of the modifying tendencies which are later brought to bear upon it, will easily account for the consistent sameness which as a rule characterizes the fantasies that are constructed around the period of childhood, irrespective of how greatly or how little experiences have contributed to them."[10]

Freud's earliest formulation of the Oedipus story takes the form of a triangular structure involving the child, mother, and father. This differs significantly from the seduction theory, which pitted the child against the adult world. Seduction came from anywhere in that world: the father's crimes were not given any particular distinction or significance. In one of his case studies in *Studies on Hysteria*—the story of Katherina's seduction—Freud transformed the paternal seducer into an uncle to protect the identities of his subjects, not realizing that the fact that Katherina's father was her seducer was a critical element in her story.

In the Oedipus story the identity of the three positions matter. The relation is instigated by the desire of the child. Until the 1920s Freud implicitly assumed that this position was occupied by the son. Although he vaguely hinted at a symmetrical triangle (with the places of the parents inverted) for the daughter, this story—the so-called Electra story, as named by Jung—was never developed, and remained incoherent in terms of the values assigned to the mother and father. In the intrapsychic world of the son's unconscious fantasy, the mother was the primal object of desire and the father, the subject who possessed that object, was the rival who must be erased in order for the son to take his place. Although Freud was certainly aware that parental desires and preferences could awaken and direct oedipal feelings, he insisted that "the spontaneous character of the Oedipus complex could not be shaken by this factor."[11] If Freud ignored the agency of the parents in the production or instigation of the oedipal crisis, he did not ignore the significance of the father-position. He assumed that infantile desire was shaped within the context of a patriarchal order in which the father claimed ownership of the object of desire and represented the political, legal, and moral authority that judged the son's desire to be a transgression deserving of radical punishment (castration), and thus productive of anxiety and guilt. "The father is the oldest, first and, for children, only authority," Freud claimed in 1900, "and from his autocratic power the other social authorities have developed in the course of human civilization."[12]

The first implication of this simplified, schematic, original form of the Oedipus story is an ethic of renunciation. In the Oedipus story, becoming a human being, achieving the position of a recognized subject of society and culture, implies renunciation of the primal object of desire. It marks the transition from wish-fulfilling fantasy dominated by the "pleasure principle" to the renunciation of unlimited gratification and recognition of the rules of the "reality principle." The story was complicated, however, by the dual aspect of this renunciation and by the means through which this renunciation was achieved. The desire to possess or "have" the mother had as its consequence and correlative the desire to displace and eventually "be" the father. But the desire to take the father's place was severely ambivalent, entailing both aggressive hatred of the father as rival and admiration for, love of, and identification with the father as model, as what the child wanted to "be." The ethical task embodied in the dynamic of the oedipal relation was thus not only to impose a renunciation of desire for the object but also to create a system of mutual regulation, recognition, and security among the desiring subjects. The threat of castration, which Freud imagined as the instigator of the child's renunciation and repression, thus had two dimensions as well: a prohibition of possession of the object and a threat to identity. As Freud worked through the implications of the Oedipus theory in his four "classic" case studies between "Little Hans" and "the Wolf Man," and in the anthropological speculations of *Totem and Taboo*, this issue of identity and the desire for recognition as a subject, as the agent of one's own activity, increasingly came to the fore. Mothers and daughters were pushed to the periphery of Freud's individual and collective histories as the story of Oedipus became focused almost exclusively on the problematic relations between sons and fathers. At the same time the Oedipus complex as a moral fable concerning the relation of the individual subject to the object of desire began to lose its prominence in favor of a story in which Oedipus's primary desire was to be like the father, to be recognized as the subject or agent of the laws that governed his relations to the object and not just as a passive "object" on whom the law was imposed by force or threat of force.

As the Oedipus complex was developed, it became less a story of renunciation than a story of emancipation, less a story of the adaptation of a desiring mechanism to the laws of "reality" than the story of the "normalization" of a subjective agent internalizing the rules governing the mutual relations of recognized human subjects. The temptation of the primal maternal object of desire lay in the surrender of one's identity as a subject, thus avoiding the self-limitations and responsibilities of living in a world that demanded mutual recognition and regulation of a plurality of subjects. The fear of the father was a fear of losing that organ—the penis/clitoris or phallus—which represented the child's claim to recognition as a subjective agent.

The shift in emphasis toward the identity problem in the story of Oedipus was accompanied by an elaboration of the story's prologue and its conclusion. In revisions of libido theory culminating in Freud's essay "On Narcissism: An Introduction" (1914), the pre-oedipal developmental stages were reworked as a story that merged, or at least joined, the organization of libido around genital pleasure and the construction of the ego as the first full object of libidinal desire. The child entered into the interpersonal relations of the Oedipus complex as a narcissistic subject that imagined its own ego as the primary object of desire and associated this "self" with the organ of genital pleasure. The moral task of the oedipal moment thus became the task of directing one's libido from self to others, from intrasubjective to intersubjective relations, and of recognizing oneself as a subject in a world of other subjects. From this perspective, the model of a successful conclusion of the oedipal story shifted as well, from an acceptance of renunciation of the object to a transformation of the prohibitive, punishing external will of the father into an internalized moral conscience and culturally representative "superego."

Although the significance of mothers and daughters in the Oedipus story often seemed reduced to that of an item of exchange and rivalry between sons and fathers, the problem of sexual and gender difference appeared within Freud's descriptions as a peculiarly central problem for the son. In three remarkable case histories produced between 1908 and 1915, "the Rat Man," "Dr. Schreber," and "the Wolf Man," Freud tied the inability of sons to resolve their ambivalent wishes toward their fathers, and thus successfully conclude the oedipal story, to an inability to free themselves from a "homosexual" and "feminine" position, that is, a position in which they submitted themselves to the father in the imagined terms of the primal feminine object of the father's active masculine desire. Freud noted that the "homosexual libido" evident in the son's identification with the father, or merger into the father, as the passive object of his active subjectivity required a displacement and sublimation that redirected the desire to be recognized and loved into an obligation to serve the "great common interests of mankind."[13] At the same time Freud returned again and again to the inner connection between the achievement of moral autonomy (the recognition of law as self-imposed due to impersonal necessity) as a repudiation of femininity—as an overcoming of the desire to seek recognition through becoming an object for the Other—and the assertion of a "masculine" subjectivity. In fact, the Freudian story of Oedipus as it had developed up to the 1920s was implicitly a story of masculine identification. The achievement of "human" moral maturity, which involved the construction of self-mastery within the context of a rational recognition of natural and social limitation, or "necessity," was perceived in terms of a struggle of the son with the father for recognition as a masculine subject. Although the dissolution of the repressed Oedipus complex entailed a rational transcendence or overcoming of its unconscious dynamics, this liberating possibility—involving an emancipation of the subject from both the mother as the primal object of desire and the father as the authority who enforced that prohibition—was only possible as a masculine project.

During the 1920s, partly in response to the work of women in the psychoanalytic movement like Karen Horney and Melanie Klein, Freud finally addressed the gendered nature of the oedipal story, especially in its prologue and its conclusion. Freud had, of course, been aware for some time that the encultured human identities emerging from the dynamic of unconscious oedipal relations were gendered identities. Before 1924 he continued to imagine this process of gender construction as proceeding in symmetrical terms from the "natural" sexual differences that preceded it. As late as 1923 (in *The Ego and the Id*), he had noted that despite the enormous complexities that had been introduced into oedipal theory since its inception, the production of masculine and feminine identities occurred in "precisely analogous" ways.[14] Desire directed toward the parent of the opposite sex was frustrated and displaced by an identification with the parent of the same sex, which led to the internalization of the parental prohibition in terms of maternally or paternally oriented superegos. Object attachments were displaced by internalized identifications on parallel tracks. In the same work, however, Freud already admitted that such symmetry could not really be correct because of the father's preeminent role in frustrating object-related desire for all children, thus producing a father-oriented superego in all children as well. The cultural production of internalized morality, or, as Kant would have said, the creation of the subjective morality of a "good will," was a patriarchally structured, male achievement, which could only have been "transmitted to women by cross-inheritance."[15] The implications of this asymmetry were articulated in important papers in 1924 and 1925 on the dissolution of the Oedipus complex and the psychical effect of sexual difference.

The first premise of an asymmetrical conception of gender construction was recognition of the primary pre-oedipal dependence on the mother in the infantile experiences of both boys and girls. As children made the critical transition from narcissism (the final phase of pre-oedipal development) to the consciousness of objects and subjective individuation, they "naturally" chose their mothers as primary objects of desire. Moreover, at this moment of primal object choice the sexual constitution of both boys and girls was organized around the active, penetrating, "masculine," and "phallic" genital organ—the penis/clitoris. "With their entry into the phallic phase," Freud wrote, "the differences between the sexes are completely eclipsed by their agreements. We are now obliged to recognize that the little girl is a little man."[16]

For the male child, entry into the dynamics of the Oedipus story was relatively unproblematic and continuous with earlier development. Pre-oedipal maternal attachment was transformed, in keeping with the phallic organization of desire, into a desire for possession of the mother as love object, creating ambivalent relations to the father as rival and model. The little girl, however, in order to gain initial entry into the dynamics of the Oedipus story, had to break her pre-oedipal attachments to the mother in order to take her father as love object and view her mother ambivalently as rival and model. Moreover, she was forced to recognize that her organ of phallic identification, the clitoris, was not a real phallus; in Freud's words, "She accepts castration as an established fact, an operation already performed."[17] Thus she must renounce not only her original object of desire but also her previous active sexual aims and assume a passive sexual position as the loved object of the father. The trauma of this radical renunciation and reversal produced inevitable psychic scars: penis envy, frigidity, inferiority feelings, contempt for her own sex. Only by accepting the necessity of this biological and social fate could the little girl enter into the oedipal triangle and become what she was destined to be: "a little woman."

> She gives up her wish for a penis and puts in its place a wish for a child: and with this purpose in view she takes her father as love-object. Her mother becomes the object of her jealousy. The little girl has become a little woman.[18]

The little girl thus established the permanent core of her feminine identity within the oedipal story. She was not forced to repress and sublimate her desires because of a radical threat to her being or identity if she persisted in her oedipal aims. Her only motivation for renouncing the wish for a penis and the desire to have a child from her father was the recognition that they were denied her by an external "fate."

For the little boy, on the other hand, recognition of the anatomical differences between the sexes produced fear, rather than acceptance, of castration. He was forced to internalize the father's command to desist from incest and patricide in order to preserve his very identity. The result was an identification with the father, the construction of a powerful superego, and a jump start into "the processes that culminate in enrolling the individual in civilized society."[19]

As Freud admitted, "the Oedipus complex . . . is such an important thing that the manner in which one enters and leaves it cannot be without its effects." Due to the absence of the dynamic that led the boy to radically renounce his object-related desire and to internalize the father's law, Freud noted that

> for the woman the level of what is ethically normal is different from what it is in men. Their superego is never so inexorable, so impersonal, so independent of its emotional origins as we require it in men. Character traits which critics of every epoch have brought against women—that they show less of a sense of justice than men, that they are less ready to submit to the great necessities of life, that they are more often influenced in their judgements by feelings of affection and hostility—all these would be amply accounted for by the modification in the formation of their superego which we have inferred.[20]

Freud's claim that the story of Oedipus was a story of identification, producing who individuals are and can be, not only what they want and can possess, amounted to a critique of femininity in which masculine identity acted as the ethical and cultural norm for "humanity."

The critique of femininity as a moral and human deficit, as the absence of sufficient "moralization" emerging from Freud's analysis of asymmetrical gender development within the structures of patriarchal culture, made explicit what had been implicit in his interpretation of the Oedipus story from the beginning. Freud's Oedipus was engaged in a struggle for emancipation, first from maternal "nature" and then from the culturally produced constraints—the paternal, symbolic, cultural identifications—that mediated the emancipation from nature through the internalized agency of the superego. When the boy finally left the unconscious dynamics of the oedipal relations behind, he brought to consciousness, and thus to completion, the process by which he recognized himself as the subject of his own history, the self-conscious master of his irrational dependencies on the maternal seductions and paternal authority which marked his struggle for maturity. The Freudian critique of femininity was a critique of failed emancipation, of incomplete detachment from the prehistorical mother/child dyad, and of seduction by the internalized figures of authority which had originally motivated that detachment. Freud's ideal Oedipus was the conscious master of his own experience, a "subject" who had overcome dependence on the illusions produced by the desire to remain in, or return to, the primal mother/child symbiosis or find consolation as the worthy object of an omnipotent father's love. Both types of illusions were ultimately "feminine": Oedipus became a moral person, a self-determining "subject," by repudiating the feminine.

With this formulation, Freud's Oedipus story entered the discursive networks and conflicts of modern cultural history and proceeded to inaugurate its own complex story of assimilation, resistance, and transformation. It was able to function as the instigator of an ongoing discourse because it articulated the structure of a moral problem rather than a clear and convincing vision of a moral resolution. It was a story of the achievement of subjective autonomy and gendered identity within a historical process in which existences were endowed with a normalizing narrative coherence, rather than a story of the evolution of biological natures, metaphysical essences, or socially enforced roles. The Freudian Oedipus story opened up a variety of emancipatory possibilities through which the subjected could renounce their subjection as the product of contingent historical constructions. At the same time, by telling this story as an archetypal, normative story of the struggle to achieve masculine identity, Freud provided not only a model but also a problematic foil for the diverse moral projects of his heirs.

Oedipus Politicus

FREUD'S PARADIGM OF SOCIAL RELATIONS[1]

José Brunner

WHAT'S LOVE GOT TO DO WITH IT?

In a footnote to *Group Psychology and the Analysis of the Ego*, Freud approvingly cites a simile from Schopenhauer that illustrates the problem of social relations by the image of a pack of porcupines crowding closely together on a cold winter day to provide each other with warmth. When they come close enough to feel the warmth of each other, they also prick one another with their bristles—hence they separate again. The cold drives them together once more, but their bristles urge them apart. Thus, Schopenhauer states, they move to and fro until they discover "a mean distance at which they could most tolerably exist."[2]

The inevitable ambivalence toward the existence of others is at the basis of social thought: others are necessary for one's physical and emotional survival since they provide one with the cooperation, protection, love, and satisfaction one seeks. But at the same time one also experiences the existence of others as an ordeal, since they may constitute a threat or burden, imposing demands and limiting one's freedom. As Freud emphasized in *Civilization and Its Discontents*, utilitarian considerations of interest and expediency are not strong enough to overcome what he called the "primary mutual hostility of human beings."[3] For even though he admitted that people acquire value for one another by working together, he claimed that even "the advantages of work in common, will not hold them together."[4] In his words:

The element of truth behind all this, which people are so ready to disavow, is that men are not gentle creatures who want to be loved, and who at most can defend themselves if they are attacked; they are, on the contrary, creatures among whose instinctual endowments is to be reckoned a powerful share of aggressiveness. As a result, their neighbour is for them not only a potential helper or sexual object, but also someone who tempts them to satisfy their aggressiveness on him, to exploit his capacity for work without compensation, to use him sexually without his consent, to seize his possessions, to humiliate him, to cause him pain, to torture and kill him. *Homo homini lupus.*[5]

Thus a force is needed which can overcome the primary hostility among people, and bind them together in spite of it. What, then, could be the force that ties individuals into a crowd? According to Freud, this force is love. For him, love constituted simultaneously the basis of authority, its instrument, and its effect. Thus he presented a complex picture of the interrelation between love and authority in *Group Psychology and the Analysis of the Ego,* claiming that "love relationships . . . constitute the essence of the soul of the group [*Massenseele*]."[6] In his words, "If an individual gives up his distinctness in a group and lets its other members influence him by suggestion, it gives one the impression that he does it because he feels the need of being in harmony with them rather than in opposition to them—so that perhaps after all he does it '*ihnen zu Liebe.*' "[7] Since Freud assumed that human beings are driven by a primary mutual hostility, he had to explain how such love could come about in a group. He did so by asserting that the tie that binds members of a group to one another derives from their submission to a father figure; it is because they share a love for the same father figure that they feel similar and close to one another.[8]

As this example implies, Freud analyzed the emotional dynamics of social relations through the perspective of the "Oedipus complex," named after the ancient Greek drama of *Oedipus the King,* in which the title figure unknowingly kills his father and marries his mother. As Freud wrote in October 1897 to his friend Wilhelm Fliess: "The Greek legend seizes upon a compulsion which everyone recognized because he senses its existence within himself. Everyone . . . was once a budding Oedipus in fantasy. . . ."[9] For Freud, all social relations, private and public alike, share a hidden oedipal typicality that underlies their various manifestations. He took this postulated unconscious oedipal core of social relations as the ultimate reference point of social analysis, to be reached by psychoanalytic investigation only.[10] Thus, toward the end of his life, when Freud recapitulated his ideas in *An Outline of Psycho-Analysis*, he declared that even "if psycho-analysis could boast of no other achievement than the discovery of the repressed Oedipus complex, this discovery alone would give it a claim to be included among the precious new acquisitions of mankind."[11]

Although oedipal themes became central to Freud's theorizing as early as 1897, he used the term "Oedipus complex" for the first time only in 1910, when he presented the combination of sexual desire for the mother and rivalrous hate of the father as the "nuclear complex" of every neurosis.[12] And even though in 1920 he declared the Oedipus complex "the shibboleth that distinguishes the adherents of psycho-analysis from its opponents," Freud never presented a systematic, authoritative account of its characteristics in any one work.[13] Rather, his thinking on the Oedipus complex went through a number of stages, in which he increasingly developed and complicated the original, simple model of social relations in the private and public spheres.[14]

This discussion of Freud's concept of the Oedipus complex and its political ramifications proceeds on three levels. On one level, I elucidate what Freud meant by this, probably the most well-known of his theoretical categories. On another, I show that his thoughts on social relations—as they can be found in his theorizing on the Oedipus complex—provide intriguing insights into the ambivalences and dialectics inherent in all social relations. Finally, I establish that Freud's understanding of social relations within the family was fundamentally political, since he conceived of the family not only as a social institution that gives rise to emotional ambivalence but also as an arena of power struggles. What makes a theory of social relations political is not its reference to the public realm, parties, or governments but rather its concern with the structures and dynamics of power and authority. Indeed, political thinkers from Plato to the present have been concerned not only with the public or governmental face of rule and domination, but also with the dimensions of power and domination that are involved in all other social relations, including those of the family.

THREE'S COMPANY

Let me start my exploration of Freud's oedipal paradigm with a close reading of his depiction of the beginning of life:

> An infant at the breast does not as yet distinguish his ego from the external world as the source of the sensations flowing in upon him. He gradually learns to do so . . . impressed by the fact that some sources of excitation, which he will later recognize as his own bodily organs, can provide him with sensations at any moment, whereas other sources evade him from time to time—among them what he desires most of all, his mother's breast—and only reappear as a result of his screaming for help. In this way there is for the first time set over against the ego an "object," in the form of something which exists "outside" and which is only forced to appear by a special action.[15]

As we see, the ego—Freud's term for the mental agent of rational and self-conscious selfhood—does not exist from the start; it has to be developed by relating to a prior existing other: the mother. To put it another way, for Freud a coherent concept of self is acquired indirectly, as it were, as a function of a concept of otherness. Moreover, in his view, the baby's ego, as it becomes conscious of its separateness and its limitations, is "first and foremost a body-ego."[16] It emerges when the baby realizes that the mother's breasts are not as completely under his control as he had at first imagined, because they belong to another person. As a result of his realization of the breasts' otherness, the baby then becomes ambivalent toward them. According to Freud, the baby seeks as much to devour the mother's breasts as to gain nourishment from them, so that they will be "assimilated by eating and . . . in that way annihilated as such."[17] By attempting to abolish the breasts' separate existence and to incorporate them into himself, the baby aims to resolve his ambivalence toward the mother's power, that is, her ability to provide or withhold food with her body.

In addition, Freud argued that the baby's emerging awareness of his physical dependence on the parents brings forth his first love, which is directed both toward "the woman who feeds him" and toward "the man who protects him."[18] If otherness and care evoke both love and aggression, according to Freud, love, in turn, creates feelings of both security and anxiety. In Freud's words: "Being loved by an adult does not merely bring a child the satisfaction of a special need; it also means that he will get what he wants in every other respect as well."[19] For this reason the child's recognition of the parents' control over his needs and wishes also turns a possible loss of their love into a dreaded prospect. Since children fear losing their parents' love and the concomitant feeling of safety, the parents can, by granting or refusing affection at will, deploy their love as an instrument of domination and control. In this fashion, the infant's feeling of dependence on another person "establishes the earliest situations of danger and creates the need to be loved which will accompany the child through the rest of its life."[20]

Out of the compound of feelings of security and anxiety which are evoked by love, authority arises. Because it serves as a vehicle of power, Freud explained, love "becomes an important, if not the most fundamental source of authority."[21] As he also put it: "For a small child his parents are at first the only authority and the source of all belief. The child's most intense and most momentous wish during these early years is to be like his parents (that is, the parent of his own sex) and to be big like his father and mother."[22]

Boys Will Be Boys

With the onset of what Freud has termed the "phallic stage," around the age of three, the penis and clitoris become the leading erotogenic zones for children. In this period, masturbation is the characteristic form of gratification. However, because Freud assumed that it is accompanied by fantasies of the mother, he did not consider masturbation a form of autoerotic sexuality at this stage.[23] As he put it, in the phallic stage there is for the first time "a sexual object and some degree of convergence of the sexual impulses upon that object."[24] Freud assumed that originally the mother constitutes the sexual object of both sexes, and that only male sexual identity exists during this period, without a corresponding independent female identity. In this phase, the antithesis is "between having a *male genital* and being *castrated*."[25] This difference in the self-conception of boys and girls, which Freud portrayed as a result of their anatomy, leads to two paths along which the Oedipus complex is said to proceed from thereon until it is superseded.

Boys desire the mother but perceive her exclusive sexual tie to the father. In the wake of more or less explicit threats of castration uttered by parents and nurses in response to masturbation, and the observation of sexual differences when they see a child of the other sex naked, they develop fantasies concerning the father's potentially castrating violence. Under the impact of such real and imagined threats of bodily mutilation, the image of the father, who appears to the child as the only obstacle preventing the fantasized incestuous union with the mother, undergoes a significant transformation. It changes from that of a benevolent protector providing security to that of a primarily restrictive, punishing figure embodying "every unwillingly tolerated social restraint."[26] Thus the father becomes hated as the person whose presence prevents pleasure and threatens to end all satisfaction of desire—and is wished dead by the little Oedipus. However, confronted with the superior power of the father, instead of realizing this lethal fantasy "the child's ego turns away from the Oedipus complex."[27]

For the baby girl, too, the mother is the original object of desire, according to Freud. However, when she realizes that both she and her mother lack a penis, she regards the mother as responsible for this absence, blames her for her disappointing anatomy, and turns away from her. Freud claimed that girls are induced to lower their sexual interests and to enter the latency period by a combination of external threats—that is, parental authority—and a feeling of humiliation in the wake of their self-conception as castrated men. However, he argued that as opposed to boys, "girls remain in [the oedipal complex] for an indeterminate length of time; they demolish it late and, even so, incompletely."[28] Thus, while boys may never completely recover from their castration anxiety, girls come to accept themselves as castrated males—or so Freud thought. Moreover, in contrast to his discussion of male development, which contains concerned comments on the potentially grave effects of an unsuccessful resolution of the Oedipus complex, Freud claimed that "it does little harm to a woman if she remains in her feminine Oedipus attitude," since this means that "she will in that case choose her husband for his paternal characteristics and be ready to recognize his authority."[29] According to Freud, problems arise when women refuse to accept male authority; in such cases "there comes to light the woman's hostile bitterness against the man, which never completely disappears in the relation between the sexes, and which is clearly indicated in the strivings and in the literary productions of 'emancipated' women."[30]

Eight decades after this questionable judgment on feminism was pronounced, it hardly needs to be dignified by serious consideration. What deserves attention, however, is the fact that Freud depicted the very first stages of life as already involving a dialectic of ambivalences, which results from a political dynamics of domination and dependence. As we have seen, in Freud's paradigm dependence evokes both love and aggression. Love leads to feelings of protection and safety on the one hand and anxiety on the other, which at first give rise to submission and obedience, and then to endeavors to gain power and become independent, as well as to hate and hostility.

DIALECTICAL SELVES

Freud presents the self as developing not only in relation to one concrete or generalized other subject—the Other, as some contemporary social theorists like to put it—but in relation to both father and mother, that is, to two separate but sexually and socially interrelated subjects, each of whom takes up a different position toward the emerging third subject. Thus Freud's perspective envisions the social condition as fundamentally triangular: each human being enters a world in which there are "always already" at least two others, related by social/sexual bonds, whose existence is a precondition for his or her very being. Each human being has to negotiate his or her position vis-à-vis their simultaneous, conflicting, and yet complementary presence, and learn to cope with the desires and anxieties, illusions and disappointments, love and hate, which their presence evokes. As Freud declared in a footnote to his *Three Essays on the Theory of Sexuality*: "Every new arrival on this planet is faced with the task of mastering the Oedipus complex."[31] By overcoming and resolving the oedipal complex, the child—that is, typically the male child—matures to a more adult stage and achieves what Freud called "the liberation of an individual as he grows up, from the authority of his parents."[32]

Freud's conception of the son's emancipation from paternal domination merits some scrutiny since, ironically, it is made contingent upon the internalization of paternal authority. In Freud's words, "The authority of the father or the parents is introjected into the ego, and there it forms the nucleus of the superego, which takes over the severity of the father."[33] Only by absorbing the father's rules—which forbid incestuous desire for the mother—and making them his own can the son become autonomous.

The resolution of the Oedipus complex leads to the establishment of the superego, as Freud called the mind's own internal, law-enforcing, and adjudicating agency. In administering and implementing moral standards—i.e., acting as conscience—which originated outside the subject, but which have become part of the son's self-conception, the superego may become harsh and cruel in pursuit of guilt and shame. However, the superego's aggression need not necessarily be derived from that of the father; mild and moderate parents can give rise to a severe conscience in their child. Freud explained that "[b]y means of identification [the son] takes the unattackable authority into himself. The authority now turns into his superego and enters into possession of all the aggressiveness which a child would have liked to exert against it."[34] In addition, Freud complicated the picture by emphasizing that the superego's "relation to the ego is not exhausted by the precept: 'You *ought to be* like this (like your father).' It also comprises the prohibition: 'You *may not be* like this (like your father)—that is, you may not do all that he does; some things are his prerogative.' "[35]

As a result of the dangers and anxieties that the Oedipus complex evokes, the child represses all sexual desires into the depths of the unconscious around the age of five. With the onset of the latency period, the radical internal otherness of the unconscious is sealed, and the fundamental opposition between pleasure on the one hand and the demands of social reality on the other is entrenched in the soul and accepted as fundamental to human life.

Freud's portrayal of the dissolution of the Oedipus complex depicts a dialectical *Aufhebung* both of desire and paternal authority, which are simultaneously abolished in their original form—i.e., consciously or externally—and preserved as well as transformed internally, that is, unconsciously. The German philosopher G. W. F. Hegel used the term *Aufhebung* to describe the result of dialectical processes; it denotes a transition whereby something is simultaneously abolished and maintained, where an affirmative moment is preserved and contained in its negation. In this sense, Freud's discourse on the Oedipus complex also delineates stages in a political dialectic of obedience and emancipation, where dependence leads to autonomy, but where autonomy not only abolishes submission but also internalizes and preserves it. To put it somewhat differently, through the Oedipus complex the child learns not only to abandon his or her desires in the face of authority but also to cope with the presence of authority by identifying with its demands. Where desire is opposed by authority, authority is internalized and made one's own.

The political dialectics entailed by the Oedipus complex became part of Freud's model of all encounters of individuals with society and authority. In Freud's vision of self and others, there are no simple human beings and no social relations without ambivalence. A variety of psychic mechanisms—such as repression and reaction formation—can unpredictably turn an emotion into its opposite. Thus he claimed, for instance, that "[t]hose who as children have been the most pronounced egoists may well become the most helpful and self-sacrificing members of the community; most of our sentimentalists, friends of humanity and protectors of animals have been evolved from little sadists and animal-tormentors."[36] Moreover, for Freud love always also involves hate; hence he described a typically oedipal mechanism such as the son's identification with the father as "ambivalent from the very first; it can turn into an expression of tenderness as easily as into a wish for someone's removal. . . . The cannibal . . . has a devouring affection for his enemies and only devours people of whom he is fond."[37] We have already seen that at an earlier stage, when suckling at the mother's breasts, the baby may wish to devour them as much as to feed on them.

Freud's vision of the child's relations to his or her parents opposes pious notions of the self and family bonds. It also contradicts common images of the subject and social relations which underlay most liberal and utilitarian thinking, where essentially rational, atomistic, transparent, unified, or static selves are presupposed. In his view, the self originally lacks unity and develops by splitting itself off from the mother until it finally incorporates the father. In the dialectics of the Oedipus complex and its resolution, some boundaries between subjects shift, and others are (mentally) cannibalized. However, the result of such processes of identification and internalization is that the cannibalized father becomes an essential and defining aspect of the son, whose very identity may be dependent on the continued internalized presence of the former. Although social relations and the authority of others can be abolished in their actual, external form, they are not thereby obliterated. Instead, they are transposed into an inner, unconscious realm, where the past is preserved and continues to have an impact on the present and future.

Thus the Oedipus complex turns the father into the archetype of all bearers of the law and of all later figures whose acts may unconsciously be perceived as castrating. He becomes the prototypical authority figure, opposing wild, anarchic desires that refuse to respect boundaries and differences. Moreover, not only are there no self-contained subjects for Freud, there are no self-contained oedipal units, either. Each oedipal triangle forms part of a web that extends across time, back to earlier generations in which past social relations have never really been annihilated. As the French analyst Jean Laplanche points out:

> ... It is, in fact, too often forgotten when we speak of the mother-child relation or of the parent-child relation that the parents themselves had their own parents; they have their "complexes," wishes marked by historicity, so that to reconstruct the child's oedipal complex as a triangular situation, while forgetting that at the two vertices of the triangle each adult protagonist is himself the bearer of a small triangle and even of a whole series of interlocking triangles, is to neglect an essential aspect of the situation.[38]

FATHERS EVERYWHERE

In *Totem and Taboo* (1912–13), Freud transposed the features of the oedipal dynamics from the private realm of the family and individual infantile development (ontogenesis) to the public aspects of the development of humankind at large (phylogenesis). He introduced the phylogenetic oedipal perspective by telling the puzzling story of a "primal horde," which he assumed to have existed in a primeval period and in which oedipal fantasies were supposed to have been carried out in reality. This myth of origins depicts a society governed by a primal father's bodily strength, who used the women surrounding him for his exclusive sexual satisfaction, castrating the sons when they dared to become his sexual rivals. According to Freud, the frustrated sons managed to escape from their father's control at some stage and, driven by their common incestuous desire for the mother and shared hatred for their father, they committed patricide for the sake of incest. Freud believed that this act occurred repeatedly in prehistoric times; in his view, primal sons overwhelmed and murdered their primal fathers, and, "[c]annibal savages as they were, it goes without saying that they devoured their victim as well as killing him."[39] In the cannibal act, the sons accomplished physically what according to Freud all later sons have aimed to achieve symbolically in the dissolution of the oedipal complex: they internalized the father, so that each of them acquired some of his strength.

After the patricide, the sons realized that none of them could actually take the place of the father without provoking a war of all against all. This was the beginning of civilization in Freud's mythology, starting with the transition from an original state, in which obedience was imposed externally by the paternal, physical coercion, to a new form of obedience, based on the internalization of rules. This transition was made possible by a social contract concluded by the sons; they pledged to renounce despotism, declaring that "no one could or might ever again attain the father's supreme power, even though that was what all of them had striven for."[40]

Moreover, by exaggerating the power of the dead father to imaginary, limitless dimensions, the sons infinitely extended the scope of his posthumous authority, so that "[t]he dead father became stronger than the living one had been."[41] Freud depicted the social contract as resulting from posthumous obedience to the father's authority, aimed at the latter's symbolic restoration in order to allay feelings of remorse and guilt. Thus, in the Freudian social contract, the sons not only bound themselves to one another as members of a community, they also concluded a "covenant with their father" after his death.[42]

If we are to believe Freud's theory, the memory of the primal patricide entered into a collective unconscious shared by the whole of humankind, which was thereby turned into an eternal son, as it were. Freud claimed in *Moses and Monotheism*, for instance, that "men have always known (in this special way) that they once possessed a primal father and killed him."[43] Freud's discourse presents this unconscious memory of the murder, as well as the concomitant unconscious guilt, as if it were part of a human instinct leading people to seek father figures, fear them, and then to revolt against them. He declared in *Moses and Monotheism* that "[w]e know that in the mass of mankind there is a powerful need for an authority who can be admired, before whom one bows down, by whom one is ruled and perhaps even ill-treated. . . . It is a longing for the father felt by everyone from his childhood onwards."[44]

In his view, the dead primal father also inspired the monotheistic construction of a paternal deity. He argued that monotheistic religion aimed to resurrect, on a cosmic scale, the dependence and submission of the sons to paternal authority. By immortalizing the primal father and enthroning him in a kingdom in heaven, monotheism nullified the universal unconscious guilt over his murder. Freud elaborated and expanded various political assumptions and implications of his phylogenetic oedipal myth in *Group Psychology and the Analysis of the Ego* in 1921, *The Future of an Illusion* in 1927, *Civilization and Its Discontents* in 1930, "Why War?" in 1932, and *Moses and Monotheism* in 1939, where he recapitulated the entire myth of the primal horde. In his eyes, all those who become authorities and elicit obedience from others— including deities—are to be seen as father figures.

As has been illustrated in the introductory passages to this essay, Freud inevitably depicted society as divided into masses/sons on the one hand and leaders/fathers on the other. He decoded large-scale social conflicts as expressing an underlying unconscious intergenerational conflict, which centers on requests of leaders/fathers for the masses'/sons' obedience and the masses'/sons' reluctance or refusal to submit to their leaders'/fathers' demand. In this conflict, Freud regularly took sides with the leaders/fathers (even though he always opposed religion); for as he argued in *The Future of an Illusion*:

> It is only through the influence of individuals who can set an example and whom masses recognize as their leaders that they can be induced to perform the work and undergo the renunciations on which the existence of civilization depends. All is well if these leaders are persons who possess superior insight into the necessities of life and who have risen to the height of mastering their own instinctual wishes. But there is a danger that in order not to lose their influence they might give way to the mass more than it gives way to them, and it therefore seems necessary that they shall be independent of the mass by having means to power at their disposal.[45]

Nowhere in Freud's writings can one find an instance where people rebel against despots because their lives and property, rights and interests have been threatened or violated by autocratic leaders. In Freud's discourse, rebellions invariably appear as the deed of masses/sons who refuse obedience to leaders/fathers because they cannot tolerate the restrictions that the latter impose on them. This authoritarian approach is the logical outcome of the oedipal analytical grid, which presents submission and obedience to father figures as necessary for social existence and which discounts the dangers of authoritarianism. Moreover, the oedipal vision exhibits a distinct patriarchal bias: it reduces politics to an activity of fathers and sons while relegating women to the role of passive objects of male desire.

However, at the same time Freud's work has contributed much to contemporary methods of unmasking leaders and their postures by drawing attention to unconscious wishes, fantasies, fears, and anxieties, which are part of human nature. After all, the leader was once a little Oedipus as well. Despite its authoritarian bias, Freud's oedipal paradigm has provided a useful vocabulary for critical thinkers such as Wilhelm Reich and Herbert Marcuse, by means of which hidden motives, mechanisms, and strategies of political repression, domination, and subjugation have been revealed and articulated. It has allowed the conceptualization of the intrusion of society into the individual mind and the formulation of critiques of alienation, discontent, guilt, shame, frustration, exploitation, and inequality—not least gender inequality. Indeed, much of contemporary feminist thinking has grown out of, and in reaction to, Freud's analysis of the dialectics of sexuality and politics.

CONCLUDING AMBIVALENCE

To sum up, Freud's oedipal paradigm conjoins complexity with reductionism and thereby evokes the very emotion, ambivalence, which it seeks to explain. On the one hand, it provides critical insights into social relations, revealing the dialectics underlying all their manifestations and tracing them to the complex duality of antagonism and complementarity between body and society, sexuality and civilization, love and hatred, authority and autonomy, child and parent. On the other hand, Freud's paradigm constitutes a reductionist theoretical construct, which turns masculine development into the norm, is strongly phallocentric and authoritarian, and slides into mythical universalization. Hence this discussion of Freud's oedipal paradigm of social relations has been both critical and sympathetic—that is, ambivalent. Without neglecting its shortcomings and prejudices, I have tried to show that even today it can still provide much food for thought.

From Suggestion to Insight, from Hypnosis to Psychoanalysis

Harold P. Blum

IN MANY WAYS, psychoanalysis emerged from hypnosis, a tool of the physician as well as the magician. Europe was fascinated by the experiments and demonstrations of Franz Mesmer, "mesmerized" by the remarkable phenomena of hypnosis, which became a popular fad, an instrument of magic and mysticism, and a mode of medical and nonmedical treatment of illness. Because of its associations with magic, hypnosis was shunned by many physicians. Freud, still a clinical and research neurologist, not only was impressed by hypnotic phenomena but developed a psychological explanation for hypnosis and its seemingly strange, yet often very powerful influence.

Until the twentieth century, the understanding and treatment of the psychologically disturbed and the mentally ill had remained limited and undeveloped. Considering neuroses as functional, rather than anatomical or physiological, disturbances of the nervous system, most medical doctors scorned to treat hysterics and other neurotics. Other physicians still subscribed to the Greek belief that hysteria was biologically caused, due to a malfunctioning uterus, although hysterical symptoms had occasionally been reported in men.

When Freud's patient Dora started treatment in October 1900, Freud noted that she had been subjected to the prevalent treatments of the time for her hysterical symptoms. At that time hysterics were treated with hydrotherapy and electrotherapy; for example, electrical current might be applied directly to the vocal cords for treatment of aphonia. These treatments, often accompanied by rest, recreation, work cures, exhortations, and remonstrations, were far from reliable. Suffering from the treatment as well as the disease, neurotic patients, not entirely irrationally, developed negative attitudes toward their physicians, as well as antagonism and pessimism regarding their treatments. Physicians, too, were frustrated by the lack of therapeutic effect and ready relapse. The physician used his authority to give imperious orders, sometimes through the medium of hypnosis, suggesting and directing the thoughts, feelings, and activities of the patient.

Freud studied in Paris with Jean Martin Charcot from October 1885 to February 1886. This experience facilitated the shift in his thinking from neuropathology to psychopathology. Charcot classified various hysterical manifestations and showed that hysteria was commonly found in both sexes and various nationalities; hysteria became a "respectable" illness. While he still invoked hereditary degeneration as a primary etiology, Charcot demonstrated that hysterical symptoms could be induced down to the last detail under hypnosis. For Freud, that the symptoms could be elicited or removed by means of a psychological technique was indisputable proof of the psychological root of hysteria. He understood both hysteria and hypnosis as mental phenomena representing the power of "mind over matter." Without abandoning the notion of individual genetic predisposition, Freud, in regarding hysteria as a psychogenic illness, believed that a cure could be effected through psychological means.

Charcot's appreciation that hypnotic phenomena occur outside of conscious awareness provided encouragement and inspiration for Freud's own research. Hypnosis indisputably demonstrated the existence of unconscious mental processes, contributing to Freud's growing understanding of the significance of unconscious motivation and conflict, initially in their relation to psychopathology.

Let us now consider a patient of Dr. Josef Breuer, Freud's mentor and close colleague. Breuer's attempts to treat the patient were apparently an exercise in futility, and he recommended to the patient and her family that Sigmund Freud be summoned for consultation. Freud described this patient as a case of successful cure through hypnosis. He may well have had this and similar cases in mind when he later stated of hypnosis, "We psychoanalysts may claim to be its legitimate heirs and we do not forget how much encouragement and theoretical clarification we owe to it."[1]

This hypnotic treatment preceded the publication of *Studies on*

Hysteria by Breuer and Freud as well as Freud's self-analysis, which probably began with the Irma dream and proceeded more systematically following his father's death in 1896. This neglected, classic case report has relevance to the problems of parenthood and depression, and reveals extraordinary insights into the psychology of motherhood, even before Freud had turned particular conscious attention to this topic or to the mother-infant relationship.[2]

The patient was a young woman between twenty and thirty years of age, very distressed following the birth of her second child. Freud had been acquainted with her since childhood, and she remained under his observation for several years after the hypnotherapy. She was suffering from what would now be called postpartum depression and was unable to feed her child. The situation was of great concern since formula substitutes for breast milk were not then available, and if a mother could not nurse, a wet nurse had to be sought. Freud noted that similar symptoms had occurred with the birth of the patient's first child, when, despite her intention to feed the infant herself, she had been unable to do so. There had been a poor flow of milk, and the new mother had lost her appetite and become agitated and sleepless. After a fortnight of suffering and unsuccessful attempts to nurse the baby, the child had been transferred to a wet nurse, whereupon all the mother's symptoms had immediately disappeared. One year after Freud's crisis intervention, the same disorder appeared yet again and was similarly treated. Experiences with an earlier and a later child provided controls for the case, which Freud described as more convincing and lucid than the majority of successful treatments.

With the birth of her second child, three years after the first, the mother's attempts at nursing the baby seemed even less successful, provoking even more distressing symptoms. The mother was again in an agitated depression, unable to eat or sleep, her distress compounded by her incapacity to care for her child.

Her physicians recommended against further efforts at feeding her baby and suggested that Freud should be consulted for a final treatment attempt through hypnotherapy. When Freud met the patient, she was lying in bed, furious at her inability to feed her baby, an inability that increased at her every attempt. She had vomited all her food and had taken no nourishment the whole day. Her epigastrium was distended, and she complained of having a bad taste in her mouth. In her agitated distress, Freud was hardly welcomed as her savior in the hour of need. Not daunted by the patient's lack of confidence in him, Freud promptly hypnotized the patient, recording the following hypnotic suggestion: "Have no fear! You will make an excellent nurse and the baby will thrive. Your stomach is perfectly quiet, and your appetite is excellent, and you are looking forward to your next meal."[3] Her husband had been worried that his wife's nerves might be totally ruined by hypnosis, but Freud reported that the patient slept peacefully, took nourishment herself, and "fed the baby irreproachably."[4] The next day, however, her symptoms returned, and she could not put the child to her breast. Freud, now acting with even greater energy, induced a second hypnosis and reported the following extraordinary intervention: "I told the patient that five minutes after my departure she would break out against her family with some acrimony: what happened to her dinner? Did they mean to let her starve? How could she feed the baby if she had nothing to eat herself? and so on."[5]

When Freud returned the third evening, the patient refused to undergo further treatment, stating that there was nothing more wrong with her. She had an excellent appetite and plenty of milk for the baby. He learned that after his previous visit, the patient had indeed clamored violently for food and had very atypically remonstrated with her mother.

A year later, when a third child was born, the patient succumbed to the same postpartum depression and responded again to the same type of hypnotic "psychotherapy." Freud observed that although the mother wanted to carry out her conscious intentions to nurture the child, she was unaware of her "counter-will." This concept was, in fact, a forerunner not so much of Breuer's "hypnoid state," as has been previously proposed,[6] as of the formulation of unconscious intrapsychic conflict. The patient was conflicted about feeding her baby and herself, but the conflicts were outside of her conscious awareness.

Freud's work with this patient became a creative process of insight and discovery, but he later stated in his case report, perhaps wishing for some "feeding" for himself, that he found it hard to understand that no reference had ever been made to his remarkable achievements. The first intervention had been classic hypnotic reassurance, with the posthypnotic suggestion that the patient's symptoms would disappear and she would be fine. The authority and power of the hypnotist would magically heal the patient and cause the symptoms to vanish. Freud's second intervention, however, was by no means a simple hypnotic suggestion; in fact, although cloaked as such, it represents a break with the entire tradition of hypnotic suggestion. In other words, it was a precursor of psychoanalytic interpretation couched in hypnotic terms, with the hypnotic magic replaced by psychoanalytic insight. It was as though Freud recognized that the hypnotic suggestion, composed of wishful denial and reassurance, only increased the patient's underlying recalcitrance and regressive tendencies.

Disappointed with the effect of hypnotic symptom removal, Freud gave the patient permission to experience and express her anger. He intuitively detected and accepted her anger as well as her oral neediness and regression. In authorizing her to awaken crying to be fed, comforted, and cared for, he implicitly recognized her envious identification with her infant, her own dependent longings, and her rage over her own unsatisfied infantile hunger. How could the mother nurture her infant when the infant within her so much insisted on being nurtured? Unlike his first hypnotic intervention, and unlike the hypnotic and psychotherapeutic interventions of the day, Freud's second intervention confronted a major root of the patient's problems: her anger. Instead of concentrating solely on eliminating the symptoms, he told the patient that she would awaken angry. The patient was in an agitated depression, and Freud evidently recognized that a depressed patient was unconsciously angry. He realized that the patient needed to express the anger associated with her depressive conflicts.

Freud appeared to have intuitively recognized the presence of unconscious fantasies of rivalry, envy, and identification with the infant that lay at the core of postpartum depression. The patient's guilt over her repudiated wish to replace her infant and be the infant probably contributed to her depression and anorexia. It was not so much that she was furious because she could not nurse, but that she could not nurse because she was furious, and vented the fury on herself through her depression.

The case report represents a confluence of Freud's burgeoning insight into the origins of depression and his understanding not only of a very important dimension of female psychology but also of the primary object relationship of mother and infant. Freud's suggestive interpretation of the woman's hostility toward her own infant and her mother was a precursor of the dynamic appreciation of conflict and symptom formation. Of course, what was conveyed to the patient, and then expressed by her, was not the conscious verbal insights that might be achieved in a contemporary psychoanalysis or dynamic, insight-oriented psychotherapy. Nevertheless, Freud's second intervention is a lucid example of how instrumental a therapist's insight into unconscious conflict is, and demonstrates the application of psychoanalytic intuition in a brief psychotherapeutic encounter. Contemporary psychoanalytic psychotherapy applies analytic understanding to a wide scope of disturbances and may be aimed toward either insight or auxiliary ego support or, most often, combinations of suggestion, support, and insight. Even in a brief psychotherapy or in crisis intervention, a little understanding may go a long way.

Freud used hypnosis in his own treatment of patients from 1887, shortly after starting his own practice, until about 1896, when he abandoned hypnosis for free association and the initiation of the psychoanalytic method. He had earlier asserted, "Neither the doctor nor the patient can tolerate indefinitely the contradiction between the decisive denial of the disorder in suggestion and the necessary recognition of it away from suggestion."[7]

Freud's interest in psychopathology had been sparked by the extraordinary research and treatment carried out by Breuer, a prominent internist and medical researcher. Fourteen years older than Freud, and a physician to Brahms and many other of Vienna's leading personalities, Breuer told Freud about his treatment of Anna O. from December 1880 to June 1882, prior to Freud's experience with Charcot.

Anna O. was a twenty-one-year-old woman with all the symptoms of grand hysteria: she suffered from hysterical paralyses, contractures, anesthesias, perceptual and speech disturbances, and altered states of consciousness. She had a pan-neurosis, sometimes including the inability to drink and eat, sometimes accompanied by frightening fantasies and hallucinations. In the evening she would talk to Breuer of her disagreeable day, and as she related the details of her symptoms, they disappeared. Anna O. called the method of treatment the "talking cure" or "chimney sweeping." Breuer began to visit the patient as often as twice a day, inducing hypnosis during morning sessions and continuing the exploration of her symptoms. This intense daily treatment, in which the patient talked about her disturbances and attempted to trace her symptoms both with and without hypnosis, was termed the "cathartic" method. Unfortunately, Anna O. ultimately developed a phantom pregnancy, ending with hysterical symptoms of childbirth.

She was calmed by hypnosis and sedatives, and Breuer terminated this landmark psychotherapy. His report percolated in the back of Freud's mind as he observed Charcot and others practice hypnosis, translated Charcot's and Hippolyte Bernheim's publications and lectures, and gave his own lectures on hypnosis. It was to have a profound influence upon his subsequent theory and therapy.

Freud had inferred that it was the transference love of Anna O. for Breuer which had led Breuer to retire from the treatment. Freud had had a similar experience with a patient, "with whom hypnotism had enabled me to bring about the most marvelous results, and whom I was engaged in relieving of her suffering by tracing back her attacks of pain to their origins. As she woke up on one occasion, she threw her arms around my neck . . . [and] from that time on there was a tacit understanding between us that the hypnotic treatment should be discontinued."[8] He observed that the treatment could be drastically affected by the relationship of patient and doctor; brilliant results could be swept aside if the relationship was disturbed or improvement restored if the doctor-patient relationship was reestablished.

During hypnosis, the subject is actually in an altered state of consciousness, neither asleep nor awake, and may experience neurophysiological alterations. Hypnosis, or even conscious suggestion, may subjectively modify the subject's experience, sensation, and perception. The altered state of consciousness may permit symptom induction and removal, access to memories and fantasies, ability to make associations, etc., not available to the subject in the ordinary waking state.

While he was aware of the phylogenetic, neurobiological aspects of hypnosis, Freud explained the phenomena of suggestion and suggestibility psychologically, as manifestations of transference. Transference is the transfer or displacement of an intrapsychic representation of a childhood love (or hate) object to the representation of a current person. The significant figures of childhood are reanimated within current relationships; patterns of thought, feeling, and behavior, modes of reacting and relating to parents and siblings, are displaced onto the present figure. The transfer of unconscious fantasies to a current person indicates that our reactions to others are never totally realistic or objective. The process of transference is unconscious, and the subject is not consciously aware that childhood fantasies of love and hate, obedience and defiance, are repeated in disguised, distorted forms in the relationship with the hypnotist or psychotherapist. There are transference fantasies associated with a readiness for or resistance to hypnosis, as well as to specific hypnotic commands and post-hypnotic reactions. A fantasy of masochistic submission, for example, may be associated with defensive awakening or erotic excitement. The transference itself could be understood as a powerful agent of therapeutic change, although one hardly capable of achieving a resolution of the underlying, unconscious conflicts. Symptom relief through suggestion is a form of "transference cure," and transference improvement accounts for much of the successful outcome of brief psychotherapy.

Transference is ubiquitous, though psychoanalysis creates the conditions in which transference can be concentrated, recognized, and explicated to the patient. The analysis of the transference relationship is a major aspect of psychoanalysis, helping the patient to understand and resolve childhood conflicts and childish attitudes.

Prior to Freud's insights, it was not known to how great a degree the patient's recovery from neurotic suffering was dependent upon the relationship with the hypnotist, the physician, or the psychotherapist. Breuer had not understood the powerful effect of his intimate relationship with Anna O. on her hysterical disturbance and whatever therapeutic progress and improvement occurred during her treatment. In contemporary psychoanalytic terms, he lacked the understanding of the patient's evolving, erotic transference and his own countertransference.

For Freud, listening to the patient became not only an art but a science. He listened for the content of his patients' conflicts but also for their criticisms of his technique. After Freud's[9] insistent questioning, his patient Emmy von N. (Baroness Fanny Moser) demanded that he stop asking her where this or that came from and let her say what she had to say. Refractory to hypnosis, Elisabeth von R.[10] remained in the recumbent position and was asked to concentrate her attention on a particular symptom and try to recall any memories concerning its origin. To enable further progress, following a technique of Bernheim's, Freud pressed her forehead with his hand. After several attempts, the patient said she could at first have told him something he deemed significant, but she didn't think it was what he wanted. This led Freud to request the patient to ignore all self-imposed restraints on what she told him, and to state everything regardless of whether she considered it to be unimportant or unpleasant. Similar to Emmy von N., Elisabeth von R. also reproached him for interrupting her with questions, considerably helping him to refine and improve on Breuer's earlier talking treatment of Anna O.[11] He had only to listen and learn that whatever occurred to the patient was in some way ultimately connected with unconscious conflict. The technical change to unencumbered waking conversation represented a further transition from hypnotic suggestion to free association, and from the cathartic method to psychoanalysis. Superseding hypnosis, psychoanalysis transformed its application as analytic formulations became the framework for psychoanalysis and derivative psychotherapies. Psychoanalytic theory became the unifying mode and foundation of various psychotherapies, including analytic group therapy.

In his work with his patients, Freud continued to learn from errors and blind alleys, from silences and other forms of what he came to understand as "resistance." Resistance was not simply a patient's uncooperativeness; it served to ward off anxiety and the awareness of unpleasant thoughts and feelings. Resistance itself could be understood and overcome by eliciting comprehension on the part of the patient, which would later be designated as interpretation. Invoking an archaeological metaphor, which he continued to use for psychoanalytic work, Freud compared the therapeutic procedure to the technique of excavating a buried city.

In terms of political and social metaphor, the psychoanalytic situation was far more democratic and egalitarian than the autocratic structure of hypnosis. The patient was not reduced to a subject who had to unquestioningly obey the hypnotherapist's commands. Rather than assuming a position of abject dependency and submission, the patient retained complete freedom of thought and expression and could critize any authority figure, including therapist or parent, without being threatened by rejection or retaliation. Love and hate, eros and aggression, exalting or denigrating thoughts and feelings, could be admitted into conscious awareness and openly expressed to a nonjudgmental analytic therapist.

In contrast to the hypnotist, the psychoanalyst eschewed deliberate attempts to suggest, direct, or indoctrinate the patient, or to engage in "friendly persuasion." Psychoanalysis attempted to limit the analyst's influence upon the patient, though it was recognized that the analyst's own personality inevitably influenced the analytic process. Elements of suggestion were unavoidable, but analysis aimed to minimize and interpret such suggestive influence, whereas in hypnosis, the outcome was dependent upon unanalyzed transference to the hypnotist and his intentional influence. In hypnosis, the transference fantasy of magical power and omnipotent command usually remained unconscious, whereas in psychoanalysis such fantasy was interpreted to the patient and in the analyst's self-analysis of countertransference.

In hypnosis, the patient regressed to a childlike helplessness and dependency upon a parent figure in whom omnipotent power and authority was invested; the psychoanalytic approach returned to the patient his or her own responsibility for thoughts, feelings, and behavior. The psychoanalytic approach promoted growth and fostered self-knowledge and understanding, whereas hypnotherapy achieved its results through transference love and submission to a parental authority. Moreover, the delegation of important reality and regulatory functions to the parental figure of the hypnotist is ordinarily neither enduring nor complete. The hypnotic subject will generally not carry out a command that is totally unacceptable to the waking personality.

Freud, always interested in the wider sphere of society and culture, applied his psychoanalytic theories to group formation. Hypnotist and subject could be described as a group of two; a special situation in which the childish regression of the hypnotized subject leads to dependence and to a lack of individually based thought, feeling, and action. In a regressive group, the individual, "hypnotized" by a charismatic group leader, is ruled by that leader and the attitudes of the "group mind." Gustave Le Bon considered the condition of an individual in a group as hypnotic, and Freud[12] cited him thus:

> We see, then, that the disappearance of the conscious personality, the predominance of the unconscious personality, the turning by means of suggestion and contagion of feelings and ideas in an identical direction, the tendency to immediately transform the suggested ideas into acts; these, we see, are the principal characteristics of the individual forming part of a group. He is no longer himself, but has become an automaton who has ceased to be guided by his will.[13]

Freud found, apart from the group reinforcement of ideals, values, and attitudes, similar dynamics in group formation as in hypnosis. The hypnotist is the group leader who exercises parental authority and power over the individuals in the group, who are symbolic children. These insights help explain the hypnotic power of the orator and charismatic leader. The herd, horde, or mob has lost individuality and may behave in a manner inconsistent with, or even contradictory to, an individual's usual standards and values. The individuals react as though they have been "hypnotized," i.e., they function like subjects in a hypnotic transference regression. Freud interpreted the contagion of thought and feeling in a group, previously attributed to suggestion, as due to transference and the interidentification of the members of the group with each other and with the leader. Analysts later formulated the group as a new family: the group and its leader could function as benevolent or destructive parent, or as a collective object.

Psychoanalysis opened new paths to the understanding of mob violence, gang activity, and the everyday phenomena of social bigotry, racism, power politics, and institutional and national myths. The emergence of psychoanalytic thought on the relationship of hypnotic phenomena to some group phenomena contributed to an expanding knowledge of the dynamics of brainwashing, cults, and mass hysteria. The further development of psychoanalytic theory allowed new comprehension of group processes and group therapies, as well as of the role of the individual within the new family of the group.

Freud's "Dora" Case

THE CRUCIBLE OF THE PSYCHOANALYTIC CONCEPT OF TRANSFERENCE

Hannah S. Decker

URING THE early years of his career as a psychoanalyst, Sigmund Freud published five case histories that have become famous. The cases are familiarly known as Little Hans, Dora, the Rat Man, Schreber, and the Wolf Man, and in each one Freud disclosed something new he had learned about human psychology or psychotherapeutic technique. Even though it has been almost one hundred years since they were written, analysts in training continue to use these cases to master Freud's findings. However, that is not the only reason why interest in these cases persists: they remain popular because they make compelling reading, magnetizing the reader and drawing her or him in. It was for a very good reason that Freud won the 1930 Goethe Prize for literature awarded by the city of Frankfurt.

Freud himself recognized early on—even before he coined the term "psychoanalysis" to describe his new kind of therapy—that he was doing something special in writing up his case material. "I have not always been a psychotherapist," he wrote in discussing the situation of "Fräulein Elisabeth von R." in 1895,

> Like other neuropathologists, I was trained to employ local diagnoses and electro-prognosis, and it still strikes me myself as strange that the case histories I write should read like short stories and that, as one might say, they lack the serious stamp of science. . . . The fact is that local diagnosis and electrical reactions lead nowhere in the study of hysteria, whereas a

detailed description of mental processes such as we are accustomed to find in the works of imaginative writers enables me, with the use of a few psychological formulas, to obtain at least some kind of insight into the course of that affection.[1]

In particular, the case history of "Dora"—officially the "Fragment of an Analysis of a Case of Hysteria"—has long been known among analysts for its vivid illustration of the phenomenon of "transference." Transference occurs in psychoanalytic treatment when patients "transfer" feelings they have for important figures in their lives onto their analyst. The story of Freud's patient Dora (his pseudonym for Ida Bauer) not only illumines the concept of transference but also shows how Freud missed the all-important transference that occurred during Dora's treatment, an omission that may have had significant consequences in her life.

Recently, this case history has drawn a great deal of attention, overshadowing, in some circles, its traditional role as a learning tool and its ability to captivate. Dora's case owes its current fame, indeed notoriety, to feminists and literary critics who have found in Freud's treatment of his patient an overweening masculine bias, grossly unsympathetic treatment, and significant errors of technique. However, regardless of why the case commands attention, the story it tells is absorbing.[2]

IN OCTOBER 1900 Dora, just short of eighteen, was brought to Freud by her father, Philipp Bauer, a forty-seven-year-old prosperous textile manufacturer. Dora had been depressed for two years, eating little, not wearing her usual jewelry, and frequently staying home. She occasionally attended lectures for women, studied on her own, or went to art galleries, but fundamentally she was dissatisfied with herself, found it difficult to concentrate, was often fatigued, and had withdrawn from social contact. She was on bad terms with her thirty-eight-year-old mother, Käthe Bauer, and refused to help with the housework. Dora also fought a lot with her father, to whom she had previously been close. Things began to come to a head after her parents found a suicide note in her desk. Soon after, in the middle of an argument with her father, she had fainted, had convulsions, and later could not remember the entire incident. Her parents had lived with her depression and irritability, but these latest events propelled them to seek medical attention. Freud had successfully treated Philipp for syphilitic symptoms six years earlier, so it was to this neighborhood neurologist that Dora's father now brought his daughter for treatment. Dora had not wanted to go, but Philipp had insisted.

Encounters with physicians were not rare occurrences for Dora; they went back to her childhood. She had been treated for late-onset bed-wetting at age seven or eight, and then for a case of "nervous" shortness of breath that had lasted six months (though episodes of troubled breathing continued to recur from time to time). At eight, it was noted, her whole personality had changed, going from that of a "wild creature" to that of a quiet, well-behaved child. At twelve, she began suffering from migraines, lost her voice for weeks at a time, and developed a hacking, metallic cough. Numerous doctors had been consulted to no avail. The migraines gradually lifted, but the loss of voice, hoarseness, and cough clung tenaciously.

Attempting to rid herself of her disabling and enervating symptoms, Dora tried the standard cures of the day: electrotherapy and hydrotherapy. In electrotherapy, currents of electricity were run through the body or applied to local areas, often with disagreeable side effects of pain, skin blistering, minor burns, nausea, dizziness, trembling, and involuntary defecation. Hydrotherapy ordinarily involved being sprayed with jets of cold (45° F) water.[3] None of these treatments was of any help to Dora, and she became contemptuous of the physicians from whom she sought relief.

Soon after Dora began seeing him, Freud learned of the reason for the depression she had been suffering with for the past two years. Dora had been born in Vienna, but when she was six her father became ill with tuberculosis and her family had moved to Meran (Merano), an area of low-lying mountains in what is now northern Italy. Meran was widely renowned as a place for rest cures because of its mild winter climate and the supposedly curative local grapes that grew in its radioactive soil. Within two years, Philipp recovered sufficiently to begin making business trips, but for the sake of preserving his health, the Bauers remained in Meran. It was at the time when Philipp started traveling again, disrupting a close relationship that had sprung up with Dora while he was an invalid, that the eight-year-old girl had undergone her personality change.

In Meran, Dora's family became friendly with the "K.s," a somewhat younger family. When Philipp developed serious symptoms of tertiary syphilis a few years later, Mr. K. recommended that he see Freud for treatment, and Mrs. K. became his primary nurse. The onset of Dora's headaches, voice problems, and cough occurred in these circumstances. After an interval, Philipp recovered enough to resume his business activities. Dora became a sort of nursemaid/teacher to the K.s' two young children, one of whom had a heart condition.

Within a short time, it became common knowledge that Philipp and Mrs. K. were having an affair. During the same period, Mr. K. grew friendly with Dora, going for walks with her and buying her presents. After a while, he began to spend a lot of time with her and sent her flowers daily when his business kept him in town. When he was traveling, he sent her picture postcards, letting her alone know when he was expected back. During this period Dora and Mrs. K. drew closer, and Dora often spent nights sleeping over at the K.s' in their bedroom, at which times Mr. K. removed himself. Dora appeared to have an adolescent crush on Mrs. K, referring to her "adorable white body."[4] On these sleep-overs, the two discussed many intimate matters.

One day, when Dora was thirteen, Mr. K. invited her to his place of business to view a church festival with him and his wife. When she arrived, she found that Mrs. K. and all the clerks had gone. After Mr. K. had closed the shutters, he drew Dora to him at the office door and attempted to kiss her on the lips. She wrenched herself free and ran down the stairs and into the street. She told no one of this incident and for a while made sure she was not alone with Mr. K., but soon their relationship resumed.

Two summers later, when Dora was fifteen, she accompanied her father to the K.s' summer house in the Alps, where Philipp was to remain for a few days and Dora for a stay of several weeks. One day Dora and Mr. K. went on a boat trip on a lake, and when the boat had docked, they took a walk. Mr. K. began talking to Dora earnestly, and she soon realized he was making a sexual proposition. Later, all she remembered was that he had said: "You know I get nothing out of my wife."[5] As soon as it dawned on her what Mr. K. was saying, she slapped his face and rushed away. Later that day, while taking a nap in the bedroom, she awakened to find Mr. K. standing beside her and felt threatened. When her father prepared to leave as planned, Dora refused to stay on and insisted on leaving with him. For a week she wondered what to do and then told her mother, who told her father.

Philipp confronted Mr. K. with Dora's account, but he denied the entire incident, saying Dora must have imagined the episode. Mr. K. added that he understood from his wife that Dora had been reading books on sex which must have overexcited her. Much to Dora's distress, Philipp told her that he believed Mr. K., clearly implying that he felt his daughter to be in the grip of some mental aberration.

Dora sank into despair and rumination. Over the next two years, she begged her father to break off his friendship with the K.s, to no avail. When feeling especially embittered over her situation, such as when Philipp would leave home to be with Mrs. K., she would sink under the weight of the thought that "she had been handed over to Mr. K. as the price of his tolerating the relations between her father and his wife."[6] Rage at Philipp overcame her. Brooding over the fact that her parents did not believe her, that Mr. K. had lied, and that Mrs. K. had betrayed the confidences they had shared, Dora plunged into a depression that did not remit in the two years prior to her father's bringing her to Freud.

Dora's situation commands attention today because of our awareness of the gravity of sexual advances made to young girls and teenagers by older men, especially when compounded by adult refusal to believe the victim's accounts. It is obvious that in Dora's case, she became seriously ill after her father's denial of the reality of her experience. Though readily acknowledged today, these aspects of Dora's circumstances went ignored by psychoanalysts for many decades after Freud first published the case in 1905. Instead, analysts focused on what Freud—who admitted that he had failed to help Dora—said was the main lesson he had learned from her treatment: the significance of transference. Although Freud failed his patient, his discovery turned out to be of immense importance to the development of psychoanalysis, and indeed to all psychotherapy.

FEELINGS THAT the patient "transfers" onto the analyst are for the most part unconscious. The most common transferences are either "erotic" or "negative," and one or both may occur. That is, the patient "falls in love" with the therapist, duplicating a past love feeling, or develops a hostility toward the analyst, based on previous angers. The analyst must not take these "transference neuroses" as reality and reciprocate in that vein, but instead must get the patient to recognize the full, upsetting extent of his or her past longings and animosities, which, since they are usually not conscious, often adversely affect the patient's social relationships. The transference situation is complicated by the phenomenon of "countertransference," the feelings and attitudes the analyst brings to the relationship between him or herself and the patient.

Freud had begun to be aware of the transference—and of the power it had as an obstacle to the treatment if the patient was not taught to recognize it—about five years before he treated Dora.[7] In his writings, we see occasional mentions of the phenomenon.[8] Then, just six months before he took Dora into treatment, he expressed his dawning awareness of the importance of the transference and his still shaky mastery of it. In a letter, he wrote to his close friend in Berlin, Wilhelm Fliess, about the conclusion of an analysis of a patient of several years, a "Mr. E." E. had gotten a great deal better, but not entirely, and Freud had an inkling as to why. "I am beginning to understand that the apparent endlessness of the treatment is something that occurs regularly and is connected with the transference. . . . Since [E.] had to suffer through all my technical and theoretical errors, I actually think that a future case could be solved in half the time. May the Lord now send the next one."[9] But the Lord sent only two new patients (and one of them lasted just a month) before Dora entered treatment. Freud had little chance to sharpen his knowledge of the transference before she showed up.

Dora began to see Freud in a daily analysis (only Sunday was excluded) at the beginning of October 1900. On New Year's Eve she abruptly departed without prior warning, much to Freud's shock. He had been feeling that the analysis was going very well and expected it to be a success within a year's time. In a postscript tacked onto the case presentation, he mulled over what had gone wrong. Why had he not seen Dora's departure coming? He came to the conclusion that he had "not succeed[ed] in mastering the transference in good time."[10] We also see today that issues of sex and anger dominated the analysis in ways that Freud, in his inexperience as a psychoanalyst, scarcely suspected.

To some extent Freud had been aware of one aspect of the transference: his correspondence, in Dora's eyes, to her father. Freud recognized that Dora saw the two men similarly because they were close in age—Freud was forty-four years old and Philipp forty-seven—and both smoked cigars. She even worried that Freud was not being

"straightforward" with her because her father, she said, "always pre-
ferred secrecy and roundabout ways."[11] But Dora's paternal transference to Freud went even further than Freud saw. He did not recognize
the transference resistance from Dora based on the fact that he knew
the Bauer family (they had moved back to Vienna from Meran and
lived three blocks from each other) and had met Philipp's older
brother and younger sister. Moreover, Freud had treated Philipp for
syphilis before Dora was brought to him against her will. So Dora
came to Freud suspecting that he was an ally of her family.

There was another aspect of the transference which Freud missed.
Dora believed that she had been sexually used by her father to facilitate
his love affair with Mrs. K., both by baby-sitting the K.s' children
whenever Philipp and Mrs. K. wanted to be alone together and by
being her father's gift to Mr. K. as a means of keeping him quiet about
his wife's affair with Philipp. Freud, too, was sexually using Dora,
through his repeated questions and interpretations to her about her
sexual fantasies and sexual knowledge. In a society where such matters
were not openly discussed, where girls did not reach puberty until fifteen or sixteen and where eighteen-year-old girls were supposed to
know little about sex, Freud, from the moment the analysis began,
talked to Dora about masturbation, fellatio, intercourse, and her sexual
yearnings. Today, psychoanalysts conclude "that the discussion of sex
in [Dora's] analysis had the transference significance of a defloration
[which] was . . . elaborated into [an unconscious] transference fantasy
of Freud—the purveyor of sexual information—forcing his way into
Dora."[12]

In addition to Freud's failure to perceive the full extent of Dora's
paternal transference, he almost totally overlooked the feelings she
transferred from Mr. K. to him. Freud early on had a hint that Dora
might leave the treatment when she related to him a dream she initially
had after the incidents occurring during her stay with the K.s in the
Alps. The dream was about her being in a house on fire from which her
father had rescued her; during the psychoanalysis she had the same
dream. Freud interpreted its recurrence to mean that Dora had
decided to flee the treatment as she had fled the K.s' house.[13] But,
Freud later wrote, he neglected to say to her, "It is from Herr K. that
you have made a transference on to me."[14]

Furthermore, the rest of the transference from Mr. K. went unnoticed. Dora felt that Freud, with his great emphasis on sexual matters,

was symbolically doing to her what Mr. K. had done physically when he grabbed and kissed her in his office and when he suggested a sexual liaison the day at the lake. Beyond this, there lay the fear that Freud might actually attempt such an assault. After all, he had told her, in interpreting a dream, that she must want a kiss from him since he was an avid smoker like Mr. K. and her father.[15]

There was yet a third transference that Freud overlooked. This one was from all the doctors Dora had seen throughout her life, but particularly from those who in recent years had subjected her to a variety of therapies, often painful and distressing, but who had been totally unable to help her. Freud himself wrote that "it was in such circumstances as these that the child had developed into a mature young woman of very independent judgement, who had grown accustomed to laugh at the efforts of doctors, and in the end to renounce their help entirely."[16] Yet he did not recognize how strongly Dora applied the doubts and ill feelings about physicians to her relationship with him.

Anger was a key factor in Dora's life, and Freud recognized only a small part of it. At the conclusion of his postscript, he talked about Dora's "cruel impulses and revengeful motives" regarding men, which had "become transferred on to the physician during treatment."[17] He was aware, then, that Dora was enraged at her father and at Mr. K. Dora, however, was possessed by other angers as well, to which Freud seems to have paid no attention. In 1900 he was focused on the role sexuality played in human psychology, but not particularly on the part played by anger. This was an element he only came to appreciate fully twenty years later.

Dora also transferred onto Freud negative feelings arising from a series of events that had disillusioned and embittered her, poisoning all of her encounters with the adult world. She was angry at Mrs. K., who had seemed to be a warm and concerned substitute for her cold and obsessive mother (this is the way Käthe Bauer is depicted in the case and in historical sources). Mrs. K., however, had used Dora as a nursemaid for her children and had spent many close hours with her and then had betrayed their intimate friendship by giving her husband ammunition (disclosing that Dora had read sex books when visiting her) to counter Dora's accusation against him. Moreover, as in her relationship with Mrs. K., Dora was hurt when she discovered that a governess who she thought had liked her was only interested in her as long as the woman thought she had a chance at a love affair with Philipp.

There were other disappointments and grievances particularly affecting Dora's future. A stark difference existed between her life and that of her slightly older brother, Otto. She and Otto had studied together until she was eight years old, and the two of them had been academic equals. Then, because of her sickness and psychological difficulties, she had fallen behind him. Otto had gone on to do brilliantly in high school and was pursuing a promising career at the university. Dora, by contrast, was depressed and adrift, having no plans for marriage, as she told Freud, and left to study on her own and occasionally attend lectures for women.

Looming over everything, affecting her consciousness and self-worth, was the fact that she was a Jew and a woman living in a society both anti-Semitic and misogynist. Since she had been born, she and her family had experienced increasing anti-Jewish sentiment, and in spite of the beginning of calls for female equality in Austria, still stronger voices preached women's inherent inadequacy. It was the general consensus that women were inferior, and anti-Semites insistently proclaimed that the proof of the Jews' deficiency lay in their exhibition of traits commonly associated with women. Antifeminism and anti-Semitism were thus intertwined at the turn of the century.[18] Dora was so resentful over the enmity Jews had to suffer that when her son was born in 1905 she converted to Protestantism so that he would not have to endure what she had.

One of the reasons Freud did not fully recognize the sources of Dora's anger was his countertransference, that is, the beliefs and emotions he brought to the analysis and applied to his relationship with Dora. The countertransference is an aspect of psychoanalytic treatment that Freud never pondered closely, but that modern psychoanalysts take very seriously.

ERNEST JONES, a founding member of the psychoanalytic movement and one of Freud's most noteworthy biographers, was a young neurologist when the Dora case was first published in 1905. He was immediately captivated and converted into an avid Freudian. "I well remember," he wrote a half century later, "the deep impression the intuition and the close attention to detail displayed in it made on me. Here was a man who not only listened closely to every word his patient spoke but regarded each such utterance as every whit as definite and as in need of correlation as the phenomena of the physical world. At the present day it is hard to convey what an amazing event it was for anyone to take the data of psychology so seriously."[19]

Almost a century after it was published, the Dora case lives. Dora's story is inherently absorbing and provocative, raises timely and pertinent questions for feminists, and teaches all psychoanalysts that to ignore the transference is to doom the treatment. Learning about the transference has not only revolutionized psychotherapy but has made it clear that transference is a ubiquitous phenomenon. Since every relationship we have is a compound of reality and transference, consciously recognizing our strong feelings about the important individuals of our formative years is essential to happy and productive living.

Freud failed to help Dora substantially because he was limited by his incomplete knowledge in the years he was developing psychoanalysis. Later on, as a sophisticated analyst, he was to write several papers on technique in which he acknowledged his early errors and showed he had made many significant advances. But they were too late to help Dora; from all available evidence it seems that she remained an unhappy individual and continued to suffer from multiple physical symptoms.

Freud did, however, help Dora temporarily, mainly by showing her that he took her words seriously, which no other adult at the time was willing to do. As imperfect as Dora's relationship to Freud was, his interest in her enabled her to tell another person for the first time about Mr. K.'s upsetting kiss when she was thirteen. Freud believed Dora's claim that her father was having an affair with Mrs. K., something Philipp vehemently denied, and Freud concurred in Dora's belief that her father was using her to advance his personal agenda. As a result, Dora's long-lived depression lifted and she was able to summon the courage to confront the K.s. She wrested from Mr. K. the admission that he had indeed made her a sexual proposal by the lake and from Mrs. K. that she was having an affair with her father. We know today that such acknowledgment of reality by the complicitous adults is psychologically important to a child's self-esteem. We also know that understanding the phenomenon of transference, like all of psychoanalysis itself, is about finding meaning through an exploration of concealed wishes, something that great thinkers and poets have always taught us.

Sigmund Freud's birth certificate, May 6, 1856.
Sigmund Freud Collection, Manuscript Division, Library of Congress.

The Freud family, Vienna, 1876. From left to right, standing: Paula,
Anna, unidentified girl, Sigmund, Emanuel (Freud's half-brother),
Rosa, Mitzi, and Simon Nathansohn (Amalia's cousin).
Seated: Dolfi, Amalia, unidentified boy, Alexander, and Jacob.
The Freud Museum, London.

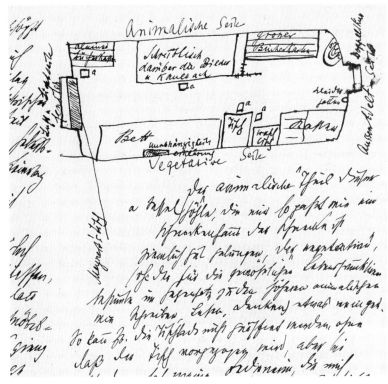

One of Freud's letters to Martha Bernays, with a sketch of
his quarters at the General Hospital. October 5, 1883.
Sigmund Freud Collection, Manuscript Division, Library of Congress.

Studio photograph of Freud,
Atelier Engel, Vienna, 1885.
Sigmund Freud Collection,
Prints and Photographs Division,
Library of Congress.

Engagement album photographs of
Martha Bernays in 1880 and of Freud
and Martha in 1886.
*Sigmund Freud Collection, Prints and
Photographs Division, Library of Congress.*

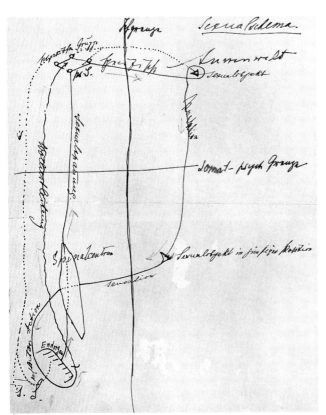

"Sexualschema" sketch in draft manuscript of "Melancholia," included in correspondence from Freud to Wilhelm Fliess, January 7, 1895.
Sigmund Freud Collection, Manuscript Division, Library of Congress.

Letter from Freud to Wilhelm Fliess, September 21, 1897, stating, "I no longer believe in my theory of neurosis." In this revealing letter Freud gives Fliess an account of why he lost confidence in the seduction theory, an important turning point in his work.
Sigmund Freud Collection, Manuscript Division, Library of Congress.

Freud with three of his five sisters and his mother at the grave of his father, Jacob Freud, Vienna, 1897.
The Freud Museum, London.

Freud (front row, fourth from right) at Clark University, Worcester, Massachusetts, September 1909, where he presented a series of lectures that introduced psychoanalysis to America. Also shown in the photograph are, front row, Franz Boas (far left), William James (third from left), Carl Jung (third from right); second row, Ernest Jones (fourth from right), A. A. Brill (third from right); third row, Sándor Ferenczi (fifth from right).
Sigmund Freud Collection, Prints and Photographs Division, Library of Congress.

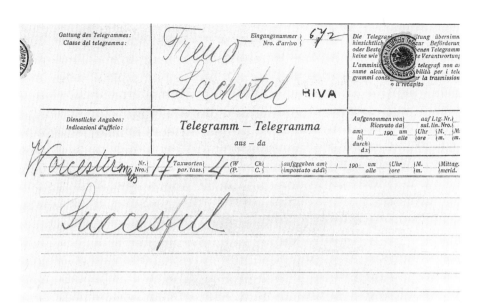

Gattung des Telegrammes: / *Classe del telegramma:*

Freud Lachotel RIVA

Eingangsnummer } 672 / Nro. d'arrivo }

Die Telegra... ...tung übernimm... hinsichtlich... ...enen Telegramm oder Beste... ...te Verantwortun keine wie... L'amminis... telegrafi non as sume alcun... ...bilità per i tele grammi conse... ...r la trasmission o il recapito

Dienstliche Angaben: / *Indicazioni d'ufficio:*

Telegramm — Telegramma
aus – da

Aufgenommen von } *auf Ltg. Nr.* } / *Ricevuto da* } *sul. lin. Nro.* } am } / 190. um {Uhr {M. {M il } alle {ore {m. {m durch } da }

Worcester Nr. } 17 Taxworten } 4 (W Ch {aufgegeben am} / 190 um {Uhr {M. {Mittag. Nro.} par. tass.} (P. C.} {impostato addi} alle {ore {m. {merid.

Succesful

Telegram sent by Freud to his wife, Martha, from Worcester, Massachusetts, in 1909, referring to his reception in America.
Sigmund Freud Collection, Manuscript Division, Library of Congress.

Sergei Pankejeff, the "Wolf Man" (right), and his family in Odessa (undated).
Sergei Pankejeff Papers, Manuscript Division, Library of Congress.

Sigmund and Anna Freud on holiday in the Dolomites, Italy, 1913.
Sigmund Freud Collection, Prints and Photographs Division, Library of Congress.

Manuscript for "The Moses of Michelangelo," with accompanying sketch. Published in 1914.
Sigmund Freud Collection, Manuscript Division, Library of Congress.

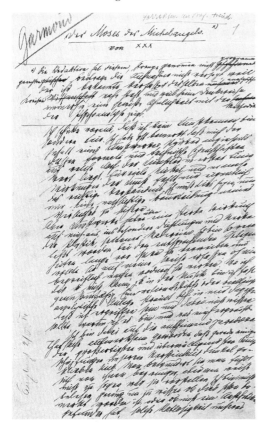

Freud with sons
Ernst (left) and
Martin. Salzburg,
August 1916.
Carl Ellinger, photographer.
Sigmund Freud Collection,
Prints and Photographs
Division, Library of
Congress.

Freud at a psychoanalytic congress
in The Hague, 1920.
Henry Verby, photographer.
Sigmund Freud Collection, Prints and
Photographs Division, Library of Congress.

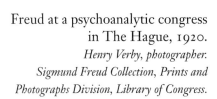

The "Committee," a group of Freud's intimates who were
united in their devotion to psychoanalysis and who promised
to watch over its development and practice. Left to right,
seated: Freud, Sándor Ferenczi, and Hans Sachs.
Standing: Otto Rank, Karl Abraham, Max Eitingon, and
Ernest Jones. Berlin, 1922.
*Sigmund Freud Collection, Prints and
Photographs Division, Library of Congress.*

Manuscript page from *The Ego
and the Id*, published in 1923.
*Sigmund Freud Collection, Manuscript
Division, Library of Congress.*

Freud and his mother, Amalia, in her apartment in Vienna, May 5, 1925.
Sigmund Freud Collection, Prints and Photographs Division, Library of Congress.

Freud next to his analytic couch in an unidentified summer residence, 1932.
Sigmund Freud–Museum, Vienna.

Freud's consulting room, with the famous analytic couch. Vienna, 1938.
© *Edmund Engelman. Sigmund Freud Collection, Prints and Photographs Division, Library of Congress.*

A page from Freud's short-entry diary, April to September 1934, in which he noted current events, visits, appointments, and work progress.
Sigmund Freud Collection, Manuscript Division, Library of Congress.

Freud on the balcony
of his summer home,
Hohe Warte, in 1933
with the family's dogs.
© Edmund Engelman.
Sigmund Freud Collection,
Prints and Photographs
Division, Library of
Congress.

Freud's study at Berggasse 19, Vienna, 1938.
© Edmund Engelman. Sigmund Freud Collection,
Prints and Photographs Division, Library of Congress.

Berggasse 19 with a swastika above the door. Vienna, May 1938.
© *Edmund Engelman.*

Freud en route to exile in London, with Princess Marie
Bonaparte and William Bullitt. Paris, June 13, 1938.
New York World-Telegram and Sun Collection,
Prints and Photographs Division, Library of Congress.

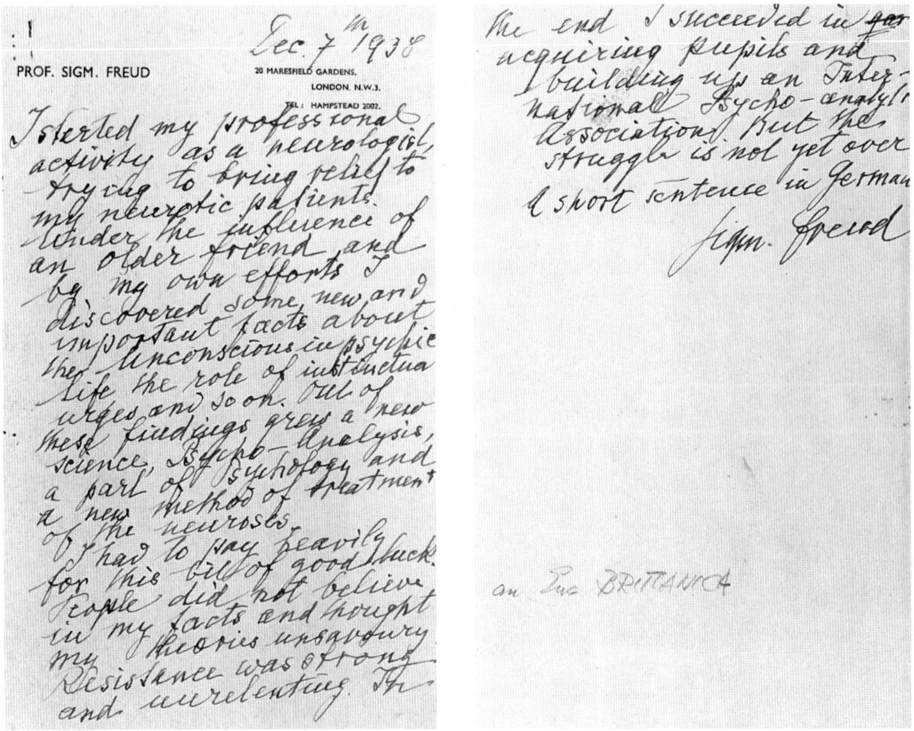
PROF. SIGM. FREUD
20 MARESFIELD GARDENS,
LONDON, N.W.3.
TEL: HAMPSTEAD 2002.

Dec. 7th 1938

I started my professional
activity as a neurologist,
trying to bring relief to
my neurotic patients.
Under the influence of
an older friend and
by my own efforts I
discovered some new and
important facts about
the Unconscious in psychic
life the role of instinctual
urges and so on. Out of
these findings grew a new
science, Psycho-Analysis,
a part of psychology and
a new method of treatment
of the neuroses.
I had to pay heavily
for this bit of good luck.
People did not believe
in my facts and thought
my theories unsavoury.
Resistance was strong
and unrelenting. In
the end I succeeded in
acquiring pupils and
building up an Inter-
national Psycho-analytic
Association. But the
struggle is not yet over
a short sentence in German
Sigm. Freud

an Enc BRITTANICA

Manuscript of Freud's BBC interview statement, December 7, 1938.
Sigmund Freud Collection, Manuscript Division, Library of Congress.

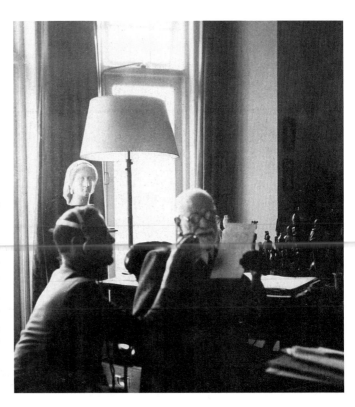

Freud recording an interview for broadcast on the BBC in his London home on December 7, 1938. He spoke of his life and work and closed by stating that "the struggle is not yet over."
The Freud Museum, London.

Manuscript page from *Civilization and Its Discontents*, published in 1930.
Sigmund Freud Collection, Manuscript Division, Library of Congress.

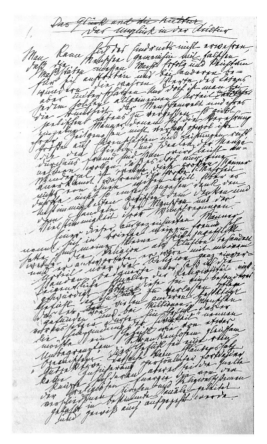

Freud in his study at Maresfield Gardens, his home in London, 1938.
Oliver Freud Papers, Manuscript Division, Library of Congress.

Freud during the last year of his life, at Maresfield Gardens, 1939.
Oliver Freud Papers, Manuscript Division, Library of Congress.

PART III

Absorption and Diffusion

Freud's influence was not to be found in specific texts or arguments but, as Auden wrote in his "In Memory of Sigmund Freud," in "a whole climate of opinion." The founder of psychoanalysis often noted the "splendid isolation" of his early years, when lack of attention seemed to be punctuated only by occasional outbursts of hostility. Perhaps Freud needed to believe that he was struggling against the world in order to maintain his commitment to his ideas and methods. By the end of his life, however, he could see that his work had not only spread across the globe, but that it was being used for purposes far beyond what he had intended for it. Psychoanalysis had become a key currency for elite and popular culture, for politics and romance, for paintings that aimed to express the unconscious, as well as for cartoons that targeted the whole enterprise for ridicule.

Freud and psychoanalysis have been one of the main areas of Peter Gay's historical research; he has also used psychoanalytic ideas in his approach to other historical subjects. In his essay in this section, however, Gay notes the widespread indifference and even antagonism among historians to Freud's theories. Despite the fact that historians and analysts are often addressing similar problems, productive interactions between these groups have been few and far between. The rest of the essays in this section describe how Freud's style of thinking spread by means of both the institution of psychoanalysis and the capillaries of popular culture. Edith Kurzweil's subject is the remarkable diffusion of psychoanalysis in the United States, beginning with Freud's 1909 trip to Massachusetts. The Second World War was the great accelerator in the professional domain, as refugee analysts found a home for themselves and their families (and sometimes for their ideas) in America. Robert Coles examines the reverse side of this process: the Americanization of psychoanalysis. As the vocation became a profession, it normalized its practitioners, creating its own kind of orthodoxy in contrast (and sometimes in opposition) to "the Pope in Vienna." E. Ann Kaplan is interested in yet another route of diffusion—the powerful medium of film. Even in Freud's own time, filmmakers were eager to bring his ideas to the screen. He was skeptical, however, that any of the unconscious processes could be represented through the cinema. Psychoanalysis appears in film framed and reframed in different cultural contexts, and Kaplan notes that in our own time the analyst is less a figure of authority or even intrigue and more likely a figure of fun. The comic possibilities of psychoanalysis are endless, and in the last essay of this section Art Spiegelman suggests why, while demonstrating still new possibilities in his "comix." Jokes may be symptomatic, but good ones can instruct even as they amuse.

Psychoanalysis and the Historian

Peter Gay

UNLIKE OTHER human sciences—sociology, economics, or anthropology—history has never enjoyed a cordial relationship with psychoanalysis. There was a brief flicker of interest, and we can date it precisely: early 1958. In January the *American Historical Review*, the house organ of the profession, published William L. Langer's presidential address, "The Next Assignment," delivered the previous December. Three months later, the psychoanalyst Erik Erikson brought out *Young Man Luther*, a biographical essay promisingly subtitled *A Study in Psychoanalysis and History*.

Langer argued that historians' next assignment should be the application of psychoanalysis in historical investigations. His talk generated widespread, respectful interest among historians largely because Langer was a professional with impeccable credentials, earned in such traditional, wholly respectable fields as diplomatic history. If this honorable, seasoned craftsman, a most improbable recruit for the Freudian dispensation, commended it to his colleagues, perhaps there was something to psychohistory after all.

Erikson for his part offered a gracefully written psychoanalytic biography that showed a gratifying, far from condescending familiarity with earlier lives of Martin Luther—a sizable literature. Erikson's was a text preaching by example. It was also, as time would reveal, a flawed work, heavily dependent on anecdotes of dubious authenticity. Although Erikson confronted some skeptical assessments from the outset—indeed, *Young Man Luther* was never reviewed in the *American*

Historical Review—for a time it appeared that, given Langer's prestige, psychoanalytically informed history might be on the historian's agenda.

This hope has largely faded. A few historians continue to rely on the Freudian corpus of ideas in their work; occasionally—very occasionally—they manage to find periodicals willing to publish articles indebted to psychoanalytic thought; and there is still a tiny handful of periodicals in rather precarious condition bravely attempting to keep alive the psychoanalytic approach in the profession. But by and large the critics of psychoanalytic versions of history, rarely bland and usually savage, have carried the day. Even historians who are not shy of deploying technical terms such as "repression" or "family romance" and the like will not commit themselves to the discipline that originated those terms.

This requires some explanation. To be sure, those who view psychoanalytic theories as a fraud, or nonsense, or a failed psychology, have no doubt as to why the historical profession has not embraced Freud. The reasons why Freud has so rarely persuaded historians, they are bound to argue, lies in the bankruptcy of his thinking—entirely. Why utilize a discredited auxiliary discipline? But if one is not quite so certain of the case against psychoanalysis, the aversion of historians does seem somewhat surprising. After all, psychoanalysis, like history, concentrates on understanding the past, works to make illegible clues legible, and digs beneath surfaces to hidden layers obscured and distorted by the passage of time, or by the writers'—or the public's—need to deny unpleasant truths. Psychoanalysis, like history, is an empirical inquiry that, though guided by theory, and for all its mysterious methods of procedure, is wedded to the conscientious search for evidence. What is more, the most sophisticated practitioners in either field have shown themselves to be critical rather than naïve realists, aware that while they rely on the reality of what they are searching for, this reality is never obvious.

Yet nearly all historians, professional and lay, even those who find in Freud's map of human nature a set of usable generalizations, are, if not indifferent or hostile to the very idea of availing themselves of psychoanalysis in their work, at least nervous about it. They have justified their anxieties and rebuffs by drawing up a list of obstacles that, in their mind, must confront the historian interested in deploying psychoanalytic knowledge, obstacles that must make it useless, if not damaging, to their inquiries. To sum up the most important of the arguments: psychoanalytic history seems virtually guaranteed to be impermissibly reductionist, as well as reckless, in its way of dealing with scanty or elusive evidence. What is more, the technical terminology that psychoanalytic historians like to smuggle into their writings is an insult to the literary heritage of their craft, a heritage in which most historians still take much pride. At best the psychoanalytic perspective on human nature is an impoverished thing, based, if the truth were known, on a highly selective, highly unrepresentative sample of humanity: late-nineteenth-century upper-class Viennese Jewish women. Nor does the subject matter of psychoanalytic investigation appear to be of immediate interest to historians, concentrating as it does on such subjective phenomena as fantasies and dreams. Historians deal with realities remote from those confessed on the couch. Worse still, psychoanalysis is severely individualistic and thus unable to accommodate the collective experiences that make up the bulk of the historian's material. We cannot psychoanalyze the dead.

It is impossible in a short essay to undertake a detailed exploration of these challenges. Nevertheless, a rapid review of Freud's ideas, of his legacy—and of his travail in the marketplace of ideas—is not out of place. Freud, we must recall, after years of pondering the nature and treatment of neurosis, returned to his original life's ambition to solve some of the mysteries of human life. Certainly by the late 1890s, when he was completing work on *The Interpretation of Dreams*, he had convinced himself that he was developing a psychology that would account not only for the mental life of neurotics but also for that of so-called normal persons. It is precisely the ambitiousness of his thought, a thought that by its very nature professes universal validity, that makes it relevant to the tough-minded questions historians ask and to the tough-minded answers they attempt to supply.

The most cursory survey of the psychohistorical literature demonstrates that its critics have a point. At least some of that literature has been reductionist or reckless or both. Intoxicated by the heady promise of a refined psychological instrument able to penetrate to the heart of the matter, psychohistorians have been known to carelessly oversimplify. One could cite texts that give historic events, and historic lives, what we might call the "nothing but" treatment. One cannot, and should not, reduce a revolution to an enlarged, spectacular version of the Oedipus complex in action, or the pronouncements and excited lives of religious reformers to certain traumatic deprivations in their childhood. True, the charge of bad writing among psychohistorians has been much exaggerated. While jargon is unlovely at all times, the most articulate among historians indebted to psychoanalysis—for example, the eminent American historian Richard Hofstadter—have shown in their work that it is possible to be a brilliant stylist and a receptive student of Freud at the same time.

Moreover, defenders of psychohistory should have no trouble acknowledging that we cannot possibly psychoanalyze the dead. Even after we have set aside skeptics who insist that we cannot psychoanalyze the living, either, we must recognize that this statement does point to some significant differences between the procedures of the psychoanalyst and those of the historian. The analysand speaks, does almost nothing but speak; in sharp contrast, Clio is silent, resisting analysis, almost defying the investigator to discover the truth about her. Historical personages dream, and have at times left in their diaries or writings tantalizing fragments of their manifest dreams. Except in some extremely rare instances, these personages, unlike analysands, have almost never supplied any evidence of having interpreted their dreams, or of having followed strands of their dream elements wherever they may lead. In short, Clio cannot respond to the analyst's—or the historian's—interpretations and thus can neither deepen nor complicate insights. The historian is bound to make guesses, one hopes well-informed guesses, to fill in the gaps in the evidence.

All of this is beyond dispute, but does not automatically discredit all attempts to apply psychoanalytic categories to individuals and groups that are no longer accessible to direct analytic treatment. Since Thucydides (one thinks of his analysis of the plague in Athens and its traumatic effects), there has been no question that all historians act as amateur psychologists. They are bound to attribute motives, describe inner conflicts, trace the tortuous path from intentions to actions. Yet there is no question that any psychological system to which the historian might apply is bound to include a measure of speculation. What is at issue, then, is not whether historians should give up conjecturing about motives for action—it is something they cannot afford to give up—but, rather, which psychological theory is most likely to get results. Even if we acknowledge the distance between the analytical situation and the work of the historical investigator, whether in an archive, at his desk, or in the field, psychoanalysis may claim enough utility to deserve consideration, a utility that goes to the bedrock of the Freudian dispensation. However psychologists, psychiatrists, and biologists may revise details of that dispensation, its essential elements remain intact and reach deeper than any other psychology. It recognizes the gap between conscious mentation and unconscious wishes, the central significance of conflicts, the urgent pressures of the drives and the maneuvers of psychological defenses to control them, the schedules of human development.

Indeed, what is implied in these key propositions of psychoanalysis transcends what has often been considered Freud's narrow evidentiary base. As we have noted, he himself took his discoveries to apply to all of humanity, present and past. Like the philosophical historians of the Enlightenment, unmistakably his intellectual ancestors, Freud was confident that such universal urges as love and hatred, and such universal responses as repression and anxiety, were not the monopoly of his time and his class but had been indispensable endowments ever since the human animal began to stand on two legs. It is intriguing to note in this connection that while we have no complete repertory of Freud's patients—at least none that is publicly accessible—we know that he analyzed Americans, Russians, Englishmen, and Frenchwomen, as well as Austrians, men as well as women, Christians as well as Jews. Beyond this, he made imaginative forays into fictional characters, Italian artists dead more than three centuries, and other "analysands" quite remote from what is generally supposed to have been his exclusive clientele.

More important still, there is no validity in the objection that Freud's ideas do not touch those realities that are the historian's bread and butter. In the first place—and it is the merit of psychoanalysis to have made this point forcefully—fantasies are realities, usually potent realities in fact, which require quite as intensive study as the more obvious bits of evidence. It was no discovery of psychoanalysis that humans are not wholly rational, that neurotic preoccupations are not specific to this individual or that. It did not uncover the fact that collective national or racial prejudices, or religious passions, compel humans into attitudes and acts that would remain altogether inexplicable if they were studied under the reasonable rubric of raw self-interest alone. This is an insight that is very old, going back at least to Thucydides. What Freud did with this insight was to systematize it, to show how fantasies arise and how they are most likely to have consequences. Granted, fantasies are shadowy things that are hard to track down, often leaving barely visible traces, but the historian who does find them at work may feel himself fortunate. He is on his way to historical truths. He is obliged to take historical realities into account. "If men define situations as real," as the sociologist W. I. Thomas famously said long ago, "they are real in their consequences."

This is not all. Widely accepted convictions to the contrary, psychoanalysis is neither remote from, nor antagonistic to, day-to-day, garden-variety—let us call them "hard"—realities. Concentrating as they do on more intangible phenomena, psychoanalysts have weakened their position by failing to stress this point, of such central importance for historians. In Freud's final theory of mind, the so-called structural theory developed after World War I, the id is wholly unconscious, the ego and the superego partially so. This means that both ego and superego, but especially the ego, persistently face the external world. So intimate and private a conflict as the Oedipus complex is, to Freud's mind, significantly shaped by outer forces, by experiences in school, at play, through reading. The external culture, even if it only occupies the background of most psychoanalytic sessions, is always there. The ego calculates, judges, and makes predictions as it works through multitudinous signals from the environment: signals from parents, nursemaids, siblings, teachers, and priests; from class, religious, and national loyalties.

The way the mind works through these impulses does not necessarily distort the material that pours in on the individual. "We expect from normal people," Freud once noted, "that they will keep their relation to money wholly free from libidinal influences and regulate them by realistic considerations." In the symbolic scheme of psychoanalysis, money may stand for feces, but by no means is this always the case. To paraphrase the most frequently quoted sentence that Freud never uttered, sometimes a dollar is just a dollar. In fact, it follows from his view of the human ego that a full analysis of a human being, or of human groups, cannot do without the interactions of inner and outer life. And this is where the historian enters the scene.

This interaction plainly complicates Freud's individualistic perspective. True, the encounter between analyst and analysand locked into the hermetic psychoanalytic situation seems the very epitome of that individualism: one lonely sufferer talking to one isolated healer, their communications symbolically and actually protected by the double doors to the latter's consulting room. Yet, again, the Other, the world, is always an invisible presence. When a couple makes love, Freud once said, there are always four persons present.

The same complex, multilayered world is the world of groups—religious congregations, political parties, racial communities, economic classes—that together make up the subjects which historians are most likely to focus their inquiry on. At this point, once again, we may fault the psychoanalytic profession for failing to throw a bridge between its insights and the needs of the historical craft. In 1977, when the American Psychoanalytic Association mounted a panel on the psychoanalytic knowledge of group processes, its chairman, Burness E. Moore, ruefully noted that the last panel to deal with social psychoanalysis had been offered in 1956, twenty-one years earlier. In fact, virtually all analysts, caught up in their specialized training and reluctant to get up from behind the couch, have been extremely slow to enter the field of history whether as executants or as critics. There may be wisdom in this modesty, but analysts, except perhaps for Erikson, have not attempted to transcend their limitations by recognizing them.

This great refusal has had the consequence that historians wishing to apply psychoanalytic ideas to "group processes" can count on very little guidance from psychoanalytic social psychology. Freud himself wrote no history and was deeply suspicious of biography; his one serious venture into collective conduct was a slender though highly suggestive pamphlet, *Group Psychology and the Analysis of the Ego* (1921). It offers fascinating insights into the erotic bonds that keep collective organizations together and link followers to leaders, but it leaves most of its vast field unexplored. Yet in general, Freud's fundamental ideas, far from being averse to such psychology, can serve as an important starting point for historians, though it looks as though the historians will have to complete the work themselves.

SUPPOSING ONE WISHED to reconcile psychoanalysis and history, how could such an accommodation be arranged, and what would be the gain? As I previously noted, historians have always occupied their own cultural universe, freely drawing on related disciplines—theology, philology, sociology, anthropology—for practical, as well as theoretical, guidance. No historian intending to write an authoritative (rather than merely anecdotal) study of the Great Depression would fail at least to explore, and if possible fully grasp, the fundamentals of economics. It is true enough that in comparison with the social sciences, rich, complex, and controversial as they may be, psychoanalysis offers far greater resistance to successful absorption and application.

Freud, in an excessively exclusive mood, more than once maintained that it is possible to understand his discipline only after undergoing psychoanalysis. But how many historians can expect for the sake of their profession to go through this elaborate, time-consuming, expensive, and upsetting kind of "schooling"? Historians have rarely resisted learning new languages, but five or six years on the couch? Even if one rejects Freud's demanding conditions for entering the sanctuary of psychoanalysis, even if one relies on books and courses, it remains true that psychoanalytic thinking will for a long time remain esoteric. Moreover, far too often its applicability to the material the historian has been able to unearth will be anything but self-evident, or even appropriate. If, as Freud maintained, the years of childhood and, later, the hidden life of adult emotions are of principal importance in securing an understanding of a historic personage's or historic group's thoughts and actions, then most psychoanalytic interpretations of the past must fail simply on the grounds that there is scanty material to work with. Even historians who reject any reductionist generalizations will find it hard to connect the manifest thoughts and actions that are their usual concern with underlying mental constellations, and to make a persuasive causal argument with such connections.

Fortunately, the commonplace that one cannot psychoanalyze the dead is more than just a severe critique of any attempt to translate analytic techniques into historical methods. It is also, largely by implication, a suggestion of what historians could possibly do with Freud's system of ideas. For the historian, in short, psychoanalysis should not be a book of recipes but rather a style of thinking. There are moments when it may be applied quite directly. After discovering an explicit and detailed diary, the historian may venture to behave much as the analyst might by offering an interpretation of dreams based on a fully detailed report or on the associations the dreamer has for some reason thought it interesting to put down. In such a scenario, the historian would be provided with an opportunity to draw plausible inferences.

In general, though, historians sympathetic to psychoanalysis are aided more by the questions that Freud equips them to ask than by the answers Freud entitles them to give. This is to say that the psychoanalytic bent enables historians to be alert to certain nuances that would probably escape their unanalytic colleagues. It would be absurd to disparage historians who lived too early, or who are now too reluctant, to equip themselves with a psychoanalytic perspective. Wisdom, that rare but splendid road to knowledge, has in the past permitted, and should in the future permit, historians to take account of what less insightful colleagues are bound to miss. To commend psychoanalysis as an auxiliary discipline to the historian does not involve feeling superior to a Jacob Burckhardt, a Theodor Mommsen, or a Marc Bloch just because they did not know Freudian theory.

THIS DISCUSSION is relevant to what is perhaps the most pervasive criticism that historians tend to level against one another: a failure in objectivity. They are on the whole confident that they understand the sources of bias in others—in others, to be sure, since they are confident that in their own work they are acting scientifically. Historians hardly expect a devout Catholic to say much that is positive about Martin Luther, a devout Marxist to praise John D. Rockefeller or Andrew Carnegie, a devout English patriot to let himself be carried away by the virtues of the German nation. Why this confidence in oneself and this skepticism about others? Professional historians generally attempt to approximate what they consider the full truth about the past by conscientiously following the rules of their craft: go to the evidence directly, do not discard evidence that contradicts your thesis, surround quotations with quotation marks, and acknowledge borrowings with footnotes. These paths to virtue are taken with a healthy fear of reviewers. And yet the march to historical objectivity seems to many a remote and unreachable ideal.

It is at this point that the technical psychoanalytic category of countertransference should prove helpful. Countertransference is the manner in which analysts respond to their analysands beyond the benevolent but strictly neutral, free-floating attention that is one of their profession's most significant demands. Psychoanalysts do not fully agree on the consequences of countertransferential attitudes. There have been those, like this author, who have argued that a historian's passionate engagement, though it bears heavy risks, may lead him to facts or qualities of character that less impassioned colleagues have simply missed. Putting this special reading aside, the classic position enunciated by Freud was that countertransference damages the analyst's ability to analyze freely.

An analyst who feels the pangs of countertransference—whether they manifest as boredom with the analysis, becoming enamored of or, just as bad, hostile to the patient—has ways out. To reduce or eliminate these interferences, he or she may undertake a brief self-analysis or consult a colleague to get to the bottom of this essentially unprofessional attitude. Even without Freud, historians have for a long time, albeit informally, tried to do something like this by confronting their loves and hatreds, their loyalties and aversions to the subject, thus going some way toward neutralizing emotional interference. Like psychoanalysts, historians are human and will never become a perfectly detached, wholly objective recording instrument of truth. However, the psychoanalytic understanding of this sort of involvement may serve to intensify the self-knowledge of the historian. This may be the first bridge we can throw between analysis and history. There should be others.

Freud's Reception in the United States

Edith Kurzweil

PSYCHOANALYSIS CAME to the United States in two major waves. The first one crested not long after Freud's 1909 visit to Clark University in Worcester, Massachusetts, and the second after the arrival of the European émigrés in the 1940s. Each wave brought enthusiastic supporters eager to explore psychoanalysis's scientific and curative potential while simultaneously appealing to a larger American public. Both times this dual reception engendered ambiguities and misunderstandings, threatened entrenched beliefs and careers, and raised unwarranted expectations that led to inevitable disappointments.

At the beginning of the century, leading American neurologists such as Morton Prince, James Jackson Putnam, and S. E. Jelliffe, and psychologists such as Stanley Hall, William James, and Boris Sidis, were following in the footsteps of the "French school"—Jean Martin Charcot, Hippolyte Bernheim, and Pierre Janet. They were using suggestion and (occasionally) hypnosis to cure neurotic conflicts caused by the so-called civilized morality.[1] When they read that Freud, a neurophysiologist, had made his patients' hysterical symptoms disappear by eliciting their unconscious memories and fantasies, they wanted to find out how his methods differed from theirs, and how he had come to realize that such symptoms might be due to sexual repression. Freud's claims also aroused much interest on the part of some American physicians and psychiatrists who were caring for psychotic patients in institutions, and who did not know how to go about treating neuroses. The doctors had observed that pathological traits often appeared in the very young, but had not been able to discern their roots. In 1904 Stanley Hall had stated that "if we knew enough about genetic psychology, the 'whole symphony of adult sexual feelings and acts' could be traced to infantile genital sensations."[2]

Most of America's leading physicians at that time had close ties to Europe and knew of Freud's works. So did some of the leading Protestant clergymen, who feared they would no longer be able to restrain their flock through the fear of God. Many intellectuals, among them William James, Edward Bradford Titchener, Franz Boas, and Emma Goldman, along with prominent psychiatrists and neurologists such as A. A. Brill, Adolf Meyer, and James Jackson Putnam, all came to hear Freud.

During his trip across the Atlantic with Sándor Ferenczi and C. G. Jung, Freud for the first time thought about how to present a comprehensive outline of his new science. These "introductory lectures" turned out to be tailor-made for his illustrious audience. In them, he stressed his hopes for the scientific exploration of the laws governing the unconscious, as well as the eventual liberating benefits such discoveries would bring to humanity. He emphasized the roles of sublimation, trauma, and catharsis. He painted a promising future, focusing on the efficacy and benefits of psychoanalytic intervention.

In spite of the disbelief and criticism expressed by some physicians and neurologists, many of them wanted to understand more about the unconscious, while feminists and other radicals saw in Freud's theories a means of combating sexual and social repression. Christian Science and New Thought practitioners, along with religious therapists of the Emmanuel movement, found that Freud was answering troubling questions and offering a method for helping ailing (as well as malingering) patients. Thus psychoanalysis became a rallying point for what otherwise were disparate spheres and disciplines, aims and interests.*

Whereas in his native Vienna and in the rest of Europe Freud's thought was mostly neglected or maligned, the sensationalist coverage of dream analysis by the American press appealed to the imagination of a broad segment of the American public, which, in turn, envisioned

---

*This attention itself was a response to the utopian and democratic ideals Freud had suggested early on and which he would expand on in *Totem and Taboo* (1912–13) and *Civilization and Its Discontents* (1930).

psychoanalysis as the new road to happiness. However, Freud did not approve of the application of his theories by clergymen, social workers, experts in child rearing, or criminologists.[3] He found that they all modified his methods for their own uses, and thereby overlooked "the gold of psychoanalysis"—the exceedingly laborious efforts to penetrate to the individual patient's unconscious. "Americans came too easily by truths others had struggled to discover," Freud stated, "and are too easily satisfied with superficial appearances."[4]

Immediately after his visit, Freud corresponded with a number of Americans. On November 19, 1909, for instance, Putnam wrote that he had already begun reading psychoanalysis with growing interest, and that he had many specific questions.[5] Less than a month later, he informed Freud that "the real psychoanalysis begins where the primary 'confessional' ends."[6] But Putnam was only one among many of Freud's American correspondents who wanted to learn more about psychoanalytic theory and therapy, about interpreting dreams and symptoms, and about ethical and personal problems. To further their research (and to distinguish themselves from the charlatans), Freud urged them all to establish an organization.

In 1911 twelve physicians founded the American Psychoanalytic Association (APA). In the same year, fifteen physicians, under the leadership of Brill, formed the New York Psychoanalytic Society (NYPS). In 1914 the Boston Psychoanalytic Society was started, with Putnam as president. These groups, as well as others in the Washington-Baltimore area and Chicago, were set up as affiliates of the International Psychoanalytic Association (IPA), which had been launched in 1910—by the forty-two persons who met with Freud in Nuremberg—in order to facilitate communication among followers who were dispersed throughout Europe.

In America the organizational initiatives were not accompanied by much clinical and theoretical research, yet, paradoxically, only in the U.S. did psychoanalysis have a general impact on the culture. Only in America would a practicing psychoanalyst such as Isador Coriat publish a primer answering questions the public might pose about psychoanalysis.[7] According to Nathan Hale:

Between 1915 and 1918 psychoanalysis received three-fifths as much attention as birth control, more attention than divorce, and nearly four times more than mental hygiene.... The unconscious had become a Darwinian Titan and dream analysis the road to its taming.[8]

Journalists were asking the Freudians about their cases. Eager to proselytize, some of them bragged of miracle cures; reporters' clichés were wedded to exaggerations and heightened the public's enthusiasm. Psychoanalysis reached mass circulation in women's magazines and was taught in extension classes, summer schools, and "girls' colleges" around New York. Max Eastman wrote, "It is a kind of 'magic' that is rapidly winning the attention of the most scientific minds in the world of medicine." In sum, simplified versions of psychoanalysis, at every level, although it had not gained much prestige among the majority of doctors, were permeating American culture.

ALREADY BEFORE the break with Alfred Adler (1911), who conceptualized psychoanalysis as a means to institute socialism, and with Jung (1913), who rooted the unconscious in a distant, genealogical past rather than in the individual, Freud wrote to Putnam of his distress about the seemingly irrevocable intellectual disagreements among his closest followers. To keep the damage to a minimum, he had entrusted the future of his movement to his six closest followers, his "Committee," who were to oversee psychoanalytic practices in the IPA's constituent societies. In other words, the IPA was to have the final word on qualifications for membership and on standards of training and therapy among all its affiliates, including those in America.

However, American and European educational backgrounds and general assumptions were considerably different. Freud and his early followers were all steeped in the classics. They were products of the Enlightenment and foresaw that the future of civilization would be dominated by discoveries that science alone could further. Hence Freud's writings are permeated by visions of scientific advances; he was intent on ascertaining the science of human psychology by uncovering the typical mental patterns, formed in response to early experiences, which would later on guide an individual's behavior. Because he assumed the human unconscious to be universal to humanity—much in keeping with the moral beliefs illustrated in the writings of the likes of Goethe, Schiller, Shakespeare, and Homer—he postulated that psychoanalysis, by penetrating the unconscious mind, would thus illuminate universal truths. Especially before they had many patients, Freud and his disciples applied psychoanalysis to the study of literary works and the personalities of writers and poets. Later, a few among them psychoanalyzed members of tribal societies and political leaders. Collectively, they expected psychoanalysis would eventually explain all human behavior, whether on an individual or group basis.

Indeed, by focusing on what is common to humanity, Freud's disciples were overlooking individual differences in rearing, education, and cultural assumptions. Moreover, unlike the European Freudians, who welcomed artists, psychologists, and philosophers into their inner circle, the Americans who had started psychoanalytic societies were self-selected, and often self-trained, doctors. Given the popularizations and heterodox practices current in American society, they felt they had to protect psychoanalysis (and their own reputations and careers) from the charlatans and "wild analysts." Yet the American Freudians realized that their knowledge of evolving theories and methods was scant, and thus went to Vienna and Berlin to be analyzed and to receive clinical training.

Altogether, the early psychoanalysts discounted the influence of cultural variables on individual psyches, including their own. In America, where popular success, however indirectly, hampered significant research and in-depth psychoanalyses, medical analysts felt they had to keep their distance from the popular practitioners. Therefore they vehemently insisted on keeping "laymen" out of their organizations, and their numbers remained relatively small. This stance, in turn, created a storm within the movement which erupted at the IPA meetings in Innsbruck in 1927. Twenty-eight papers were presented on the question of lay analysis. To distance themselves from the charlatans, American Freudians insisted on ignoring IPA rules—and Freud's advice—by restricting future access to their organizations to physicians alone. Even referring to Freud as "the Pope in Vienna," the Americans refused to capitulate. He addressed these issues in *The Question of Lay Analysis* (1926) and in its "Postscript" (1927).

Because American psychoanalysts realized that they were not keeping up with scientific advances, they set out to invite a number of Europeans as training analysts (including Freud, who refused for health reasons). This led to the formation of the Chicago Institute in 1930 under the aegis of Franz Alexander, and of the New York Psychoanalytic Institute in 1931 under Sándor Radó.

The rift between European and American Freudians continued to widen over the issue of admitting lay analysts. In 1936, to counter the IPA's insistence on the matter, the APA declared that it would veto any resolution by that organization addressing American issues in any way. By 1938 the APA formulated its own rules for "minimal training of physicians" at its affiliated institutes, spelled out what it considered proper conduct of members, and prohibited the admission of laymen. And they informed the IPA that its European members were not to accept American candidates who had not already been approved by the APA.[9]

Freud himself had anticipated some of these difficulties. He maintained that because psychoanalysis was a social and intellectual movement, a clinical therapy, and a theory of mind, these major thrusts were bound to come into conflict from time to time. Yet he could not foresee that the Nazis would seize power, that most of his disciples would move to America, and that World War II would effectively kill the practice of psychoanalysis on the European continent.

THE SECOND major wave of American psychoanalysis began with the arrival of the European émigrés. From the beginning, Freud had spoken of his disciples as pioneers who were exploring the hidden paths of the unconscious. Now, many of them were in the "country of pioneers." Psychoanalysis in America grew phenomenally as a result. The numbers speak for themselves: in 1920 the NYPS had 20 members, growing to 68 by 1936. In 1925 the IPA had had 210 members, of whom 16 percent lived in the United States; by 1931, of the 307 members, 22 percent were in the U.S.; and by 1952, of the 762 members, 64 percent were in the U.S.[10] In 1968 the APA had 1,255, with membership in local societies adding up to 1,846, but although APA participation would reach 2,000 in 1972, applications had already begun to decline.

The original reception of the (mostly Jewish) émigrés was mixed. Despite the fact that almost every American psychoanalyst had sent affidavits to guarantee financial support for European colleagues, and that Lawrence Kubie had organized an extremely efficient Emergency Committee to help get them into the country, many affiliates of the American Medical Association were afraid that the Europeans would be competing for their jobs. Legally, foreign nationals were not allowed to practice medicine in all but five states—they were required to pass medical boards before becoming psychoanalysts—yet they had to show that they would be self-supporting within a year in order to enter the country. Furthermore, prejudice against Jews, though not always explicit, was fairly widespread. The Emergency Committee overcame these handicaps by finding jobs in hospitals for many of Freud's followers.

In these hospital settings, the Freudians were able to demonstrate the efficacy of the "talking cure" to their colleagues, who were impressed enough to recommend that every aspiring physician learn the rudiments of psychoanalytic principles. Thus, by 1942 textbooks for medical students included a section about the influence of unconscious factors on their patient's behavior. Many of these students would later become interested in turning to psychoanalysis as a specialty. In this context, the émigrés offered a rich resource to their American colleagues. Soon they became training analysts and held the most prestigious positions in the new institutes that, mostly under their leadership, were springing up around the country. However, the disagreements about restricting the practice of psychoanalysis to physicians were still unresolved. Freud's death in September 1939, and then the war, took precedence; IPA business would not be taken up until much later.

FREUD'S THINKING had changed over his long working life, as he tried to understand the dynamics of the unconscious. This resulted in many different, and often opposite, emphases and interpretations while an organizational network was being built. In America, where the split between medical and lay analysts determined who was allowed into the APA and its affiliates, associations by so-called deviants began to proliferate. Moreover, after the Austrian *Anschluss* the Emergency Committee made exceptions for psychologists who had been close to Freud, sponsoring, for instance, Ernst Kris, Siegfried Bernfeld, Bruno Bettelheim, Erik Erikson, Otto Fenichel, and Theodor Reik. The latter, who did not appreciate becoming an "honorary member," by 1948 had started his own society and began to train psychologists. His graduates, in turn, taught others. Similar situations arose in cities throughout the country, especially on the two coasts. In 1941 Karen Horney left the New York Psychoanalytic Institute (NYPI) as a result of a long theoretical controversy. Basically, she argued that the ego-oriented psychoanalysis of her colleagues was culture-bound rather than universal, and that it often was more productive to address a patient's present in order to understand his or her past rather than to begin by eliciting insights into this past from the individual's history.

By then Horney's books, *The Neurotic Personality of Our Time* (1937) and *New Ways in Psychoanalysis* (1939), along with Erich Fromm's *Fear of Freedom* (1942), were introducing psychoanalytic concepts to a broad public—a public that did not really care about the theoretical disputes among psychoanalysts. These disputes arose over clinical methods, over differences in how to best reach patients' unconscious conflicts. Both Horney's and Fromm's brands of psychoanalysis were easier for laymen to understand, more oriented to social issues, and less focused on techniques and technicalities than those of the classical Freudians. In fact, Horney's and Fromm's theories, though far from simplistic, appealed to the American propensity to believe in quick fixes, and to the native optimism about the malleability of human nature. They were early proponents of the "cultural" and "applied" psychotherapies that would eventually flood the country.

AMONG AMERICAN Freudians, however, the theories Freud had postulated in *The Ego and the Id* (1923) would dominate for a long time. The division of the psyche into the structural components of id, ego, and superego lent itself more readily to scientific investigation than the earlier categorization of conscious, preconscious, and unconscious elements and the subsequent inquiries into narcissistic behavior. In fact, what would come to be called "American ego psychology" adopted the language of medicine and the scientific methodology of its practice. This is one reason why psychiatrists took to psychoanalysis so readily at first, and just as easily abandoned it when it did not prove as effective as expected, especially once mind-altering chemicals were being developed.

During the 1940s and 1950s the links between psychological and societal phenomena were being investigated by social scientists as well. For instance, in cooperation with émigré analysts, the Harvard sociologist Talcott Parsons set out to decode the links between human motivation and social institutions. The political scientist Harold Lasswell began explaining the behavior and ambitions of political figures in terms of their psychic makeup, following Freud's postulates in *The Ego and the Id.* Literary scholars such as Lionel Trilling, and art critics like E. H. Gombrich and Clement Greenberg, also responded to the intellectual challenges posed by psychoanalysis. The early explorations of literature and art, which had originally been championed by Otto Rank[11] and accepted to some extent by all of Freud's Viennese disciples, had not been pursued in America before the 1940s. At that point, however, academics began not only to introduce students in the humanities to psychoanalysis but also to enrich their own knowledge of it, often by collaborating with some of the émigrés, thereby furthering the acceptance of psychoanalytic insights by the intelligentsia.

It is important to note that the same European analysts who, in America, gave the impetus to "scientific ego psychology"—which would remain the dominant paradigm well into the 1970s—were also the ones to explore literary and social questions. In that domain Heinz Hartmann, who came to New York in 1939 after a brief stay in Paris, became a central figure. He had already wondered in Vienna why some individuals so readily adapt to changes in their surroundings while others cannot do so at all. His own "adaptive" innovation included working with physicians in hospital settings at a time when advances in technology allowed for new, precise observations of chemical and neurological reactions in patients. His concomitant investigations of the genetic relations between animal instinct and human drive, and between animal instinct and human ego function, led him to examine, also, the consequences of "Ego-Id differentiation." This inquiry, in turn, reinforced his conviction that an individual's mental health depends on a combination of cultural, emotional, *and* biological influences.

Certainly, in one way or another all the émigrés' experiences during their flight and resettlement had been harrowing, as we can perceive from the letters that are deposited in the Freud Archives of the Library of Congress and elsewhere. They had to cope with delegitimation as psychoanalysts, learning to function in a new language, and the difficulty of reestablishing themselves in a struggling profession. Additionally, on a personal level, they had to contend with exposure to a virulent, racially based anti-Semitism and sudden poverty, and were ignorant of American society and politics. To adapt to all this, the émigré psychoanalysts were turning themselves into their own foremost subjects. The variety of dangers and displacement they had experienced, the confidence they had gained from their work with Freud, and their dedication to perfecting psychoanalytic theory and practices helped propel their ideas into the maelstrom of American intellectual life.

That Freud's European disciples had come to psychoanalysis not only from the field of medicine but also from those of art (Erik Erikson and Ernst Kris), education (Anna Freud), philosophy (Robert Waelder), and literature (Henry Lowenfeld) gave them the range to appreciate American intellectuals' preoccupations. The scope of their interests, in turn, provided yet another impetus to attempts at solving the scientific, clinical, and theoretical problems associated with psychoanalysis. By 1946 Hartmann, together with Ernst Kris and Rudolph Loewenstein, wrote the paper that summarized the many theories Freudians had derived from their research and speculations, from clinical work and cooperation with intellectuals, and from increasingly differentiated observations of infants and children.[12] They synthesized all of these findings on a highly abstract, theoretical plane.

In 1944 a few psychoanalysts had been invited by the American government (together with some of the country's best minds) to a top secret conference on reeducating the German populace after the end of the war. They had been asked to cure war neuroses, provide a psychoanalytic portrait of Hitler, assess leadership qualities among American recruits in the armed forces, and contribute to countless symposia exploring the connections between social phenomena and the psychosomatic symptoms they might produce. These invitations certainly showed that psychoanalysis had gained much esteem, and that just a few years after their arrival the Freudians had made their mark in America.

In 1947 David M. Levy, who had left the NYPS—along with Sándor Radó, George Daniels, and Abram Kardiner—to form the Columbia University Institute for Psychoanalytic Training, wrote a book entitled *New Fields of Psychoanalysis*. He delineated its astounding influence on child guidance and noted that psychoanalytic terminology, such as "maternal overprotection," "maternal rejection," etc., had become part of everyday language. He also summarized the psychoanalytic data that could predict recidivism, which were used by lawyers in defense of criminals (and against them by parole boards). He also outlined the many collaborations psychoanalysts had forged with social workers, and with educational, industrial, and military psychiatrists. Clearly, Freud's disciples had become pillars of the American establishment.

The general questions the Freudians were then addressing, along with the clinical ones, would set their research agendas for the coming years. Hence it is no accident that when they reconvened on the European continent after the war, they would insist on imposing their theories and clinical methods on the Europeans, or that their practices would be referred to as "American" psychoanalysis.

Success brought prestige and research moneys to the profession. Until the 1970s ego psychology was the leading theory, but by then individuals and groups outside the APA were increasingly chafing at the bit. They resented the privileged status enjoyed by insiders, as well as the fact that through their affiliation with the IPA they had succeeded at exporting their clinical and theoretical views first to Europe and then to Latin America. Furthermore, by then the many defectors, beginning with those following in the footsteps of Horney, William Silberberg, Clara Thompson, Harry Stack Sullivan, Fromm, and Reik—those who had theoretical disagreements with the ego psychologists and their students—were doing therapy with patients in hospitals and in their offices. And they were analyzing psychologists and social workers who, sooner or later, would form their own associations. In sum, as Philip Rieff noted in *The Triumph of the Therapeutic* (1966), America had become the therapeutic society par excellence.

By that time, the patients who expected psychoanalysts to cure their neurotic symptoms, or their general malaise, were very different from the repressed hysterics who had led Freud to formulate his increasingly complex theories. In addition, the analyses by his diverse descendants were initiating more and more discussions about changing clinical pictures and problems, and possible solutions. Gradually, the clinical techniques based on the structural theory were being questioned, and no longer seemed to be as effective as they had been before.

By 1971 Heinz Kohut, a neurologist who had graduated from the Chicago Institute of Psychoanalysis after World War II and a former Viennese, was dissatisfied enough to explore Freud's theories of narcissism and then move them to the center of the debates. He had noted that children tend to make up for the "unavoidable shortcomings" of maternal care, and the concomitant primary narcissism (the infant's self-involvement at birth), either by evolving a *grandiose* and exhibitionist *self-image* or by creating an *idealized parental image.* As the approval in the mother's eye mirrors the child's exhibitionist display, he found, the child's self-esteem and grandiosity are inflated. This necessitates different techniques in conducting a psychoanalysis, more empathic and demanding interactions with patients, and abandonment of the emotional abstinence that had been one of the classical analysts' accepted techniques. Kohut's so-called self-psychology, focusing on the interactions between mother and infant, became accepted among some Freudians. Soon thereafter another clinical theory, based on object relations (the specific affinity created between a mother and her infant), which had been advanced primarily by Melanie Klein in London, was further developed by Otto Kernberg, another émigré psychoanalyst.

Whether this search for new approaches was due to changing symptomatology alone or to the fact that the acceptance of psychoanalysis itself had made promises for cures it could not achieve is a debatable issue. Certainly, changing cultural trends, contact with psychoanalysts from Europe and South America, advances made by the interrelationists (mostly Horney and Sullivan), and many other elements were contributing to the development of clinical theories and methods. The psychoanalysts themselves were both products and creators of their culture.

The reception of psychoanalysis has gone through many phases, in line with changes in the culture, breakthroughs in drug and behavioral therapies, and advances in psychoanalytic knowledge. Throughout all the shifts, there has been a constant tension—and much misunderstanding of the connections—between what practicing analysts do and the place accorded Freud's ideas either in the culture at large or in academia. The various aspects of psychoanalysis that are stressed or denied keep changing, so that its first and second major receptions have been followed by smaller waves of reaction and theories. Certainly, the fact that qualified members were accepted into the APA and the IPA as a result of the lawsuit brought by American psychologists in 1985 has reduced factionalism. Thus, when the members of the leading British and American psychoanalytic institutes met in New York on February 28 and March 1, 1998, they mostly debated the pros and cons of clinical methods. Whether this is the beginning of yet another major wave remains to be seen. But clearly the main concepts of psychoanalysis are widely accepted. At least in that respect, Freud has irrevocably altered the Western tradition.

Psychoanalysis:
The American Experience

Robert Coles

EARLY IN 1933, when Erik H. Erikson and his wife, Joan, told friends in Vienna that they were planning to leave for the United States, the reaction was by no means approving. Indeed, these two young members of the so-called Freud circle were greeted with the peculiar kind of psychological skepticism that in its worst (and all too prevalent) form becomes crude reductionism: *why* such a drastic move, for what personal reasons? Erikson had just graduated from the Vienna Psychoanalytic Institute, and a career as a child analyst awaited him— he had been analyzed by Anna Freud, trained by the likes of Heinz Hartmann and August Aichhorn, and, of course, his analyst's "supervisor" was none other than Sigmund Freud. "We left Vienna, we left Europe," Erikson told me in 1970, when I was interviewing him for a biographical study of his life and his work, "because we saw the terrible writing on the wall." He paused and lowered his bright blue eyes, focusing on the floor for a few seconds, then abruptly lifted his gaze, directed it outward, through the window of the Widener Library study, toward the rest of the building, and, beyond it, to the cloistered safety of Harvard Yard. The silence was getting to be a little too long, and I began searching for a question to interrupt it, move us forward, when he continued: "Hitler had just taken over in Germany, and the Austrians who were anxious to follow his lead were already emboldened." Another pause, as I think to myself: That last word, that verb— vintage Erik. (I had been teaching in his course, taking seminars he offered, and his writing for years had been a tremendous help to me as

I tried to connect psychoanalysis to the kind of field work I was doing. "You can call it documentary child psychiatry," he once said, so sensitively aware of the need we all have, even those of us who are wanderers, for some kind of home for our work.) Again, the awkwardness of the room's quiet, interrupted by my shifting of position, the scraping of my shoes on the floor as I lifted one foot, moved the other. Finally, a sustained lecture from this wise teacher and wise psychoanalyst, then at the height of a distinguished career:

> I tell you, the writing *was* on the wall—thugs on the streets of Vienna, and all over Germany, now in the name of the German government: the advanced guard of the murderous cohorts who would threaten the entire civilized world. Why is it that "they" can't see it? Joan and I kept wondering [that]. I'm not trying to be the smug one, looking back so that I can compliment my moment of foresight! But I remember seeing those Nazi hoodlums—a *nice* way of describing them. You could see right away that they were hateful murderers, getting ready to have the time of their life!
>
> You have to remember, I suppose, that Freud was old, in his late seventies, and sick, with the constant pain of mouth cancer—and he'd had to face anti-Semitism all his life, so it can be hard to think: *This* is different, this is something really different! Our friends in the psychoanalytic community there kept telling themselves that when the German people got to see the truth, the truth of who—and what—the Nazis were, they'd turn on them, vote them out. You see, you see there the faith of psychoanalysis—it's a part of the "liberal enlightenment": the truth will win out—will prevail over the "lower instincts," "the base side of man." I heard that often back then—and what a price we all paid, eventually, to win that victory [over the Nazis]!
>
> The hardest thing, let me tell you, is to put yourself back in time in [such] a way that you are doing justice to what was happening back then, but not with the vision that depends upon what you now know was going to happen. Back then, we saw nothing but trouble ahead. Back then, many of our [psychoanalytic] friends were worried, but they weren't *that* worried. A few years later, Joan and I would be welcoming them to Amer-

ica—and we'd all hold our breaths and hope that Hitler would eventually be beaten. For a while, that was by no means a sure thing, you know—quite the contrary. I think it was during those years [the 1930s and early 1940s] that I began to realize how important it was for us [in psychoanalysis] to understand the importance of "society," of "history," of "politics" on our thinking, our "inner life." I'm using abstractions now, but I'm thinking of the way a child or an adult is shaped by—well, I used the word "society" in the book I was working on in the 1940s [*Childhood and Society*]. I wanted [thereby] to make a statement, that's for sure, about a connection.[1]

I would hear more, of course, much more. A psychoanalyst who had learned to take "society" seriously (a major aspect of our daily life, the significance of where and how we live as powerful influences on our subjectivity, even as they help define our objectivity) was now summoning history to supply some context for the developments that defined the course of a particular mode of thought: psychoanalysis. The Freud who visited America very early in this century, but who had no great love for it, would one day exert an enormous influence on that nation's cultural and intellectual life. Since, in many ways, this has been an American century, it has also been a psychoanalytic one. In a sense, then, the Eriksons were pioneers in a movement of sorts, even though at the time they regarded themselves as vulnerable young individuals, alarmed enough to cross the Atlantic in search of a less threatening life. Soon dozens of others would arrive in cities that would nurture psychoanalytic institutes: Boston, New York, Washington, Philadelphia, Chicago, San Francisco, Los Angeles, places where a broad, educated group of people were eager to learn about themselves, become more solid and sound, more knowing husbands, wives, parents, and workers. They would ardently seek daily time on those couches, which themselves became a subject of such speculative interest and humor (the latter a measure of the former). Soon enough, as Erikson would put it at another time, "a small group of men and women, relatively obscure and not thought very highly of [in Vienna's academic world], would find everyone—so it seemed—attending their every word." Another one of his reflective silences, after which: "This [kind of development] can be very seductive—but it can also be as dangerous as it is intoxicating. Anyway, what gets built up can quickly get torn down—or abandoned: people turn elsewhere, rightly or wrongly."

There was a lot of history in such an apparently casual remark. By 1950, when *Childhood and Society* was published, psychoanalysis was well on its way to cultural ascendance in the United States—and to a deliberate, sought-after absorption into the conservative medical profession, Freud's views (expressed in *The Question of Lay Analysis*) notwithstanding. Here was one book by the "master" (as Hans Sachs called him) that even his most devoted followers were quite willing to overlook or criticize. The result, of course, was a profession that became associated with another profession. Psychoanalysts were now physicians, who placed second to none in the respect and authority granted them by a secular public interested in, well, *themselves:* what they thought, dreamed, expected, and feared in this brief span of time allotted them by fate, chance, or circumstance. In his epilogue to *Childhood and Society*, Erikson made a rather penetrating critique of his profession—so very much had happened to it in the less than twenty years he'd spent in America. He had become, even then, quite worried by the "value-free" stance of some of his colleagues, their insistent removal of themselves from any number of social, political, and economic struggles which he felt ought to be very much on everyone's mind, including those who, presumably, hear every day about the struggles of their fellow citizens to make do in a country not without plenty of social pain, cultural conflict, economic hardship, and inequity. Taking sweeping measure of a profession, he dared to say:

> The various identities which at first lent themselves to a fusion with the new identity of the analyst—identities based on talmudic argument, on messianic zeal, on punitive orthodoxy, on faddist sensationalism, on professional and social ambition—all these identities and their cultural origins must now become part of the analyst's analysis, so that he may be able to disregard archaic rituals of control and learn to identify with the lasting values of his job of enlightenment. Only thus can he set free in himself and in his patient that remnant of judicious indignation without which a cure is but a straw in the changeable wind of history.

A tough challenge indeed; a jeremiad, really, that took precise aim at what had happened to a profession now riding high, and which precisely for that reason was morally endangered by the complacency and self-satisfaction that frequently come with success. On April 16, 1968, Erikson's analyst, Anna Freud, was struggling with some of the same matters, albeit more indirectly and tactfully, when she addressed her colleagues at the New York Psychoanalytic Institute. She was giving the Freud Anniversary Lecture, reminding her listeners that for many, by then, the psychoanalyst was "no longer an outsider" but actually a very much "recognized" person—not a status without certain consequences, which she regarded with a jaundiced eye. She was making a historical contrast that had its own edge, its own implicit melancholy, for all her fair-minded, even-handed tone:

> When we scrutinize the personalities who, by self-selection, became the first generation of psychoanalysts, we are left in no doubt about their characteristics. They were the unconventional ones, the doubters, those who were dissatisfied with the limitations imposed on knowledge; also among them were the odd ones, the dreamers, and those who knew neurotic suffering from their own experience. This type of intake has altered decisively since psychoanalytic training has become institutionalized and appeals in this stricter form to a different type of personality. Moreover, self-selection has given way to the careful scrutiny of applicants, resulting in the exclusion of the mentally endangered, the eccentrics, the self-made, those with excessive flights of imagination, and favoring the acceptance of the sober, well-prepared ones, who are hard-working enough to wish to better their professional efficiency.[2]

She surely had in mind her father, herself, her best-known analysand, Erik H. Erikson, her close friends August Aichhorn and Helen Ross and Dorothy Burlingham, and others, such as Helene Deutsch—men and women who dared take on all sorts of principalities and powers in their "odd," rebellious lives, in their original-minded determination to probe appearances, look squarely at what we tend to hide from ourselves, never mind others. These were individuals interested in changing things, explorers who looked not only within but without; many of them wanted to see a vastly different social and political order than what then obtained in Europe, or, for that matter, in the United States. These were individuals who wanted to help "wayward youth"; who wanted to help schoolteachers do a better job with children, especially the hurt, scorned, misunderstood ones; who reached out to Native American children, to the survivors of the concentration camps, to children struggling under the daily threat of the blitz visited by the Luftwaffe on wartime London. "Professional efficiency" was not exactly the overriding purpose that informed the lives of such individuals—and a major transformation of sorts was under way, as Miss Freud was reminding any in that audience who cared to notice.

She was emphasizing matters theoretically rather than merely offering a few casual social observations. She was pointing out that one's motivations, one's "psychodynamics," respond to the changing rules, habits, and customs of the workplace. That word "institutionalized" has its own psychological (as opposed to sociological) significance: not only do the applicants vary, depending upon the values and preferences of particular organizations (in this case, institutes), but so do the teachers, no matter their background or even their training. As American psychoanalysis became more and more a postgraduate subspecialty, pursued by doctors who had become psychiatrists, the older psychoanalysts who had been teaching at those institutes, and conducting the training analyses, had their own adjustments to make, their own conflicts to confront and bring under control. Grete Bibring, also a member of the "Freud circle" in Vienna, talked about the shifts in the profession which she witnessed during the 1950s:

> Back then (and back there!) we were a small group, and not a very respected one—certainly in the universities. Many of us wanted to understand the way we thought, and help our patients live different lives psychologically, of course; but we also had in mind a different world. We thought—well, our fantasy, you might call it today, went like this: the more people [there were] who have been analyzed, the better things would be in general, because people would treat other people more sensitively. Freud said as much (didn't he?) in his *New Introductory Lectures*. There was this larger world out there that many of us worried about, and we hoped to change it, and we thought of psychoanalysis as part of social and political progress, not only intellectual progress. We hoped that schools

and hospitals and the prisons and the universities—we thought our knowledge would change those institutions. We thought that people in the professions, the arts and sciences, in education and law and business, not just medicine, would embrace psychoanalysis, and the result would be . . . revolutionary: society would change. Now, our sights are, shall I say, set in a different direction, or shall I say, they are [set] lower? Remember, it's not only the candidates [the applicants chosen for psychoanalytic training], it's us [the training analysts]: we do the selecting, and before that, we set the criteria—so, it's been (how is it put?) an "evolution."[3]

An evolution indeed, and one that is still taking place, as a biological emphasis utterly dominates the psychiatric profession, and rides a cultural ascendance as well. In a sense, of course, psychoanalysis first came to America with Freud's relatively unnoticed visit to Clark University in 1909. At that time psychoanalysis was an idea, a way of looking at mental life. In the late 1920s, two decades later, psychoanalysis became a profession. By then Freud had explored not only the various "agencies" of the mind but the various ways his patients, and he himself, responded to that investigative effort through transference and countertransference. Moreover, he and his first colleagues were not only welcoming others across the world as interested intellectual or medical visitors, as inquirers or potential associates, but beginning to recruit men and women for training, those who would eventually become the "candidates" Dr. Bibring mentioned of the various "institutes" that would arise across Europe and then the world, certainly including the United States. In the late 1930s, to repeat, Hitler's murderous march across a continent prompted the analysts who were skeptical of the Eriksons in 1933 to follow suit, and the result was a major boost in American psychoanalysis. By the 1950s psychiatry in the United States was very much psychoanalytic, and not inconsequentially, our culture was also enormously taken with Freud's thinking. Indeed, psychoanalytic concepts gradually became authoritative, even normative, a widespread means of judging people—those whose "defenses" are "ego-syntonic," as against those with "primitive" defenses; those who seemed "fixated" at the "oral stage," or the "anal stage"—in W. H. Auden's well-known description, "a whole climate of opinion." It is hard, under such circumstances, for any group of individuals, in any organization, to resist the consequences of widespread attention, acceptance, and acclaim.

The orthodoxy that worried Erikson as early as 1950 would only become more entrenched in the years immediately following the publication of *Childhood and Society*. In 1964, when I began talking with him and interviewing him, he would bluntly say that "we are the victims of our success," after which, unsurprisingly, came a long disquisition on such a historical irony: A band of central European outsiders, not only ignored but reviled, gradually earn a following across the civilized world, then themselves are dispersed to the four corners of that world. In no time, it seems, those men and women, in growing numbers, become "experts," if not revered figures, who possess a magical knowledge that enables access to the mind (which is all there is in a secular society, the soul having been forsaken). "Everyone turns to us for everything," a much-in-demand Erikson, then a Harvard professor, would observe, and not with triumphant pleasure but with the sure knowledge that the gullibility of those in need would more than tempt those being sought to an arrogance that would be unbecoming, to put it mildly. To call upon Erikson again, in his wonderfully blunt and earthy manner: "It is hard to say 'I don't know' when everyone seems to think you have all the answers." A few minutes later, this postlude: "Pretty soon a lot of us began to accept without reservation the faith others put in us."

This last sentence expressed a tactful yet tough social and historical observation that brings up, by implication, the matter of "faith" in a broad sense. He was really talking about a modern instance of idolatry—the passion for creedal submission that bears down upon even members of the agnostic intelligentsia. Freud's shrewd, knowing analysis of what obtains between the two who together (their lives, their rational and irrational sides, their stories) make up any given analytic situation (the regression of the analysand to a childlike dependence on the revered—and feared—parental figure, the analyst) can also be applied to that larger sphere known abstractly as a cultural moment, a historical time; hence the submission of so many to the emerging haughtiness, the self-importance, the unqualified sureness of conviction to be found in some psychoanalytic circles in mid-twentieth-century America. Inevitably, though, a responsive critique arose both from within the profession (Erikson, Anna Freud, Allen Wheelis, Leslie Farber) and without, as in Philip Rieff's extremely influential reflections not only on Freud but on the rest of us, for whom psychology has increasingly become a religion of sorts, and an all too mushy and morally rudderless one at that. In that regard, Anna Freud said, in 1970:

> In the early years of psychoanalysis we could take the Super-Ego for granted: it was *there*, a big presence in the lives of our analysands. Now, that is not always so—now many of us are almost surprised when we meet someone who wants to be analyzed and is driven by a stern conscience that won't let go. Now it is the instincts that are—how is it put these days?—all over the place, with no voice within saying no, no, or maybe I should say, a mere whisper, compared to the past [the relative authority of the conscience back then, as contrasted with the present time].[4]

It is a considerable irony, of course, that a profession intent on helping to understand (and thereby reduce) anxiety became an instrument of a new kind of anxiety. Once there was the anxiety of the intensely guilty; now there is the anxiety of those who are virtually without guilt, and at the seeming mercy of the instincts. Miss Freud, in *Normality and Pathology in Children*, wrote: "Where in its turn, the severity of the Super-Ego was reduced, children produced the deepest of all anxieties, i.e. the fear of human beings who feel unprotected against the pressure of their drives."[5]

In one sentence Freud's daughter tells of so very much that happened to her father's ideas: they were initially unknown; then they were ignored or denounced, reviled; further along, they were continuously taken into consideration, and soon enough they were embraced to the point where not only more and more people became psychoanalysts and became psychoanalyzed but millions of others, knowingly or unknowingly, came to think and act in response to notions that supposedly derived their credibility from psychoanalysis, whose credibility, in turn, had become, for a while at least, all too uncritically accepted. Needless to say, many psychoanalysts resisted this cultural idolatry, reminding themselves and others that they were learning and that they had a lot to learn. But again, it is hard for any of us to resist the lure of iconic status, an "occupational hazard" even in a particular analysis, as Allen Wheelis pointed out in "On the Vocational Hazards of Psychoanalysis," a chapter of *The Quest for Identity:*[6] a powerful warning of the distinct dangers transference presents to those of us who see troubled psychiatric patients and rather quickly become held in high esteem—too high for our own good, no matter the reasons for such an act on the part of our patients. Once more, in Erikson's wry words: "I'm afraid we sometimes can't help believing what we're told in those offices."

Such constant idolization is not without its social and political consequences. After all, in America psychoanalysis became a clinical experience chiefly for the upper bourgeoisie, those who could afford to see a physician four or five times a week for years. These analysands have been people of no mean influence, and if they are drawn into admiring postures by dint of "transference," there is always "countertransference" to tug at their doctors. We have not yet, perhaps, sufficiently "analyzed" that aspect of psychoanalytic experience—the way doctors who see only one kind of patient, from one kind of social and economic and cultural (maybe even racial) background, gradually get drawn into the assumptions and preoccupations (if not convictions) of their patients. Moreover, apart from whom we see and what happens to us, there is the question of who we are, as Sara Lawrence Lightfoot makes quite clear (politely, but also unflinchingly so) in her biography of her mother, Margaret Lawrence, who was the first black psychoanalyst to emerge from training in America, at the Psychoanalytic Clinic of Columbia University's Psychiatric Institute.[7] To be a black woman, to be, additionally, a person of religious faith (the daughter of a clergyman), was no easy experience for Margaret Lawrence. Some of the stories told by her daughter are yet another reminder that those who have been both well educated and well analyzed, and who have become teachers or training analysts, are still not immune to the temptations of parochialism, insularity, and a kind of crude ignorance that takes an all-too-familiar persecutory expression: comply with our thoughts, our ways, our habits, our beliefs, or you are *out;* or you may be branded in a reductionist way, told you are in need of more (and more and more) analysis, or, God forbid, decreed not suitable for psychoanalytic education due to "resistance" or to a "character structure" that won't bend to the requirements set up by those who have appropriated the power to make such judgments.

If the above smacks of ideological authoritarianism, of power politics masked as "scientific decision-making," or of thinly disguised name-calling, then so it can go in the academic or the medical world, where none of us lose our human weaknesses, our susceptibility to those aspects of the drive termed "aggression," or "thanatos," in the psychoanalytic literature, our meanness, spitefulness, or, in Freud's phrase, "the narcissism of small differences" that makes for petty squabbling, gossip, and organizational intrigue.

It has been a full century since the young Freud began his search (within himself as well as his patients) for the big, important truths that would eventually come his way—not without much brave and determined effort, a few missteps, and no small amount of isolation and loneliness. To the end, in exile, he fought hard on behalf of his beloved psychoanalysis. He was a skilled protagonist, able to write lucid, compelling prose and marshal convincing and persuasive arguments in the elucidation of his ideas, which he had the considerable courage to alter, revise, and even abandon in the interests of a psychological candor he knew to seek. He lived long enough to see his ideas persist, to enlist the allegiance of hundreds who would join him as psychoanalysts and many thousands who would become analysands. He lived long enough, also, to see that larger world of needy people, his fellow human beings, look with growing interest at his books, his views, the profession he initiated. Now, as this century so shaped by his genius, his force of being, thinking, and writing comes to an end, and as his own prophecy (that someday biochemistry will considerably curb the reign of psychology) comes nearer to realization, we are left with important memories of him and his followers through their books, their letters, and their deeds and words as witnessed and remembered by others. Such a legacy is great, but the greatest legacy, surely, is that known by the thousands of us who have learned ever so much about ourselves, and have thereby been spared the pain, anxieties, and fears that Freud knew us all to have.

When all the intellectual rancor generated by psychoanalytic disputation is forgotten, when all the organizational and personal tensions within and between the various institutes have ceased to matter, when new theories and formulations and modes of psychological (and psychobiological) treatment have become, one by one, more and more prominent, psychoanalysis will still stand for something precious indeed: a way a particular person can help another person along in this life through the patient, persistent, thoughtful attentiveness that is at the heart of psychoanalysis. At rock bottom, the desire to help is an aspect of our very humanity, for we are the ones who try to understand this world through language, and share what we have come to know with others. It is what happens all the time in those psychoanalytic offices between two human beings who, by mutual consent, have an opportunity to become so honestly, searchingly, committed to one another.

Freud, Film, and Culture

E. Ann Kaplan

FOR THE PAST two decades or so, the psychiatrist has become an object of humor, contrasting drastically with the pre– and post–World War II image of the psychiatrist as an imposing bearded and scholarly presence: often with a German or Slavic accent, and a Jewish valence, his (*sic*) deeply furrowed forehead attested to his being accustomed to long hours in deep thought (the old doctor in Hitchcock's *Spellbound* [1945] typifies the image). Not that alternate images were totally absent, as, for example, the arrogant, unprofessional, and incompetent Dr. Judd in Jacques Tourneur's *Cat People* (1942); or the rare female analyst played by Ingrid Bergman, also in *Spellbound*. In any era, there will be many, varied images of psychiatrists: in what follows, I focus on the predominant ones.

If the decades following the war were the "golden age" of the cinema's male psychiatrist[1] (remember the engaged, activist, and flexible therapist in *Ordinary People* [1980]), the 1990s might represent the era of the cinema's greatest ridicule of the therapist. Additionally, it may not be a coincidence that the ridiculed therapist is often *female*. If female analysts have hitherto been rare in cinematic protrayals, they now offer a kind of double opportunity: the image of a female analyst is itself likely to amuse, so the image of silly female analysts should be twice as amusing, consequently reinforcing the popular conception of psychiatry as a profession of incompetents. Think of the ridicule heaped on therapists in the TV show "Ellen": in the fall 1996 episodes, the heroine tries one therapist after another (many of them again women) to help get her life in order, but they all offer her banal or useless advice. Perhaps the most extreme 1996 image of this kind is that of the female psychiatrist in the movie *The First Wives Club*. She is a completely immoral and incompetent woman who not only cannot help her patient, played by Diane Keaton, but has all along been having an affair with the patient's husband.

How might we account for the change in the portrayal of psychiatrists? Perhaps the shadow of Freud himself loomed over the decades immediately following his death, ensuring respect for his theories. Or perhaps the plethora of alternate therapies that the 1960s spawned brought about the change, so that the increase of ridicule heaped on therapists in the post-sixties era is linked to the relaxation in the U.S.'s historically severe puritanical mores during that time. Allison Anders's film *Grace of My Heart* (1996) briefly parodies a 1960s therapist called in to help the troubled, suicidal hero. Although the doctor's unorthodox methods get him out of his isolation, the hero drowns himself soon afterward. In *Shine* (1997), the hero is not cured by the psychiatrists in the mental hospital or by the shock therapy he undergoes there, but is finally reached and helped by a female astrologist.[2]

As is clear from these recent examples, popular culture (especially as expressed in film) has been fascinated with Freud and has represented his theories in widely differing ways since the time Freudian discourse began to circulate in the United States. While the psychiatrist in some films may have been a useful narrative tool for allowing information about the protagonists' lives to be efficiently conveyed to viewers, in general it seems that psychoanalysis formalized, and opened up avenues of discovery to, something that humans have always been curious about: the knowledge of how the mind works and, more importantly, of what it means when it seems *not* to work. In many eras and cultures, mental illness has been considered something shameful, something to be hidden from public view. Just why mental illness evokes such fear and shame, when physical illness evokes the opposite response of sympathy, caring, and concern, is a complex question beyond the scope of this essay. The point is that people are at once fascinated by mental illness—hence its presence in so many Hollywood narratives—yet have strange attitudes to those whose profession it is to try to cure mental illness. In attempting to understand mental distress, psychoanalysts have opened themselves to idealization, rejection, or, in our own era, ridicule in film and sometimes in the culture more generally as well.

For many people, there is still something uncanny about mental dysfunction. However, Hollywood fascination shows that beneath the fear and rejection, American audiences do want to see stories about mental distress, about socially inappropriate behavior and strange ways of relating to others. They are curious about methods of therapy and healing, perhaps due to anxiety about their own mental functioning and to unease about aspects of themselves that Freud's theories touch upon. In other words, as always, what is repressed seeks release.

THE PROTOTYPICAL mental distress, therapy, or cure film emerged in Freud's own time in G. W. Pabst's film *Secrets of a Soul* (1926), made with advice from a Freudian analyst, and such movies were later made in Hollywood, among them Fritz Lang's *Secret Beyond the Door* (1948), Alfred Hitchcock's *Spellbound* (1945) and Nunnally Johnson's *Three Faces of Eve* (1957). Many pop Freudian explanations for characters' behaviors crop up in films in the 1950s, such as Nicholas Ray's *Rebel Without a Cause* (1955) and later films like Henry King's *Tender Is the Night* (1962).[3] In many pictures—Jacques Tourneur's *Cat People* (1942), Anatole Litvak's *Snake Pit* (1948), Hubert Cornfield's *Pressure Point* (1962), and, closer to our time, Robert Redford's *Ordinary People* (1980) and Leon Marr's *Dancing in the Dark* (1986)—the psychiatrist is called in when the protagonist's behavior becomes extreme or dysfunctional.

In these films, the Hollywood analysis often relies upon "standard" Freudian concepts such as anxiety neurosis caused by an oedipal complex, the repression of a childhood trauma preventing a wife from having a normal marital relationship, or amnesia resulting from a traumatic event evoking repressed childhood guilt; and in most there is a scene in which the protagonist's recurring nightmare is presented to viewers. In a way that condenses the inevitably slow process of cure in psychoanalysis, in Hollywood, when the dream is interpreted by the psychoanalyst, repression is lifted and the patient is cured. The most famous of these dream sequences is that produced with Salvador Dalí's help in *Spellbound*. As a master of surrealism, Dalí was able to evoke a strange, alien dream landscape, with its illogical leaps, its defiance of earth's physical laws, and its odd shapes and objects. Each element of the dream is finally shown, in somewhat improbable fashion, to allude to one aspect of the hero's trauma, and when traced back to childhood, reveals his misplaced guilt for an accident. In Hollywood dream analyses like this, American audiences have been receiving their introduction to psychoanalysis from the cinema. They have also been deriving from cinema the satisfaction of confronting their fears of the mentally ill, as well as their fascination with how the mind works.

Dreams and their meanings constitute the one element of mental life that has fascinated humans for the longest time. Humans have always dreamed and believed that dreams have significance; Freudian dream analysis was merely another form of interpretation. And humans have always created symbolic performances or artifacts which, like dreams, function as release mechanisms for the strains, stresses, fears, and desires of whatever environmental or social context humans have found themselves in. What is most interesting, however, is the special link between the "discovery" of psychoanalysis and that of the cinema—two technologies with close associations to the human capacity to dream—at about the same historical moment. What exactly it was about Freud's nineteenth century that created the environment for these linked technologies to emerge remains unclear. But it is safe to say that in capitalist contexts technologies follow closely upon (or are circularly linked to) social changes. In the West at least, "cinema" seemed inevitable once the three-dimensional perspective came to dominate visual modes in the Renaissance. Cinema's technologies, with stories about city and family life, fitted the needs of its historical period.

Meanwhile, for the German bourgeoisie, especially for their women, the strains and stresses of modern life required a different technology for their accommodation, release, and cure. The repressed wishes and longings of this class could not be healed through vicarious identification with screen heroes and heroines, as they might for the working and immigrant classes. Given its working-class (called "vulgar" by the bourgeoisie) ambience, the cinema was at first forbidden to the sons and daughters of the middle class. The strains and stresses instead spoke through the bodies of these bourgeois daughters and sons, manifesting, as they must, in hysterical symptoms and illnesses. While the strains and stresses of working-class life also spoke through male and female workers' bodies, psychotherapy was rarely an option; for them, it was the cinema or the mental hospital.

Freud developed psychoanalysis as a technology for the release of the stresses in bourgeois life: in this literal way, then, psychoanalysis was a technology that paralleled the cinema. For if cinema was where some people's dreams and fantasies found a place for their expression, psychoanalysis was a place where other people's dreams and fantasies could also be expressed, but via a different technology. Christian Metz has pointed out the similarities and differences between the "couch" dream text and the cinema dream text,[4] while others have analyzed similarities between cinema and psychoanalysis.[5] The operation of imagery in the production and circulation of desire is similar in both psychoanalytic dream theory and film, although links between cinema and culture are complex. Cinema has increasingly influenced the kinds of goods people desire and the values they hold dear. In turn, prevailing fashions and beliefs have influenced cinema's narratives and styles.

Of more interest is the relationship of Freud's own theories and texts—his case histories—to popular culture, and to cinema's melodramas in particular. Freud was one of the first to theorize that creative writing and daydreaming, as well as art itself, was one mechanism through which ordinary and gifted people could deal with, and perhaps release, their inner conflicts, struggles, desires, and fears along the lines noted above. His famous studies of great artists like Leonardo da Vinci exemplify his theories about the links between psychic strains and stresses and great art, while his essays "Creative Writers and Daydreaming" and "Family Romances" describe how the ordinary person's needs and fantasies find expression. Freud obtained many of his psychoanalytic concepts from the history of Western art and his thorough knowledge of classical mythology. It's clear from reading Freud how steeped he was in high culture and in the great books in the Western canon. Less obvious is his scorn for mass culture, for the *Kitschik*, as he would no doubt have called it. (Late in his life, Freud adamantly refused to collaborate with a studio interested in making a film about his life and work because he feared Hollywood would only trivialize everything.)

In all this, Freud was a man of his class and particular historical moment. The high/low cultural divide was at its most severe in the late nineteenth century because of the rapid development of mass culture and the enthusiasm for it being shown by the working classes and, increasingly, the lower middle classes. The upper middle and aristocratic Christian classes felt threatened by popular culture, not least because its pleasures were largely due to its images of sexuality that the upper classes were determined to repress within their official or public culture. The parents of Freud's patients were also determined to suppress their children's sexualities. The patients were often suffering from this repression and from the hypocrisy of their parents' secret sexual exploits behind a veneer of propriety (viz., the Dora case history). Freud's explicit discussion of creativity and the "family romance," or seduction fantasies, as he termed them, is particularly interesting in this context. In a sense, his theories about creativity laid the groundwork for understanding the appeal of popular culture, since the concerns of much of this culture with sex, adultery, illegitimate children, violence, incest, abuse, and so on were ironically also evident in Freud's patients' desires and fears. Popular culture is the perfect terrain for the deployment of the unconscious fantasies, wishes, and fears that are produced in humans through their various social constructs—the family, law, education, social codes, institutional mandates, and government.

The narratives of unconscious fantasies found everywhere in Freud's case histories are easily recognizable as the staple of melodramas already flooding the theatrical stage and moving into cinema plots while Freud's patients lay on his couch. It is significant that Freud presents his stories—more explicitly than do stage and cinema—from the child's point of view. However, like cinema melodrama, Freud's archetypes assume the child is male, and Freud does not explore female oedipal or pre-oedipal processes. It has taken the advent of feminist film theories (often including Lacanian as well as Freudian insights) to analyze the melodramas that *did* speak to women's oppressions.[6] Feminists have tried to understand the complexities of feminine unconscious processes by using Freudian theories and going beyond them.[7]

Given that popular film relied heavily on melodrama, and given that its themes were indeed those of the "family romance," which Freud himself had theorized as determining many of his patient's psychic woes, one might have thought that he would find in popular culture—especially in the sentimental melodrama that predated radio, and later TV, "soap operas"—precisely the terrain where his patients' troubles were being explored. Freud might have understood before anyone else cinema's function as a locus of an imaginary repertoire of fantasies and fears such as those he found in his patient's dreams. In our own period, this function of popular culture has become quite self-conscious, especially in what has been called the "therapeutic" discourse of television soap operas, where popularized Freudian concepts are taken for granted.

However, given his bias against mass culture, Freud could not make this leap. Ironically, in writing of his patient's "family romances" in case histories like those of Dora, Anna O., and the Wolf Man, he himself wrote stories close to melodrama. Like cinema and stage melodrama, he frames his often female subject's voices in his own male voice but cannot quite contain them. As in cinema, the women's voices emerge in the gaps and fissures of the case histories. For example, Dora refuses the transference, as does Freud's lesbian patient (detailed in his 1920 essay "The Psychogenesis of a Case of Homosexuality in a Woman"): she refused to be found "ill." Freud notes that although "the analysis went forward almost without any signs of resistance . . . ," it seemed "as though nothing resembling a transference to the physician had been effected."[8] In this case, unlike that of Dora, Freud is not dismissed but rather dismisses the patient, advising that if any treatment is to be pursued, it should be done by a woman.[9]

If Freud could not see the similarities between his concerns and those of cinema, the Hollywood industry certainly did. That is, Hollywood very quickly gravitated to a popularized version of Freud's theories in the post–World War II period, when, as a result of war traumas demanding psychoanalytic treatment, Freud's theories were circulated even more widely than before. Freudian ideas seemed to offer the authority of "science" for the stories the cinema was already telling, and the austere, usually Germanic figure of the psychoanalyst as "scientist" emerged. Producers saw the relationship between the dreams of their audiences and the "dreams" Hollywood put forth on the screen.

Hollywood's success depended upon the ability to exploit the desires common to all while satisfying the individual imagination. The moviemakers, whether instinctively or consciously, sought to use those of our dreams that are collective and culturally specific (dreams of finding true love; dreams of financial success and upward social mobility; dreams of the perfect children and family harmony). Collective fears—the reverse side of the dreams—follow the same dynamic.

The discussion of the invention of cinema and of Freudian psychoanalysis has assumed that the male and female spectators are white. As viewers will readily perceive, few of the clips from Hollywood films dealing with psychoanalysis show ethnic minorities either as patients or as psychiatrists. Sophisticated 1970s and 1980s feminist analyses mainly explored ways in which the figure of the "white" woman was disseminated to accommodate specific unconscious (white) male desires, fears, and fantasies. Even now, little has been done in relation to psychoanalysis, cinema, and race, although research on ethnic images in Hollywood has advanced.[10]

It's interesting to deploy Freud's own theories to help us understand the absence of black, Asian, and Hispanic analysts and analysands in Hollywood narratives and the traditionally negative racial stereotypes in Hollywood cinema. Issues need to be addressed on at least two levels. First, what are the obvious social and practical reasons for the absence of minority analysts and analysands in film? These include the social racism that prevented people in these groups from being trained as psychoanalysts; the economic plight of many minorities, which put psychoanalysis outside their reach; and, finally, Hollywood's own racism, echoing that of American culture. This racism meant that until only too recently, ethnic actors were rarely hired to play any major and serious roles in film.

Second, there is the level of unconscious cultural processes, linked to such social and economic realities, which have an impact on cinema images. Few have studied what unconscious fears and fantasies may have been calmed for white spectators through the circulation of Hollywood images of ethnic "Others" in lowly, ridiculed, or depraved roles; nor has the psychoanalytic impact of such images on black or other ethnic spectators been much researched. Finally, Hollywood's use of the psychoanalytic session as a strategy for *normalizing* African-Americans needs attention. Such sessions have been used in film to transform a black analysand (e.g., in *Home of the Brave* [1949]) into a model citizen by explaining away experiences of American racism as really about something else.

Psychoanalysis's institutional founding, like that of cinema itself, took place in the era of European imperialism.[11] Categories and concepts that justified imperialism to European leaders saturated intellectual life in this time, almost regardless of political affiliations. It would be too much to expect nineteenth-century psychoanalysis to avoid some of the racialized discourses that prevailed and were embedded in language, such as the "savage/civilized" linguistic duality that had become linked to a black/white dichotomy. Psychoanalysis, in either theory or practice, did not confront such language categories. Meanwhile, on the level of the individual, there was unconscious repression of racial (and racist) knowledge because it posed a threat of conflict and/or danger. As an institution, psychoanalysis was founded with, as Susan Handelman has argued, a Jewish identity and scholarly method,[12] in the sense that some of Freud's methods derive from the rabbinical tradition of the day. Indeed, it is possible that some of the negative images of psychoanalysts in Hollywood cinema result as much from anti-Semitism as from dis-ease about psychoanalysis per se.[13] Nevertheless, psychoanalysis was unable to confront the racism directed toward the Other characteristic of imperialism and of Western thought at least since the Renaissance.[14]

While psychoanalysis as a practice was originally linked to its founding institutional basis, since then it has been opened up to varied approaches. Bitter and intense debates have surrounded psychoanalysis in both theory and practice, beginning in Freud's own time and intensifying over the years. Wherever psychoanalysis is, there are passionate communities and rivalries; it is no longer a closed paradigm, if it ever was. Prevailing discursive paradigms impact on psychoanalytic formulations wherever they are made, so that psychoanalytic practice would seem *theoretically* adjustable to different cultures. Indeed, it can be argued that psychoanalysis is precisely the tool needed to understand racial as well as gendered thought, whether conscious or unconscious. Joel Kovel argued as much in *White Racism* as early as 1970. New research currently under way by scholars from different ethnic backgrounds will no doubt introduce fresh perspectives on psychoanalysis and race.[15]

As an example of psychoanalysis's adjustability to varied cultural contexts, we should consider Frantz Fanon's groundbreaking work. A black psychoanalyst from Martinique, Fanon used Freud's theories for ends far different from what was previously conceived. Freud's is largely a middle-class male voice that speaks from within white, Western, patriarchal culture; but it is a voice with significant hesitancies that are surely produced by his Jewish "difference" and his oppositional, marginalized position within the medical establishment. In this sense, Freud's voice has some similarities to Fanon's, although the latter's voice is self-consciously hybrid, ambivalent, and conflicted: Fanon sometimes speaks as a specifically black, also middle-class, but anticolonial male. Sometimes, in his case studies, when the focus is the individual, he vacillates between readings that evacuate race and gender as the "cause" for illness and personal neurosis and readings that account for black neurosis in social terms.

In contrast to Fanon's conceptions, Hollywood and popular culture generally have had a role in displacing the causes for mental disorder from the social order to the individual in the case of women and blacks. Many Hollywood movies try to account for neurosis as simply an individual's defect not linked to larger social matters. As noted above, Hollywood has used the psychoanalytic session, sometimes explicitly the transference, as a narrative device for producing individual change. In fact, we know that mental disorder is a very complicated phenomenon that is produced through complex interactions of family environment, genetic inheritance, social codes, norms, context, and an individual's race/class/gender. The entire network of processes has to be taken into account in dealing with any specific case of mental disorder, whether it be in the analytic session, in a film analysis, or in writings about mental illness.

While the many films depicting psychoanalysts and the psychoanalytic session are now well known,[16] those particularly relevant to World War II and to racial issues may not be. These include *Home of the Brave* (1949), *The Quiet One* (1948), and *Pressure Point* (1962). American racism could no longer be successfully hidden after the experiences of GIs in World War II, so there are some post–World War II films—from the forties through the sixties—in which the filmmakers use the psychoanalytic session to normalize U.S. male race relations. In *Home of the Brave*, the black soldier, Moss, is convinced through psychoanalytic hypnosis that his experience of racism—on the part of white members of a small combat team isolated on a Japanese island—was not the cause of his paralysis. Rather, it emerged because he was glad that his friend was killed rather than he. In the end, Moss's blackness is reduced to the level of a certain "handicap," like the literal handicap of another member of the team whose arm was blown off, and the two go off into the sunset to establish a business together.

It is, however, important that in *Pressure Point* there is a flashback story in which a black male analyst (played by Sidney Poitier) analyzes a white American neo-Nazi (Bobby Darin) and confronts the unconscious racism of the white medical staff in the prison hospital where Poitier had worked. As director of another prison psychiatric unit in charge of several analysts and many cases, Poitier faces the reverse challenges of a black patient angered by being assigned a white therapist. Having experienced anti-Semitism himself and having seen the racism in the army in World War II, producer Stanley Kramer set about the long task of introducing new images in which black characters have agency, some authority, and some control.

One much later film deserves comment partly for its having (briefly) a black male analysand, but also because it presents an unusual view of the white psychoanalyst as not at all in control. This is *The President's Analyst* (Theodore J. Flicker, 1967). The analyst is far from the would-be all-controlling, rational "scientist" figure of earlier films, such as *Cat People* (Tourneur, 1942). Indeed, he becomes increasingly out of control, the helpless victim of forces beyond him. In addition, he begins to develop the paranoid-schizoid tendencies he has been curing in his patients.

Meanwhile, Godfrey Cambridge plays the role of a CIA agent undergoing analysis while checking out the psychiatrist selected to analyze the president. In the end, the psychoanalytic session does not figure much in the narrative, since we are not privy to Coburn's meetings with the president. However, Cambridge is given one of the most serious and poignant analytic scenes in the film—indeed, he's the only one of Coburn's analysands that spectators are privy to (the others are a rushed silent series of images designed to give viewers an idea of the diversity of Coburn's patients and his analytic style).

In the scene in question, Coburn discovers that Cambridge is a CIA agent and has the license to kill. Coburn is intrigued, and partly shocked, that the folder identifying Cambridge as a CIA agent allows normal morality to be waived; but Cambridge (since it is his analytic hour) immediately associates to what he calls his "nigger" story, or "how he got to be one." This story involves his having discovered through his brother that he was the object of ridicule by his friends, when he had thought he was ridiculing an Other with his friends by calling him "nigger." His brother informs Cambridge that *he* is the "nigger," and so Cambridge wants to kill his brother. His (normal) aggression is channeled into killing through this incident. But before Coburn can comment, Cambridge hastens to tell him about his mission to enroll Coburn as the president's analyst and rushes him off to a first meeting.

Read in the 1990s, the scene is somewhat troubling in that what is perhaps the most serious moment in the film is recuperated back into comedy. Cambridge's story recalls Fanon's famous account of self-alienation in *Black Skin, White Masks* and has a Fanonian intensity. It feels as if it deserves further development, but the genre does not permit any return to Cambridge other than in his comic role as yet another agent now trying to capture Coburn, this time for the American government.

Fanon's question to psychoanalysis—is neurosis oblivious of race or is neurosis caused by racism?—remains to be answered. Hollywood most often argues for the former, depicting neurosis as caused by things other than race or racism. In relation to women, movies most often show that neuroses emerge when women step outside their prescribed roles as subordinate to men.

HOLLYWOOD CONTINUES its flirtation with psychoanalysis, only now with perhaps more ridicule than comic empathy, or by offering a somewhat heavy-handed authoritarian "scientist" figure. And even this ridicule might indicate, as Freud himself might have suggested following his theories in *Jokes and Their Relation to the Unconscious*,[17] a defensive process (similar to that which occurs in dreams) geared to warding off the distressing knowledge of mental illness in friends or loved ones and their need for methods of cure. Contemporary images offer newer, less strictly Freudian models of cure. It might perhaps surprise one to realize in how many films there is at least one (often brief) scene of a psychoanalytic session. Films in which female protagonists are in therapy or concerned with it have been mentioned,[18] but some films have males in therapy, such as Hal Ashby's *Harold and Maude* (1971), Woody Allen's films such as *Another Woman* (1988), *Ordinary People*, and so on. There is generally less serious reference to therapy in 1990s films. The turn toward comedy may reflect economic realities that have made therapy less of an option for middle-class people, or it may be a product of an increased focus on ghetto environments where protagonists seem out of the reach of therapy (Spike Lee's *Clockers* [1996]); when the therapy session does appear, it does so in a very negative way (Bernard Rose's *Candyman* [1993]).

Yet the apparently still obligatory scene that appears from time to time does fulfill some social need to understand mental and behavioral dysfunction. Indeed, testifying to the integration of Freudian theories into everyday life and American interpersonal discourse is the fact that popular culture has claimed many of the therapeutic discourses earlier confined to the psychoanalytic session. Individuals of the middle class routinely understand conflicts, differences, anger, violence, and jealousy in pop Freudian terms. They analyze one another in oedipal or "family romance" terms, and also deal with dreams in a pop Freudian manner. Had he lived to see it, Freud might have objected to the popularized and somewhat reductionist versions of his theories as promoted in popular culture, yet the penetration of his ideas into this culture does manifest a radical change in how humans think of themselves and others. We have Freud to thank for the self-understanding to which we all have access today. Indeed, if the appearance of Gus Van Sant's *Good Will Hunting* (1998), which is in some ways a remake of *Ordinary People*, is anything to go by, the next decade may witness a return to imaging the important contributions of psychoanalysis to social harmony.

Freud's long shadow still lingers over the twentieth century as it nears its end. His powerful influence is felt despite postmodern theories and contexts that seem to be producing new ideas of what it is to be human, and in so doing to have made Freud outdated. I believe, on the contrary, that Freud's innovative studies of human consciousness will come to the center of human concerns in the twenty-first century. As has often been the case, popular culture already seems to have an inkling of this: Barry Levinson's fascinating movie *Sphere* (1998), made from a Michael Crichton novel, suggests that unconscious wishes, fears, and fantasies can produce immensely destructive social and political effects if not brought under control. Attention to such unconscious motives for human projects would seem to be of the utmost social importance. Freud's shadow, then, will stretch well into the twenty-first century.

CRACKING JOKES

A Brief Inquiry Into Various Aspects of Humor — © 1975 art spiegelman

WHO HAS AN I.Q. OF 200? ...

DOWNTOWN BURBANK!

YA' HOMOS!

TOILET!

DINGBAT!!

NOW, TAKE MY WIFE... PLEASE!

LAFFS

THE AUTHOR

RAQUEL WELCH!

A Joke: SO THERE'S THIS GUY WHO THINKS HE'S *DEAD* AND HIS FAMILY CAN'T CONVINCE HIM OTHERWISE—

...SO THEY TAKE HIM TO A SHRINK, WHO SAYS...

LOOK INTO THIS MIRROR FOR 3 HOURS AND REPEAT: *'DEAD MEN DON'T BLEED.'*

THREE HOURS LATER THE SHRINK PRICKS THE GUY'S FINGER WITH A NEEDLE...

PRICK

(THE CHILD'S JACK-IN-THE-BOX PROVIDES A POTENT EXAMPLE OF THE JOKE IN ITS PRIMITIVE FORM. A MOMENTARILY THREATENING SURPRISE PROVES ITSELF TO BE HARMLESS. THE CHILD LEARNS TO MASTER ITS FEARS THROUGH LAUGHTER.)

...AND HOLDS THE BLEEDING DIGIT UP TRIUMPHANTLY...

THERE NOW, WHAT DOES *THAT* PROVE?

THE GUY LOOKS AT HIS FINGER, AND SAYS...

DEAD MEN *DO* BLEED!

Introduction~Some Humor History and Theory:

THE FOOL DOES NOT ACCEPT THE INTELLIGENCE AND LOGIC OF THE GROWN-UP WORLD. HE IS THE REBELLIOUS CHILD WHO STUBBORNLY REFUSES TO LEARN.

THERE NOW, WHAT DOES *THAT* PROVE?

MOST HUMOR IS A REFINED FORM OF AGGRESSION AND HATRED.

HYAR hee YUK HAW!

BLIND

Ⓞ OUR SAVAGE ANCESTORS LAUGHED WITH UNINHIBITED RELISH AT CRIPPLES, PARALYTICS, AMPUTEES, MIDGETS, MONSTERS, THE DEAF, THE POOR AND THE CRAZY. EVERYONE WAS YOUR POTENTIAL ENEMY WHOSE WEAKNESSES AND MISFORTUNES MIGHT BE TO YOUR BENEFIT.

Ⓘ IN MEDIEVAL TIMES THE COURT JESTER WAS SEEN AS AN IDIOT, AND MADE THE BUTT OF CRUEL JOKES. HIS DROOPING TASSLES SYMBOLIZED IMPOTENCE. HAVING GIVEN THIS REASSURANCE HE IS FREE TO EXPRESS HIS AGGRESSION IN THE FORM OF WIT.

POPPA!

IN TIME, THE JESTER WAS SUCCEEDED BY THE CIRCUS CLOWN (AND LATER, THE BURLESQUE COMEDIAN) WHOSE BAGGY PANTS MAKE THE CONTENTS SEEM SMALL AND RIDICULOUS. HE IS THE ONCE LARGE AND MENACING FATHER WHO IS NOW POWERLESS AND SILLY. THE CASTRATED FATHER FIGURE IS AT THE BASE OF MUCH COMEDY.

Ⓣ TODAY WE STILL LAUGH AT THE UNFORTUNATE, THE DEFORMED, AND THE INSANE PERSON; BUT TO AVOID A FEELING OF GUILT THAT MIGHT BLOCK THE PLEASURES OF LAUGHTER, THERE MUST BE A SKILLFUL BALANCE BETWEEN AGGRESSION AND AFFECTION.

FINGER-PAINTING IS MY LATEST HOBBY!! RIGHT, DOC ??

Stereotyped Characters in Jokes:

OUR JOKE IS ONE OF MANY THAT USES THE STEREOTYPES OF PSYCHIATRIST AND NUT. IF THESE TYPES ARE REVERSED, SO THAT THE PSYCHIATRIST IS **NOT** PORTRAYED AS AN AUTHORITY FIGURE, OUR JOKE LOSES SOME OF ITS POINT.

(THE CARICATURIST SEEKS POWER OVER THE VICTIM OF HIS AGGRESSION BY A MEANS SIMILAR TO THE WITCH DOCTOR WITH HIS VOODOO DOLLS.)

THIS GUY THINKS HE'S DEAD, SO HE'S TAKEN TO A SHRINK, WHO SAYS...

LOOK INTO THIS MIRROR FOR 3 HOURS AND REPEAT: 'DEAD MEN DON'T BLEED.'

...AND HOLDS THE BLEEDING DIGIT UP TRIUMPHANTLY...

THERE NOW, WHAT DOES **THAT** PROVE?

THREE HOURS LATER THE SHRINK PRICKS THE GUY'S FINGER WITH A NEEDLE ...

PRICK

THE GUY LOOKS AT HIS FINGER AND SAYS...

DEAD MEN **DO** BLEED!

RIGHT!

Incidentally:

THROUGH PUNNING METAPHOR THIS JOKE RELIEVES CASTRATION ANXIETIES; THE SHRINK/FATHER UNSUCCESSFULLY ATTEMPTS TO EMASCULATE THE FOOL/CHILD.

Aggression in Jokes:

THOUGH WE FEEL SUPERIOR TO THE FOOL, AND LAUGH AT HIS DISCOMFORT, IF THE JOKE'S HOSTILITY IS NOT WELL DISGUISED **WE** BEGIN TO FEEL UNCOMFORTABLE.

WOOPS!

FUNNY!

I HAVE CANCER!

NOT SO FUNNY

THIS GUY THINKS HE'S DEAD, SO HE'S TAKEN TO A SHRINK, WHO SAYS ...

LOOK INTO THIS MIRROR FOR 3 HOURS AND REPEAT 'DEAD MEN DON'T BLEED.'

THREE HOURS LATER THE SHRINK PRICKS THE GUY'S FINGER WITH A NEEDLE ...

PRICK

...AND CHOPS THE FINGER **OFF** WITH AN AXE...

CHOP

...AND SLICES HIS BELLY OPEN WITH A CARVING KNIFE!

THERE NOW, WHAT DOES **THAT** PROVE?

SLICE

THE GUY FALLS TO THE FLOOR CLUTCHING HIS INTESTINES, AND MOANS ...

D-DEAD MEN DO BLEED!

IF YOUR SUPEREGO LET YOU CHUCKLE AT **THAT**, OVEREXPOSURE TO VIOLENCE IN MASS MEDIA MAY HAVE IMMUNIZED YOU FROM FEELINGS OF GUILT.

TRY IMAGINING THE SEQUENCE WITH PHOTOGRAPHS INSTEAD OF DRAWINGS (PHOTOS OF LOVED ONES.)

A Question:

WOULD OUR JOKE BE AS AMUSING IF THE CHARACTERS WERE PORTRAYED AS WOMEN? ☐YES! ☐NO!

LOOK INTO THIS MIRROR FOR 3 HOURS AND REPEAT: "DEAD MEN DON'T BLEED."

Tips on Telling Jokes:

KNOW YOUR AUDIENCE! AN ANXIETY MUST BE MASTERED BEFORE HUMOROUS REFERENCE TO IT CAN BE ENJOYED.

PEOPLE FROM WARSAW DON'T TEND TO SAVOR POLAK JOKES...

...SO THE GUY LOOKS AT HIS FINGER AND SAYS: "DEAD MEN *DO* BLEED!"

WELL... THEY *DO*!

THIS GUY THINKS HE'S A MIRROR SO HE GOES TO SEE A SHRINK...

MEMORIZE A JOKE *CAREFULLY* BEFORE TELLING IT AT PARTIES!

?

AND HE PRICKS HIMSELF WITH A NEEDLE!...

PRICK

THREE HOURS LATER HE HOLDS HIS SHRINK UP TRIUMPHANTLY...

HAH!

...AND SAYS...

DEAD FINGERS *DO* BLEED!

THIS GUY THINKS HE'S DEAD, SO HE'S ... SHRINK WHO SAYS:

JOKES ARE DELICATE MECHANISMS; TIMING IS IMPORTANT. SWIFTNESS AND SURPRISE WILL HELP YOU GET YOUR LAUGH!

THIS MIRROR FOR 3 HOURS AND REPEAT: "DEAD MEN DON'T BLEED."

...SO THE GUY STANDS IN FRONT OF THE MIRROR FOR THREE HOURS AND REPEATS...

DEAD MEN DON'T BLEED!...

...DEAD MEN DON'T BLEED!... ...DEAD MEN DON'T BLEED!...

...DEAD MEN DON'T BLEED!... ...DEAD MEN DON'T BLEED!...

...DEAD MEN DON'T BLEED!... ...DEAD MEN DON'T BLEED!...

...DEAD MEN DON'T BLEED!... ...DEAD MEN DON'T BLEED!...

...DEAD MEN DON'T BLEED!... ...DEAD MEN DON'T BLEED!...

...DEAD MEN DON'T BLEED!... ...DEAD MEN DON'T BLEED!...

167

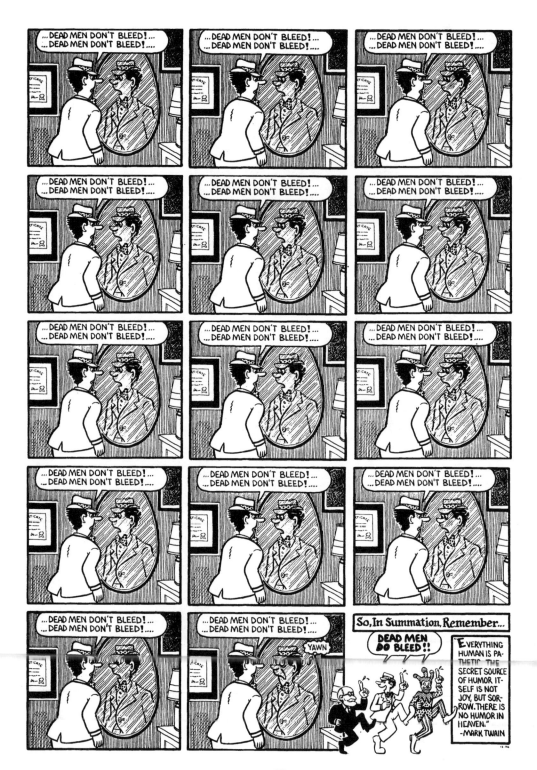

PART IV

Contested Legacies

FREUD THOUGHT THAT his work would arouse controversy because his discoveries could not easily be assimilated into our conventional self-image. We are not who we think we are, and, more importantly, we are not even in control of our thoughts and emotions, not "masters in our own house." The fact that Freud's theories provoked such criticism indicated to some that psychoanalysis was on the right track, bringing unpleasant truths to consciousness and finding ways to overcome resistance to these truths. However, as Frank Cioffi notes in his essay, so much depends on whether what is being resisted is in fact true and not just unpleasant. How can we tell? The work of Cioffi and Adolf Grünbaum point to two major strands of argument in the criticism of psychoanalysis: biographical and theoretical. Cioffi emphasizes that given the specific qualities of the theoretical claims being made, the question of Freud's (and his followers') reliability as reporters is a crucial dimension of any critical appraisal of psychoanalysis. According to the biographically oriented critics, to question a psychoanalyst's reliability is not to engage in an ad hominem attack but to explore a necessary dimension of appraisal. For Grünbaum, issues of empirical testability rather than biographical evaluation are key. Psychoanalysis makes causal claims about, for example, symptom formation, and Grünbaum focuses on whether these claims tally with what we know about the relevant illnesses. Peter D. Kramer's approach in his essay is quite different from either Cioffi's or Grünbaum's. Psychiatry has changed dramatically since Kramer (like many others, inspired by Freud's example) entered the field, a time when psychoanalysis was at the core of much of medical education. Different accounts of the genesis of an illness, of human development, and of biochemical treatment now exist. Some of these have developed in opposition to Freud, or in fields indifferent to his work. From this contemporary perspective, and under the influence of biographical criticism, what can we still learn from reading his texts? Kramer's answer has some affinities with Grünbaum's conclusion about psychoanalysis's heuristic potential in the wake of a critical appraisal. Feminist criticism of Freud's ideas has developed side by side with psychoanalysis. Muriel Dimen underscores the fundamental nature of the criticism, even as she recognizes how psychoanalytic and feminist thinking have influenced one another. The strange liaison between the two has produced creative, challenging, and disturbing offspring. Dimen notes how the liaison has also produced an attention to basic questions concerning how subjectivity and sexuality have been related in the cultural contexts of patriarchy, and how they may play a critical role in regard to those contexts. The final essay in this volume returns to the beginning of Freud's professional career, and considers it in the context of contemporary neuroscience. Oliver Sacks is interested in how the neurologically oriented Freud was already moving toward a dynamic view of the nervous system, a view that would serve him well as he shifted his concentration to the psychological sphere. Freud's rejection of the doctrine of localization (that specific functions were tied directly to specific anatomical locations) was the crucial move in his original neurological work, and the foundation for his later development of psychoanalysis. Everything that has been constructed on that foundation has been highly contested, but the constructions have also served as a legacy to, and an inspiration for, some of the most significant cultural developments of the twentieth century.

The Freud Controversy

WHAT IS AT ISSUE?

Frank Cioffi

WE ARE EITHER approaching the centenary of the birth of psychoanalysis or have recently passed it, depending on whether its birth date is taken as 1895, the date of publication of the *Studies on Hysteria*, or as 1899, when Freud's masterwork *The Interpretation of Dreams* appeared. In either case there is a problem. Why, after almost a century of debate, has no consensus emerged as to the authenticity of Freud's achievement?

The solution might be in part that those who take opposing views do not share the same conception of achievement. For example, in L. L. Whyte's judgment, "Freud changed, perhaps irrevocably, man's image of himself. Beside this it is of secondary import that some of his valid ideas were not new, his special conceptions questionable, and his therapeutic methods uncertain."[1] There are those for whom it is of far from "secondary import" that Freud's "special conceptions were questionable," and for whom changing "man's image of himself" is of little moment if the new image does not correspond better to an independently existing reality.

Suppose we take the precaution of confining the dispute to a sense of the term "knowledge" close to Freud's own, would we then attain consensus? Apparently not, since while some hold that Freud added more to our knowledge of humanity than any other thinker of our time, others are just as sure that psychoanalysis "is the paradigmatic pseudo-science of our epoch,"[2] and that it is "the most stupendous intellectual confidence trick of the 20th century."[3]

This range of opinion is much less surprising if we consider that it is unlikely that the same thing is meant by the word "Freud" or "psychoanalysis" by the contending parties. T. S. Eliot once said of Christianity that it is constantly modifying itself into something which may be believed. Something similar can be said of Freud's psychoanalysis. If we take the precaution of avoiding indefinite terms like "psychoanalysis" and substitute a determinate thesis, it becomes easier to say what is really at issue.

Let us take one of the most important theses that Freud ever advanced, which he repeated at intervals over a period of forty years, which was widely taken as the distinguishing feature of his theory (Freud himself called it his "shibboleth"), and which made its way into general works of reference as an established fact, like the height of Everest or the source of the Nile—the Oedipus complex. The core of this complex is the male child's need to resolve the conflict created by his sexual desire for his mother and his fear of punitive castration by his father. Its status has an additional claim to interest in that its validation would simultaneously certify Freud's claim to have discovered a novel technique for recovering the forgotten formative episodes of early life through the interpretation of his patients' dreams, and of their behavior in the analytic situation. One common complaint against the oedipal theory is that it is unfalsifiable—nothing is permitted to count against it. The grounds for this complaint is that often when Freudians are confronted with reported falsifications of the theory, these are rejected and imputed to the distress that acknowledgment of the theory's truth would cause, i.e., to resistance.

Is the Resistance Argument an Example of Falsification-Evasion?

In "On the History of the Psycho-Analytic Movement," Freud analyzed the objections of his critics: "It was not surprising that they should be able to justify on intellectual grounds rejection of my ideas, though it was actually affective in nature. The same thing happened with patients . . . the only difference was that with patients one was in a position to bring pressure to bear. . . ."[4] Adolf Grünbaum has argued in Freud's defense that Freud only invoked resistance when he had independent grounds for believing that his theses were true, but this immediately raises the question of whether Freud's judgment in such matters was sufficiently disinterested to settle the issue.

The resistance argument has been particularly invoked in defense of Freud's conception of infantile sexuality (oedipal cravings, castration anxiety, penis envy, etc.). For example, Charles Brenner's entry on classical psychoanalysis in the *International Encyclopedia of the Social Sciences* explains why we must ignore those who deny "the paramount role of infantile sexuality": ". . . Each adult individual, as a result of having passed through the conflicts of the Oedipal period himself, has stubborn defences within himself against his own childhood wishes."[5] It is probably arguments like Brenner's which provoked Thomas Szasz's jibe that the Oedipus complex plays the same sort of role in the beliefs and practices of the faithful psychoanalyst as the Eucharist played in those of medieval Catholics.[6] How is this issue to be settled? Do we have in Szasz someone who has been unable to come to terms with his own incestuous inclinations and thus derides a proven fact, or is it rather Brenner who has so heavy an ideological investment in the oedipal theory that he will resort to the most deplorable ad hominem arguments to defend it? Furthermore, it is not only professional analysts but even Freud's lay admirers who can be suspected of ulterior motives for their convictions. It was the philosopher Ludwig Wittgenstein who suggested that although Freud attributes the skepticism his sexual theories encountered to their repugnance, this was also the reason why they often received such a warm welcome. "It may be the fact that the explanation is extremely repellent that drives you to adopt it."[7] Freud seems to have been privately aware of this, since, early in his career, he wrote to a friend, "The sexual business attracts people. They all go away impressed and convinced after exclaiming: 'No one has ever asked me that before.' "[8] But it isn't necessary to rely on the appeal of the repellent to make a plausible case for the infatuated character of Freudian partisanship. Freud has become a symbol for so much that is liberating that it is almost impossible to criticize him without provoking passionate resentment. The literary critic Alfred Kazin's observation that Freud has replaced the Bible as a source of counsel and comfort suggests why it is so difficult for dissident views to get a fair hearing. It is true that the fact that a theory is a source of counsel and comfort to some doesn't preclude its arousing an irrational antagonism in others. But though the invocation of resistance need not be a proof of falsification-evasion, neither does it resolve the issue in Freud's favor; rather it leads to an impasse.

Does the Suggestibility of Patients Make Freud's Theory Falsification-Evading?

Another common ground for the charge of falsification-evasion is that the psychoanalytic method itself limits the possibility of encountering falsifiers. The suggestibility of Freud's patients was held to account for the apparent consistency between his infantile sexual etiology and his clinical data. To the objection that the validity of the data produced by patients under analysis was contaminated by his own preconceptions as to the role of sexuality, Freud replied that he had formed no preconceptions and so could not have contaminated the data. This assurance was quite baseless. In 1888, several years before he began the practice of analysis, he wrote, "Conditions related functionally to sexual life play a great part in the etiology of hysteria (as of all neuroses), and they do so on account of the high psychical significance of this function, especially in the female sex."[9] Yet as recently as 1992, in an ostensibly authoritative work on Freud, the very paper I have just quoted from is invoked as documentation of how "slowly" and "reluctantly" Freud came to his conviction of the role of sexuality in the neuroses.[10] Although Richard Wollheim's rewriting of history suggests how disturbing the argument from suggestibility has been found to be, the failure to take precautions against suggestion, because it would be such an arduous thing to do, does not justify the charge of deliberate falsification-evasion.

Does the Abandonment of the Seduction for the Oedipal Theory Show That Freud Was Responsive to "Adverse Evidence"?

Adolf Grünbaum believes he has rebutted the falsification-evasion charge against Freud by demonstrating that Freud actively solicited falsification. Grünbaum argues that Freud's abandonment of his "previously cherished" seduction theory—the theory that no one could suffer from neuroses who had not been sexually molested when a child—demonstrates his "receptiveness to adverse evidence."[11] Even if Grünbaum were correct in holding that the seduction theory was abandoned because it was falsified, which is doubtful, his argument would still not show that Freud was responsive to adverse evidence because he ignored Freud's failure to respond to the likelihood that what the seduction mistake demonstrated was that he could not, as he had claimed, arrive at correct accounts of the infantile history of his patients by interpreting the data of the analytic hour. It is this which provided the basis for the most telling accusation of falsification-evasion. Instead of questioning the validity of his reconstructive technique, Freud responded by replacing the seduction theory with a theory that a century later there is still no means of assessing empirically since it gives a pathogenic role not just to public events, like molestations, but to the infant's fantasies. The result is that alternative psychoanalytic accounts of what happens in infancy to predispose adults to neuroses proliferate. In abandoning the seduction theory, Freud went from an epidemiologically testable theory to an epidemiologically untestable one. Seductions distinguished neurotics from non-neurotics; incestuous fantasies did not. Seductions had prophylactic implications; fantasies did not. Seductions had a spatiotemporal location; fantasies did not. The moral of Freud's transition from seductions to incestuous fantasies is thus the opposite of that which Grünbaum assigns it. Nevertheless, this move toward unfalsifiability is not sufficient to warrant the more extreme denunciations of Freud's post-seduction oedipal theory.

Clinging to a Theory Must Be Distinguished from Spurious Claims to Have Confirmed It

Over eighty years ago, R. S. Woodworth objected that the oedipal theory was untestable since, while "the open expression of sexual interest by a young child is clear evidence in favour of infantile sexuality, the absence of such expression is evidence of repression."[12] Half a century later, the immunity of the theory to falsification was conceded by one of its upholders, Sibylle Escalona, although she did not conclude that the theory was pseudoscientific on that account. She argued that though it was "self-evident" that nothing the little boy could do would overthrow the oedipal theory "since the hypothesis would still be applicable if he had done the opposite instead," the moral to be drawn was that novel means of assessment must be developed. This would make the theory protoscientific rather than pseudoscientific.

It is important to distinguish between those who regularly reported the confirmation of this unconfirmable theory, i.e., held that it was testable, had been tested, and had survived testing, and those who, like Escalona, candidly concede the theory's current unfalsifiability but merely express confidence in its ultimate falsifiability. We must take account of the difference between our inability to test a theory due to the crudity of our observational powers and spurious claims that observation has repeatedly confirmed that theory. It is only the latter that warrant so extreme a denunciation as Medawar's "stupendous intellectual confidence trick."

Why the Oedipal Etiology, Though Less Testable Than the Seduction Theory, Is Not on That Account Pseudoscientific

Whereas the seduction theory implied the challenge "Show me neurotics who have not been sexually molested in infancy and I will admit that the seduction theory is false," in the case of the post-seduction oedipal theory, epidemiological assessment of this kind was not feasible. Before he gave up the seduction theory, Freud had an answer to the question "What stands to neuroses as insulation from the tubercle bacillus stands to tuberculosis?"—a sexual molestation in infancy—but after Freud replaced the seductions with the child's own sexual activities it was no longer clear what we would need to prevent to ensure that a child did not become neurotic. But there was an alternative way of assessing the post-seduction oedipal theory. Freud's challenge had now become: "Show me a neuroses of which you can make as much sense as can be made of it by deploying my theory of infantile incestuous and polymorphous perverse sexuality." Freud thought of this "making sense" as like jigsaw-puzzle solving. In the original seduction papers Freud wrote, "Just as when putting together children's picture puzzles we finally, after many attempts, become absolutely certain which piece belongs to the gap not yet filled . . . so the content of the infantile scenes proves to be an inevitable completion of the associative and logical structure of the neurosis."[13] After Freud abandoned the "infantile scenes" that this procedure had led him to postulate, he replaced seductions with other scenes—ones in which the child was lusting rather than lusted after. But these were supported by the same argument. Freud says of the infantile sexual fantasies that succeeded seductions as the cause of neuroses just what he had said of the seductions: "What makes [the analyst] certain in the end is . . . like the solution of a jigsaw puzzle . . . so that there is no gap anywhere in the design and the whole fits together. . . ."[14]

But many of those to whom the jigsaw rationale is acceptable in principle share the doubts of the philosopher of science Paul Meehl: "Freud's jigsaw puzzle analogy does not really fit the psychoanalytic hour because it's simply not true that all of the pieces fit together. . . ."[15]

Why the Credibility and Authority of the Analyst Are of Central Importance

Some Freudians are aware—as Freud himself was—of the inadequate circumstantiality of the evidence produced in Freud's case histories. They have, however, a reply to objections such as those of Paul Meehl. They argue that there is further supporting data of a kind that is only available to the analyst actually treating the patient and so not transmissible to the reader. Ernest Jones appealed to imponderable data of this kind to account for the unpersuasiveness of many published cases: "A given interpretation, which can be put in a sentence, may be based on several hours of detailed observation, most of which—the individual utterances of the patient, the tone, the emotional gestures, etc., are impossible to reproduce—although it is just those that inevitably convince one of the validity of the inference drawn."[16] We should no more expect Freud, or any of his followers, to supply overwhelmingly persuasive circumstantial support for his infantile etiology than we ought to expect Bernard Berenson to give compelling grounds for his judgment that a painting is a genuine Raphael. If this is so, then it is our confidence in an analyst's astuteness and disinterestedness which will determine our acceptance of his claims—not the evidence he produces but the evidence he says he has.[17] But what confers on Freud authority such as connoisseurs like Berenson have? The Freudians' answer is that just as chemical analysis or other independent means of validation establish the authority of a Berenson, so independent investigation of infancy has established Freud's ability to reconstruct the formative events of childhood from his patients' dreams, associations, and behavior in the analytic situation. But Freud's seduction error shows this to be untrue. Why did the proof of the fallibility of Freud's judgment as to what happened to his patients in infancy not undermine Freud's authority? For a reason that has been held to demonstrate the disingenuousness or credulity of those who transmitted Freud's claims to the general public—because the grounds Freud had originally advanced for crediting that his patients had suffered molestation as infants have been consistently misrepresented. We are told that Freud came to grief through trusting his patients' analytically recovered memories of having been sexually molested and that the lesson he learned was not to depend on such "memories" but to devise independent means of determining what had happened in the patients' infancy; and that this is what Freud did. But this contradicts the account Freud gave at the time.

For example, Janet Malcolm, in her *New Yorker* articles on psychoanalysis, wrote, "Freud had happened on the Oedipus Complex back in the eighteen-nineties while coming to terms with his disconcerting realization that his patients' stories of childhood seduction, on which he had confidently erected his theory of the etiology of the neurosis in childhood trauma, were largely untrue."[18] The instructiveness of this passage consists not in the fact that it inertly recycles the standard view of the discovery of the Oedipus complex. (No one else has asked how Freud could "happen" on the theory that men lust after their mothers by discarding a theory in which women had been abused by their fathers, so why should Malcolm?) It is because a journalist of Malcolm's credentials should produce an account of Freud's abandonment of the seduction episode that a moderately attentive reading of Freud's original papers would have shown to be false. (And this in spite of the services of the famous fact-checkers at *The New Yorker*.) When we find that the same mythical account has been recycled by almost everyone who has written on the topic, we are entitled to suspect a very general incapacity among commentators to notice anything that might reflect on the truthfulness of Freud's retrospective accounts—accounts that are so blatantly inaccurate and self-serving that Han Israëls and Morton Schatzman entitle the concluding section of their paper on the seduction theory "Why Did No One See?"[19]

Is this then the solution to the longevity of the Freud controversy? Have we only to stand the resistance argument on its head and recognize that the facts impugning the reliability of Freudian method were always there to be seen but were ignored due to the tendentiousness of the producers of psychoanalytic discourse and the docility of its consumers? Have we only to wait for the truth about episodes like the seduction error to be more widely disseminated for the dispute to be resolved in favor of Freud's critics? I think not.

Can't Genuine Discoveries Be the Subject
of Tendentious Reporting Practices?

There are those who concede the prevalence of tendentious reporting practices among Freud and his followers but think that this still leaves the case against Freud's status as a discoverer open. It is argued that those who advance specious evidence in favor of a theory may be "lying for truth," to use the expression coined by William Broad and Nicholas Wade, two scientific journalists, in their book on scientific fraud.[20] Their argument for the inevitability and occasional beneficence of tendentiousness and fraud consists of a list of great scientists who are shown to have tampered with evidence or dealt disingenuously with objections. Would it be unforgivable if some overardent heliocentrists issued spurious reports of having observed parallax, or if some Newtonians announced the discovery of an extra-Uranian planet long before they were in a position to do so? If Freud, convinced as he was of the momentousness and emancipating power of his discoveries, resorted to taking liberties with the truth, is it really so blameworthy? Even so astringent a critic as R. S. Woodworth conceded that Freud's intuitions might be sound even if his evidence was not. And similarly with his followers. Of course, there are critics of Freud for whom this trade-off is unacceptable, but for those who are willing to consider it, the question then becomes whether there are indisputable psychoanalytic achievements to which we could point as post hoc vindication of the Freudians' premature celebration of their explanatory triumphs.

However, there are those who insist that this is *not* the issue to be addressed. For them the central issue is not whether the evidence for psychoanalytic claims is specious but the investigatability of such claims "in principle."

Is It Its Untestability That Makes a Theory Pseudoscientific or
Spurious Claims to Have Confirmed It?

Among both detractors and defenders of Freud's theory there are those who argue that its logical character, rather than the conduct of its advocates, should be the focus of discussion. But what those who condemn the theory, because they believe it untestable, overlook is the comparative innocuousness of an untestable theory when presented as candid speculation rather than as invariably confirmed or frequently verified. What those who think a theory's testability proof of its scientific status overlook is that even where its untestability is introduced into the argument for condemning it as pseudoscientific, the reason is not its untestability alone but the necessary spuriousness of the claims that it has been confirmed in the light of this untestability. You can't confirm, i.e., successfully test, an untestable theory. Moreover, even where the theory is testable, this does not show that it is not pseudoscientific since this will depend on the rigor and disinterestedness with which it is investigated. This view is put by Malcolm Macmillan in his *Freud Evaluated*: "No discipline exists apart from its practitioners. It is their attitudes which determine whether they use their methods to gather data and develop and test theories in an objective way . . . attitudes matter." What is at issue is thus not just a theory but a practice.

On the other hand, Morris Eagle, who is both an analyst and a critic of the methodological weaknesses of psychoanalysis as generally practiced, takes a different view. He charges Frederick Crews with failure to distinguish "between the methodological practices and attitudes of individual analysts (including Freud) and the independent logical structure of psychoanalytic theory. . . ."[21] Yet historically, the scientific value of Freud's theory has turned on the question of the "methodological practices and attitudes" of Freud and his advocates, and there are good reasons why it should continue to do so. Of course, there are contexts in which the sentiment expressed by Eagle (and by B. A. Farrell, Adolf Grünbaum, Neil Cheshire, and a host of others) would be unexceptionable, but not in a debate over the validity of Freud's claims. An analogy: If we reject the reported sightings of UFOs, it is disconcerting to be assured that nevertheless, the statement that earth has had recent visitors from outer space is investigatable "in principle."

Why the Judiciousness of Those Who Relate Psychoanalytic Narratives Matters

Doesn't the credibility of stories of patients having come to grief due to the resurgence of infantile struggles over incestuous and perverse desires bear on their "scientific value"? Consider one of the most contested and tenaciously maintained components of Freud's oedipal etiology—the castration complex. In his last statement on the subject, Freud described the castration complex as "the central experience of the years of childhood, the greatest problem of early life and the most important source of later inadequacy. . . ."

On one occasion Freud dealt with skepticism regarding the ubiquity of the castration complex with the following downright assertion: "I can only insist that psychoanalytic experience has put these matters beyond doubt and has taught us to recognize in them the key to every neurosis."[22] Is it not disconcerting that a decade earlier, in the course of a polemic against Adler's theory that neuroses were to be explained in terms of a flight from femininity, in which Adler used Freud's own findings on the centrality of the castration complex in support, Freud had written: "I find it impossible to base the genesis of neuroses on so narrow a foundation as the castration complex. . . . I know of cases of neurosis in which the castration complex plays no pathogenic part or does not appear at all."[23] How then could Freud later insist that he had found in the castration complex "the key to every neurosis"?

In the light of this revelation as to the laxity (to put it at its most charitable) of Freud's reporting practices, would it be sensible to expend resources in determining whether Freud's castration complex is investigatable "in principle," or to strive to make it so? And can't this doubt be generalized to other psychoanalytic propositions once the credibility of those who maintain them has been brought into question? Isn't the natural response to this objection that of attempting to assuage such skeptical doubts, or at least to circumscribe them? For unless they are, and it is shown that we have some prima facie grounds for believing that Freud's claims have some chance of being true, we will have lost our grounds for continuing to take a serious interest in them. An analogy: There is, of course, an important difference between the question "Is there a monster in Loch Ness?" and "Were those who reported sightings of a monster in Loch Ness either drunk or attempting to entice tourists?" But if the answer to the latter question is "I'm afraid so," is it sensible to go on looking for a monster in Loch Ness? Why not in Lake Michigan?

It now becomes clear why we can't bring the Freud controversy to a successful conclusion. The major disagreement as to the value of Freud's theories is not between those who hold them falsifiable and those who do not; not between those who think Freudians have wantonly clung to their views in spite of reported falsifications and those who do not. The division is rather between those who credit the prolific reports of corroboration of Freud's claims and those who suspect them. And of those who suspect them there are those who question only the judgment of Freudians and those who question their candor. Put in more familiar terms, we can say that the ultimate division in the Freud controversy is between those who would be happy to purchase a used car from Freud or his advocates and those who would not.

Psychoanalysis is a testimonial science.

A Century of Psychoanalysis

CRITICAL RETROSPECT AND PROSPECT

Adolf Grünbaum

INTRODUCTION

The most basic ideas of psychoanalytic theory were initially enunciated in Josef Breuer and Sigmund Freud's "Preliminary Communication" of 1893, which introduced their *Studies in Hysteria*. Three years later, Freud[1] designated Breuer's method of clinical investigation of patients as "a new method of psycho-analysis."

By now, the psychoanalytic enterprise has completed its first century. Thus, the time has come to take thorough critical stock of its past performance qua theory of human nature and therapy, as well as to have a look at its prospects.[2]

THE "DYNAMIC" AND "COGNITIVE" SPECIES OF THE UNCONSCIOUS

Freud was the creator of the full-blown theory of psychoanalysis. But he was certainly not the first to postulate the existence of unconscious mental processes of some kind or other. Over the centuries, a number of other thinkers—such as Plato, Gottfried Wilhelm Leibniz, and Hermann von Helmholtz—had done so earlier in order to explain conscious thought and overt behavior for which they could find no other explanation. Indeed, Freud had additional precursors who anticipated some of his key ideas with impressive specificity.[3] As he himself acknowledged,[4] Arthur Schopenhauer and Friedrich Nietzsche had speculatively propounded major psychoanalytic doctrines that he himself claimed to have developed independently thereafter on the basis of his clinical observations of his patients.

There are major differences between the unconscious processes hypothesized by current cognitive psychology, on the one hand, and the unconscious contents of the mind postulated by psychoanalytic psychology, on the other.[5] Freud's "dynamic" unconscious is the supposed repository of repressed, forbidden wishes of a sexual or aggressive nature which recklessly seek immediate gratification without regard to the constraints of external reality, but whose reentry or initial entry into consciousness is prevented by the defensive operations of the ego. Indeed, according to Freud,[6] we would not even have developed the skills needed to engage in cognitive activities if we did not rely on them to gratify our instinctual needs.

However, the psychoanalyst Heinz Hartmann was driven, by facts of biological maturation discovered nonpsychoanalytically and presumably already known to Freud, to acknowledge in his "ego psychology" that such functions as cognition, memory, and thought can develop autonomously by innate genetic programming, independently of instinctual-drive gratification.[7]

In the cognitive unconscious, there is great rationality in the ubiquitous computational and associative problem-solving processes required by memory, perception, judgment, and attention. By contrast, as Freud emphasized, the wish-content of the dynamic unconscious makes it operate in a highly illogical way. Furthermore, the dynamic unconscious acquires its content largely from the unwitting repression of ideas in the form they originally had in consciousness, whereas neither the expulsion of ideas and memories from consciousness nor the censorious denial of entry to them plays any role at all in the cognitive unconscious.[8] Freud reasoned that the use of his new technique of free association could lift the repressions of instinctual wishes, thereby bringing the repressed ideas back to consciousness unchanged. This Freudian technique calls on the patient to express freely, without omissions, any and all thoughts, feelings, wishes, or whatever came to mind apropos of any given idea.

In the case of the cognitive unconscious, there is typically no such awareness of, say, the elaborate scanning or search process by which someone rapidly comes up with a half-forgotten name when asked for it. Some psychoanalysts have claimed the compatibility of the two species of unconscious within the same genus,[9] yet Morris Eagle[10] has articulated the extensive modifications required in the Freudian notion of the dynamic unconscious if it is to be made compatible with the cognitive one. More importantly, some Freudian apologists[11] have erroneously claimed support for the psychoanalytic unconscious from the cognitive one, although the existence of the latter does not confer any credibility on the former.

We must likewise beware of the bizarre argument, recently put forward by the philosopher Thomas Nagel,[12] that the pervasive influence of Freudian ideas in Western culture vouches for the evidential probity of the psychoanalytic enterprise and for the validity of its doctrines. Yet Freud's widespread cultural influence no more validates his tenets than Christian cultural hegemony warrants belief in the virgin birth of Jesus or in his resurrection.[13] Even Nagel's premise that Freudian theory has become part of the intellectual ethos and folklore of Western culture cannot be taken at face value. As Henri Ellenberger[14] has stressed, the prevalence of vulgarized pseudo-Freudian concepts makes it difficult to determine reliably the extent to which genuine psychoanalytic hypotheses have actually become influential in our culture at large.

For example, the purview of Freud's psychoanalytic motivational elucidation of slips or bungled actions ("parapraxes") was avowedly confined to lapses whose *motives* [are] *unknown to consciousness*,"[15] and which are thus thought to be prima facie psychologically unmotivated. Yet all psychologically motivated slips or bungled actions—even those whose promptings are both conscious and transparent—are commonly but incorrectly called "Freudian." Hence Freud disclaimed any credit for the explanations of those slips that are motivationally transparent.[16]

CRITIQUE OF FREUDIAN AND POST-FREUDIAN PSYCHOANALYSIS

Let us now turn to my critique of the core of Freud's original psychoanalytic theory, and, thereafter, to a verdict on whether my objections to this core are overcome by the two major post-Freudian sets of hypotheses called "self-psychology" and "object relations theory." I have often been told by psychoanalysts that they no longer accept Freud's formulations, as if this disavowal vouched for the probity of one or another of the post-Freudian doctrines. Moreover, when Freud is *not* under attack by outside critics, these same revisionists continue to cite him very frequently with biblical deference.

As Freud told us, "The theory of repression is the corner-stone on which the whole structure of psycho-analysis rests. It is the most essential part of it."[17] The three principal branches of the theory of repression are sets of hypotheses pertaining to the unconscious causation and psychoanalytic treatment of psychopathology, the theory of dreams, and the previously mentioned theory of slips (parapraxes). In each of these three branches, the repression of mental contents is asserted to play a *causally necessary* role: it is deemed crucial to the production of neuroses and psychoses by unconscious sexual motives, to the formation of dreams by latent, forbidden infantile wishes, and to the generation of bungled actions by diverse hidden motives of displeasure (German: *Unlust*).

In Freud's view, our neurotic symptoms, the manifest contents of our dreams, and the various sorts of slips we commit are each constructed as "compromises between the demands of a repressed impulse and the resistances of a censoring force in the ego."[18] Therefore, Freud can be said to have offered a unifying "compromise-model" of neuroses, dreams, and parapraxes. And psychoanalysts have pointed to the explanatory virtue of such unification to claim validity for it, a claim that I shall challenge.

But what, in the first place, is the motive or cause that initiates and sustains the operation of the unconscious mechanism of repression *before* it produces its own effects? Apparently, Freud assumed axiomatically that distressing mental states, such as forbidden wishes, trauma, painful memories, disgust, anxiety, anger, shame, hate, guilt, and sadness—all of which are displeasurable—typically actuate, and then fuel, forgetting to the point of repression.[19] Thus repression presumably regulates pleasure and displeasure by defending our consciousness against various sorts of negative affect.

As Freud put it dogmatically: "The tendency to forget what is disagreeable seems to me to be a quite universal one,"[20] and "distressing memories succumb especially easily to motivated forgetting."[21] Yet he was driven to concede that "one often enough finds it impossible, on the contrary, to get rid of distressing memories that pursue one, and to banish distressing affective impulses like remorse and the pangs of conscience." Furthermore, he acknowledged that "distressing things are particularly hard to forget."[22] Thus, some painful mental states are vividly remembered while others are forgotten or even repressed. Yet Freud's account is vitiated by the fact that factors *other than* the degree of their painfulness determine whether they are remembered or forgotten.

For example, personality dispositions or situational variables may in fact be causally relevant to memorial success or failure. Freud never came to grips adequately with the negative import of the phenomenon of obsessive recall of distressing experiences for his central tenet that negative affect drives repression. Incidentally, the psychologist Thomas Gilovich at Cornell University is now doing valuable work on the sorts of conditions under which painful experiences are *remembered*, and on those kinds of *other* conditions under which they are *forgotten*.

Another basic difficulty, which besets all three branches of the theory of repression alike, lies in the epistemological defects in Freud's "fundamental rule" of "free association." It is a cardinal thesis of his entire psychoanalytic enterprise that this method of free association has the twofold major capability of being both causally investigative and therapeutic. It can identify the unconscious causes of human thoughts and behavior, both abnormal and normal, and by overcoming resistances and lifting repressions, it can remove the unconscious pathogens of neuroses, thereby providing therapy for an important class of mental disorders.

We are told that by using his unique method to unlock the floodgates of the unconscious, Freud was able to show that neuroses, dreams, and slips are caused by repressed motives. For brevity, I shall use the legal term "probative," and will say that a supposed method for identifying causes correctly is "causally probative." And, using medical terminology, I shall speak of the causes of an *illness* as the "etiology" of that illness.

Employing these locutions, I now ask: What was Freud's evidence that free association is causally probative for etiologic research in psychopathology? As he tells us very clearly,[23] his argument for this investigative tribute to free association is essentially a therapeutic one going back to the "cathartic" method of treating hysteria, which had been pioneered by Freud's senior mentor Josef Breuer. In the cathartic method, the hypnotized patient is asked to retrieve the memory of a repressed trauma and to verbalize the previously suppressed emotion felt when he/she had the traumatic experience. Such an emotional release or "catharsis" becomes possible after the hypnotic recall of the trauma.

What then was Freud's *therapeutic argument* that free association can uncover the causes or pathogens of psychopathology? Freud inferred the key therapeutic hypothesis that the remedial disappearance of the neurotic symptoms is *not* a placebo effect, but is causally attributable to the cathartic lifting of repressions by means of the method of free association. According to Breuer and Freud, in a placebo-cure, the patient's expectation of improvement ("suggestion") is responsible for the cure. Assuming, to the contrary, that the cathartic lifting of the patient's repressions is the operative therapeutic agent in getting rid of his/her neurotic symptoms, Freud[24] then drew two additional major theoretical inferences, as follows: (1) The presumed cathartic removal of the neurosis by the associative lifting of repressions is good evidence for postulating that ongoing repressions, accompanied by affective suppressions, are *causally necessary* for the very existence of a neurosis.[25] After all, he reasoned, this postulate then permits the valid deduction of the stated key therapeutic hypothesis that the cathartic removal of the presumed pathogen of the neurosis would issue in its disappearance (cure). Furthermore, he concluded: (2) If repressions accompanied by affective suppression are the essential causes of neurosis, the presumed unique ability of the method of free association to uncover them vouches for its capacity to identify the causes or pathogens of the neuroses. However, his therapeutic argument for the cogent etiologic probativeness of free associations fails in multiple respects, no matter how revealing the associative contents may be otherwise in regard to the patient's psychological preoccupations or personality dispositions.

In the first place, the durable therapeutic success on which the argument was predicated at the outset did not materialize, as Freud was driven to admit both early and very late in his career.[26] For example, contrary to Breuer's own report,[27] his treatment of his famous first patient, Anna O., was a complete therapeutic fiasco.[28] And Breuer knew it when he sent a letter referring her for further treatment elsewhere.

But even insofar as there was a transitory therapeutic gain, Freud failed to rule out the stated rival hypothesis of placebo effect, which undermines his attribution of such a gain to the insightful removal of repressions by free association: this ominous hypothesis of placebo effect asserts that treatment components other than insight into the patient's repressions—such as the mobilization of the patient's hope by the therapist—are responsible for any resulting improvement.[29] To rule out that rival hypothesis cogently, it would have been necessary to show that in a control group of similar patients whose repressions had *not* lifted, the treatment outcome was worse than in the psychoanalytically treated group. No such data have become available during the past century.[30] Thus, the viability of the rival hypothesis of placebo effect rightly challenges Freud's insight-dynamics of therapeutic gain.

Moreover, even if we grant the assumption that the neurosis is removable by cathartically lifting repressions, this outcome does not provide cogent support for postulating etiologically that repressions, accompanied by affective suppressions, are causally necessary for the existence of a neurosis. This lack of support for the crucial foundation of the entire theory of repression can be made apparent from the following analogous fact: The remedial action of aspirin for tension headaches does not lend any support to the outlandish etiologic hypothesis that a hematolytic aspirin deficiency is a causal sine qua non for having tension headaches. Yet if an aspirin *deficiency* in our blood *were* causally required for tension headaches, then it would follow that the removal of that deficiency by taking aspirin will issue in the removal of the tension headache. But that is just not good enough to warrant the inferred etiologic role of the aspirin *deficit.*

Similarly, supposing that repression-accompanied-by-affective-suppression is causally necessary for neurosogenesis, then it follows validly that the *cathartic removal* of the repression will issue in the *removal* of the neurosis. But again, that is not enough to infer the *pathogenic* role of repression-cum-suppression. Thus it is unavailing to the purported etiologic probativeness of free associations that they may lift repressions, since Freud failed to show that the latter are actually pathogenic. The upshot is that Freud's stated therapeutic argument multiply forfeits its foundation. Furthermore, it is a red herring to claim, as some psychoanalysts have done in rebuttal, that this fundamental difficulty is overcome by Freud's subsequent theorizing.

Yet, as we learn in Freud's opening pages on his method of dream interpretation, he extrapolated the role of free associations from being only a method of etiologic inquiry aimed at therapy, to serving likewise as an avenue for finding the purported unconscious causes of dreams.[31] In the same breath, he reports that when patients told him about their dreams while associating freely to their symptoms, he boldly, if not rashly, extrapolated his "compromise-model" from neurotic symptoms to manifest dream contents. In that model, both symptoms and manifest dream contents are regarded as "compromises between the demands of a repressed impulse, and the resistances of a censoring force in the ego."[32] Later, Freud carried out the same twofold extrapolation to include sundry slips or bungled actions.

What, in Freud's view, do free associations tell us about our dreams? Whatever their manifest content, they are purportedly always wish-fulfilling in two logically distinct ways: at least one usually unconscious infantile wish is required as the motivational cause of any and every dream,[33] and the manifest content of the dream graphically displays, more or less disguisedly, the state of affairs desired by the wish. As Freud contends:[34] "When the latent dream-thoughts that are revealed by the analysis [via free association] of a dream are examined, one of them is found to stand out from among the rest . . . [and] the isolated thought is found to be a wishful impulse. . . . This impulse is the actual constructor of the dream: it provides the energy for its production. . . ." Furthermore, Freud claimed[35] that a preconscious universal wish-to-sleep explains why we dream at all, as distinct from why our dreams have the specific manifest contents they do.

Quite independently of Freud's unsuccessful therapeutic argument for the causal probativeness of the method of free association, he offered his psychoanalysis of his own 1895 "Specimen Irma Dream" as a separate, *non*therapeutic argument for deeming the method of free association to be a cogent means of identifying hypothesized hidden wishes as the motives of our dreams. In my detailed critique of that unjustly celebrated analysis of his Irma Dream,[36] I have argued that Freud's account is regrettably no more than a piece of false advertising: it does not deliver at all the promised vindication of free association; it does nothing toward warranting his foolhardy dogmatic generalization that all dreams are wish-fulfillments in his stated twofold sense; and it does not even pretend that his alleged "Specimen Dream" is evidence for his compromise-model of manifest-dream content. Nonetheless, Freud's analysis of his Irma dream continues to be celebrated in the psychoanalytic literature as the paragon of dream interpretation.

Moreover, his wish-fulfillment theory of dreaming was deeply flawed from the outset. As it now turns out, he did not heed a patent epistemological consequence of having abandoned his 1895 *Project*'s neurological energy-model of *wish-driven* dreaming. By precisely that abandonment, he had forfeited his initial biological rationale for claiming that at least all "normal" dreams are wish-fulfilling, which left him without any kind of energy-based warrant for then universalizing the doctrine of wish-fulfillment to extend to any sort of dream. Yet, unencumbered by the total absence of any such warrant and of any other justification, the universalized doctrine, now formulated in psychological terms, rose like a phoenix from the ashes of Freud's defunct energy-model. As I have argued elsewhere,[37] his neuroenergetic argument for wish-driven dreaming was dead in the water *at birth*.

Once he had chained himself to the universal wish-monopoly of dream production, his interpretations were constrained to reconcile wish-*contravening* dreams with the decreed universality of wish-fulfillment.[38] Such reconciliation demanded imperatively that all other parts and details of his dream theory be obligingly tailored to the tenability of his governing wish-dogma. Yet Freud artfully obscured this contrived dynamic of theorizing while begging the methodological question.

Indeed, since there are innumerable distressing, prima facie wish-contravening dreams, Freud's idée fixe of universal wish-fulfillment dictated nothing less than the following three major *artifactual* doctrines of his dream theory. First there is the distinction between the conscious, manifest content of a dream—which is topically polymorphic—and the repressed, latent content, which Freud claimed to feature invariably a repressed, infantile wish.[39] The manifest content is allegedly just a façade for the forbidden, latent wish-content: the former purportedly resulted, in the service of disguise, from the distortion of the forbidden wish by a process that Freud designated as the "dream-*work*"; but this *hypothesized distortion* must *not* be confused with the *familiar bizarreness* of dreams.

A second artifact of Freud's "wish-imperialism" was the related tenet that the manifest dream content, no less than a neurotic symptom, is the product of a conflict and compromise between a repressed wish clamoring for expression—a so-called latent dream-thought—and the censorship exerted by a repressing ego.[40]

Finally, the insistence on the universality of wish-fulfillment in dreams also imposed a methodological exigency. As Clark Glymour[41] has noted, Freud's method of dream interpretation by free association was antecedently constrained by his exigency to weave together the ensuing associations selectively so as to yield a wish-motive as standing out from the others. But Freud[42] misrepresented this preordained result as a straightforward empirical finding, unencumbered by prior theory-driven regimentation of the products of the patient's associations.

Advocates of psychoanalysis have proclaimed it to be an explanatory virtue of their theory that its compromise model gives a unifying account of such disparate phenomena as neuroses, dreams, and slips, and furthermore that the theory of repression also contributes to Freud's theory of psychosexual development. In fact, some philosophers of science have hailed explanatory unification as one of the great achievements and desiderata of the scientific enterprise. Yet, in other contexts, unification can be a vice rather than a virtue. For example, Thales of Miletus, though rightly seeking a rationalistic, rather than mythopoetic, picture of the world, taught that everything is made of water—a cosmic chemical unification. But a later chemist could have said to Thales, across the millennia: "There are more things in heaven and earth, Horatio, than are dreamt of in your philosophy."[43]

As I have argued, the same moral applies to Freud's dubious psychopathologizing of normalcy; by unwarrantedly assuming the causal cogency of the method of free association, his compromise model has generated a *pseudo*unification of neurotic behavior with dreaming and the bungling of actions.

The French philosopher Paul Ricoeur[44] endeavored to parry quite different criticisms of psychoanalysis from philosophers of science during the 1950s and 1960s.[45] In concert with the other "hermeneutic" philosophers Karl Jaspers and Jürgen Habermas, as well as with Ludwig Wittgenstein, Ricoeur retorted patronizingly that Freud himself had "scientistically" misunderstood his own theoretical achievement, such that the scientific failings of psychoanalysis were actually virtues. Mind you, scientism is a form of intellectual malfeasance. It is the supposed misguidedly utopian, intellectually imperialistic, and exclusionary worship of the scientific way of knowing the world, and it is often linked as a whipping boy with what is untutoredly denigrated as "positivism." The hermeneuts offer their own reconstruction of psychoanalysis.

But elsewhere[46] I have contended that all of the misunderstandings and confusions with which they charge Freud are actually their own, not his. Thus they champion the muddled doctrine that Freud's theory of the unconscious *"meaning"* of symptoms, dreams, and slips is a contribution to *semantics!* Accordingly, Ricoeur speaks of Freud's supposed "semantics of *desire.*" And the English psychoanalyst Anthony Storr stated misguidedly that "Freud was a genius whose expertise lay in semantics."[47] But the Freudian meaning of a symptom is *etiologic*, unlike the semantic meaning of language. The etiologic meaning of a symptom is its latent motivational cause. No wonder that the methods of the hermeneuts have deplorably failed to spawn a single new clinically or explanatorily fruitful psychoanalytic hypothesis. Instead, their proposed reconstruction is just a negativistic ideological battle cry that leads nowhere.

POST-FREUDIAN DEVELOPMENTS

What have been the contemporary post-Freudian developments insofar as they still qualify as psychoanalytic in content rather than just in name? Are they on firmer epistemological ground than Freud's original major hypotheses?[48] The well-known clinical psychologist Morris Eagle[49] has given a comprehensive and insightful negative answer to this question. As he tells us:[50] "In the last forty or fifty years there have been three major theoretical developments in psychoanalysis: ego psychology, object relations theory, and self-psychology. If contemporary psychoanalytic theory is anything, it is one of these three or some combination, integrative or otherwise, of the three."

As we already had occasion to note, Heinz Hartmann's ego-psychology departed from Freud's instinctual anchorage of the cognitive functions. More importantly, both Heinz Kohut's self-psychology as well as the object relations theory of Otto Kernberg and the British school fundamentally reject Freud's compromise-model of psychopathology: indeed, self-psychology has repudiated virtually every one of Freud's major tenets.[51] Similarly, the object relations theorists deny that the etiology of pathology lies in Freudian (oedipal) conflicts and traumas involving sex and aggression, claiming instead that the quality of maternal care is the crucial factor. However, besides diverging from Freud, these two post-Freudian schools disagree with one another.

But what about the evidential merits of the two post-Freudian developments that are usually designated as "contemporary psychoanalysis"? Do they remedy Freud's epistemological failings? Eagle argues that the verdict is clearly negative:[52] "The different variants of so-called contemporary psychoanalytic theory . . . are on no firmer epistemological ground than the central formulations and claims of Freudian theory. . . . There is no evidence that contemporary psycho-analytic theories have remedied the epistemological and methodological difficulties that are associated with Freudian theory."

Since Jacques Lacan avowedly forsook the need to validate his doctrines by familiar canons of evidence, I shall not comment on them except to mention his willful, irresponsible literary obscurity and notorious cruelty to patients,[53] which he justified as satisfying their alleged masochistic needs.

Finally, what are the prospects for the future of psychoanalysis in the twenty-first century? The noted psychoanalysts Jacob Arlow and Charles Brenner[54] reached the following sanguine conclusion about both its past and its future:

> Psychoanalysis will continue to furnish the most comprehensive and illuminating insight into the human psyche. It will continue to stimulate research and understanding in many areas of human endeavor. In addition to being the best kind of treatment for many cases, it will remain, as it has been, the fundamental base for almost all methods that try to alleviate human mental suffering by psychological means.

By contrast, a dismal verdict is offered by the renowned American psychologist and psychoanalyst Paul E. Meehl.[55] Since one of my main criticisms of psychoanalysis figures in it, let me explain first that apropos of my critiques of Freud's theories of obsessional neurosis (the Rat Man) and of transference, I had demonstrated the fallaciousness of inferring a causal connection between mental states from a thematic ("meaning") connection between them.[56] Meehl refers to the latter kind of shared thematic content as "the existence of a theme" and writes:

> His [Grünbaum's] core objection, the epistemological difficulty of inferring a causal influence from the existence of a theme (assuming the latter can be statistically demonstrated), is the biggest single methodological problem that we [psychoanalysts] face. If that problem cannot be solved, we will have

another century in which psychoanalysis can be accepted or rejected, mostly as a matter of personal taste. Should that happen, I predict it will be slowly but surely abandoned, both as a mode of helping and as a theory of the mind [reference omitted].

Accordingly, in regard to the last one hundred years, Arlow and Brenner's rosy partisan account is very largely ill founded, if only because, as we saw, the lauded comprehensiveness of the core theory of repression is only a *pseudo*unification. Among their glowingly optimistic statements about the future, only one is plausible: the expectation of a continuing heuristic role for psychoanalysis. Such a function does not require at all that its current theories be correct.

As an example of the heuristic role, one need only think of the issues I raised in connection with Freud's dubious account of the relation of affect to forgetting and remembering, issues that range well beyond the concerns of psychoanalysis. In this vein, the Harvard psychoanalyst and schizophrenia researcher Philip Holzman observes:[57] "This view of the heuristic role of psychoanalysis, even in the face of its poor science, is beginning to be appreciated only now." Holzman[58] mentions three areas of inquiry as illustrations: (1) the plasticity and reconstructive role of memory as against photographic reproducibility of the past; (2) the general role of affect in cognition; and (3) the relevance of temperament (e.g., shyness) in character development, as currently investigated by Jerome Kagan at Harvard. These are topics that will very probably be explored further in the years to come.

Freud: Current Projections

Peter D. Kramer

LIKE MANY PSYCHIATRISTS of my generation, I entered the profession because of Sigmund Freud. While a graduate student in literature at University College London, I underwent psychoanalysis with a Freudian associated with the Hampstead Clinic.[1] The treatment was utterly orthodox—it aimed at uncovering and influencing my Oedipus complex—but the analyst was humane and the process compelling. Among my friends at the university, psychoanalysis was a way of understanding social relationships; the standard of worth in those relationships was authenticity, which meant both taking responsibility for unconscious motivation and discussing that motivation openly. In my spare time, I sat in the college library in Bloomsbury, plowing through the James Strachey translation of Freud's *Collected Works*. It was then that I chose my profession. My hope was to emulate Freud, seeing patients afternoons and in the morning writing speculatively about the nature of mind.

I was not unaware of objections and alternatives to Freud's theories. Several colleagues were in Kleinian analysis, through the rival Tavistock Clinic. I sat in on Richard Wollheim's philosophy seminars on the emotions (he was a biographer of Freud and something of a Kleinian), and I discussed the merits of psychoanalysis with friends in medical training. But the alternative schemata we considered were embellishments or elaborations, more or less successful, of the Freudian framework. The universe of psychiatry, insofar as I was acquainted with it, was a "hub and spokes" affair, with Freud at the center and other theories interesting only as offshoots of the central truth.

Far from disturbing this perspective, medical school in the States reinforced it. Child development—this was in the mid-1970s—was taught along Freudian lines. (We learned that four-year-olds may be afraid of shoe stores because trying on shoes arouses castration anxiety—will the foot return?) Even during my residency, where the breadth of the psychiatric world became apparent, individual psychotherapy was grounded directly in the teachings of Freud. Psychoanalytic metapsychology was taught in the same fashion as orthopedic anatomy or cardiac physiology: as material to be mastered.

Freud, the man, was, in those innocent times, a grand if imperfect figure. According to the available biographies, he was contentious, sectarian, suspicious, self-pitying, pessimistic, capricious toward followers, and prone to an unworthy wish to distance himself from his own roots; but these were the idiosyncrasies of a giant, a member of the pantheon that included Marx, Darwin, and Einstein. Even as it became apparent that Freud had missed a good deal—about cultural relativism, the two-person or group perspective, the importance of attachment and empathy, and the development of women—and that neurobiology had bypassed certain of Freud's theories, Freudianism continued to be regarded as the foundation on which any serious understanding of the modern psyche would be built.

I came late in the tide of Freudians; my classmates in psychiatric training included geneticists and monkey-spinal-fluid researchers. Residency introduced a host of perspectives to compete with Freud's. Yet my experience typified that of many psychiatrists now in practice. We were drawn to training because we admired Freud the man, and because we found in the texts much that explained our own behavior.

Now, for the past twenty years, we have had to consider how to react to historical revision. Freud, aspects of whose personality had always been unclear, went entirely out of focus. Perhaps it should come as no surprise that a person is hard to know; Freud himself taught that so apparently straightforward a matter as a diagnosis may remain obscure until the end of an extensive psychoanalysis. After a century, it seems that the analysis of Freud will be of the interminable variety.

The problem is not our understanding of one or another detail of Freud's life or practice. "Great Doctor, are you savant or charlatan?" was the question posed seventy years ago by an anguished husband,

Abraham Bijur, whose wife left him on Freud's advice.[2] Now we can choose biographical accounts that lead to either conclusion. In some readings, Freud remains the heroic figure that W. H. Auden made him out to be in the famous elegy.[3] Just as often, Freud is portrayed as a hypocrite who in his quest for fame betrayed or misunderstood the people he purported to analyze, beginning with the early hysterics and Dora. He is the progenitor of a great intellectual tradition, unless he is the most dishonest of scientists. His is a new key to understanding the self, one of the few ever granted the human race, except that every detail of his theory—child development, structure of mind, psychopathology—is gravely flawed. Our vision of Freud is composed of extreme images that barely intersect.

I am not a Freud scholar, I never did become a psychoanalyst, and though I discuss Freud in each of my books, my writing concerns psychoactive medications and an eclectic array of psychotherapies. The Freud controversies reached me largely through publications with "New York" in the title: the *New York Times, The New Yorker,* the *New York Review of Books.* My intimate response to this material was relief. My own theory and practice had moved away from Freudianism, and the historical revision provided belated absolution for this infidelity. Still, there was a sense of loss and dislocation.

The faults of which Freud has recently been accused are not incidental but essential to his character: dishonesty, moral timidity, credulousness, venality, cruelty, and an almost willful intellectual shortsightedness. To his critics, these traits are embedded in Freud's theory: Freudianism is said to have blighted untold lives, though the lives in question (those of abused children disbelieved, of parents falsely accused, or of women misdiagnosed) are not always the same ones. The accumulation of charges has led me, as a working psychiatrist and also as a general reader, to wonder how convincing Freud's theories remain.

RECENTLY I HAD occasion to return to the *Works.* The passage I consulted (I was researching the origins of "projection" as a concept) was a case vignette from Freud's correspondence in 1895 with Wilhelm Fliess.[4] What struck me as I reread it was how effective the attacks on Freud have been, even vaguely considered, and how profound an influence they have had on the way we are likely to read Freud today.

In the letter, Freud is developing the concept of projection as a defense characteristic of paranoia. He defines projection as a disowning of "an idea that is incompatible with the ego" and which must then be attributed to another person. Freud illustrates his theory by describing a patient. She is an unmarried woman in her thirties who believes that the neighbors are observing and deriding her—spreading the story that she was jilted by a former boarder in the family home. The patient's sister has recounted an incident involving this boarder, which Freud relates to Fliess: "[The younger sister] had been doing out the room when [the boarder] was still lying in bed. He had called her up to the bed, and, when she had unsuspectingly obeyed, put his penis in her hand. There had been no sequel to the scene. . . ."[5]

The younger sister's paranoid symptoms began when the boarder left town. By the time Freud interviews her, she denies having been approached sexually, and though he tries, Freud fails to bring the patient's mind back to the episode with the boarder. Nonetheless, Freud considers the mental process causing the illness to be self-apparent: "[S]omething was repressed. And we can guess what that was. She had probably in fact been excited by what she had seen and by recollecting it. So what she was sparing herself was the self-reproach of being 'a bad woman.' " The younger sister has projected her self-accusations onto the neighbors. Freud writes Fliess that a like process underlies all other cases of paranoia.

To a modern audience, no element of this chain of argument will do. Repressed and projected thought is hardly likely to be the basis of paranoia. Ours is an era in which evolutionary psychology holds sway, an era that therefore attends to animal ethology; and quite simple traumatic or pharmacologic stressors can make animals hypervigilant and anxious in the manner of paranoia. In humans, the mental content of paranoia seems to be a way of attempting to organize overwhelming sensations whose cause lies elsewhere, perhaps in a neurological dysfunction. True, that organization comes from within, but people suffering with paranoia are hardly transparent in the way Freud describes. If anything, their stereotyped responses make them opaque. A paranoid person can be suspicious without reference to any particular ego-threatening accusation against the self.

Regarding the story of the younger sister and the boarder: What are we to make of it? Presumably the memory is not "recovered" (the repression or denial of the memory occurs after it has been shared); still, in light of the controversy over "false memory," we are likely to be less eager than Freud was to take the account at face value. The sister's illness may predate the boarder's sojourn; paranoia may be the cause, rather than the result, of the bedroom story. Or perhaps the problem lies in the opposite direction. From the contemporary perspective, the boarder's approach appears abusive rather than inviting. We may wonder whether he had been more intrusive than the younger sister initially indicated, and whether for the victim the experience constituted a return to an earlier trauma. Entertaining the other side of the memory debate, we may want to ask whether the woman was, for example, molested in childhood as well, and whether her paranoia is the result of repeated psychic injuries. Far from taking Freud's account at face value, the contemporary reader is likely to generate a host of scenarios, with various parts played by the family and the neighbors. Freud's version—that the genesis of illness can be traced back to a single event—is the least likely scenario.

These modern perspectives concern the utility of Freud's account as psychiatry. We are unlikely to believe that the younger sister's paranoid productions are important indicators of the etiology of her ailment (the concept of psychosis as a defense is altogether out of favor), and we are unlikely to share Freud's confidence that the alleged encounter with the boarder caused the illness. In this critique, Freud's theories are being judged according to standards or prejudices that postdate his writing by a century. Nonetheless, our opinion of Freud's science has a decided effect on the way we are likely to read the letter. If Freud's analysis is faulty—if we believe he was unable in any objective sense to use his data to reconstruct the history or mind of the patient—then the vignette speaks primarily to Freud's own mental processes.

Freud's speculation does not cast him in a flattering light. Of the young woman he says, "She had probably in fact been excited. . . ." Humiliated, perhaps, or terrorized—we can generate any number of alternative accounts. In attributing a guilty mind to his patient, Freud seems cruelly blind not only to her circumstances but also to those of women in general, in precisely the way that critics charge. Rapidly, this vignette transforms itself from a story about a young woman and her projections into a story about Freud and his.

We no longer automatically accord Freud the virtues he was for decades assumed to possess: clinical acumen, wisdom in human affairs, dedication to his patients and to the truth. Once we adopt any degree of skepticism, we will judge that Freud's observations and conclusions are too conveniently affirming of his theory. In particular, how can he construe his failure to elicit the memory from the younger sister to be a confirmation of his suspicions? It is often said that a person must be judged separately from his work. But in Freud's case, the distinction is difficult to maintain. It is precisely our doubt about his theory—its lack of accord with contemporary opinion about paranoia and post-traumatic stress disorder—that turns the vignette into an occasion for judging Freud's character. In a broader sense, if his work is an invaluable contribution to human knowledge, then Freud must be allowed the genius's quota of peremptoriness; but if the work is misguided, then its arbitrary quality reveals the man to be one more ideological despot.

Reciprocally, attacks on Freud's character diminish the work. In the end, theory must be judged on its own account; it is not only the personally admirable who produce good science. But any evaluation of Freud's theory will be complicated by the nature of the evidence he adduces: his subjective reporting of his own observations. The way we read the work, the way we accept the evidence, is colored by our estimation of the man: are these stories rendered in good faith? Are they reliable? Or have the facts been doctored more than the patients? In terms of the current value of Freud's theories, if he was profound and self-searching, then his ideas merit testing or revision as part of a historical scientific progression; but if he was merely a relentless self-promoter, then even if a few of the concepts are useful, the collection can be dismissed as hypnotic patter. The accusations of bad science and bad character interact synergistically to Freud's detriment. We can no longer recall why the sort of vignette Freud provides in his letter was once valued as revolutionary and liberating, why Freud was celebrated for taking seriously the unspeakable thoughts of the outcasts of society.

ADMITTEDLY, THE LETTER to Fliess is intimate writing, not meant for publication. Modern readers might be more sympathetic to Freud's first published vignette regarding paranoia, the case of a paranoid mother who has shameful memories of a sexualized childhood involvement with her brother.[6] However, much of Freud does read today like the vignette of the paranoid younger sister. I am hardly qualified to enter the well-elaborated controversy over the Schreber case,[7] Freud's most prominent discussion of paranoid projection and a work of his maturity, but surely it serves today more as a study of Freud's projections than of Schreber's. Like the younger sister's supposed excitement over the boarder's behavior, the hidden content that Freud ascribes to Schreber's delusions—latent homosexuality—grounds illness in the patient's guilty mind rather than in the trauma inflicted on the patient by others. In truth, discomfort in reading Freud—in finding that his interpretations act as judgments upon him, in realizing how hard it has become to take him generously—might arise in response to almost any of Freud's writings.

PERHAPS IT IS best to confront this discomfort, and to try in each instance to disaggregate the flawed theory from the flawed man. From the modern standpoint, Freud is often simply wrong. In particular, we doubt his explication of psychosis, and we disagree with almost everything he had to say about sex and gender at any stage in his career. Penis envy, castration anxiety, latent homosexuality, the universality of the Oedipus and Electra complexes, the detrimental effects of sexual abstinence or withdrawal, the prevalence of fantasy over fact as regards molestation in childhood, the unique role of sexual drives (as opposed, say, to drives for attachment or mastery), the inscrutability of women's desires—on every issue we are likely to find Freud misguided. This large realm of disagreement might seem devastating to psychoanalysis—after all, Freud based his psychology on a theory of psychosexual development—but in practice it is not. Alternative psychoanalyses flourish; it turns out that it is possible to incorporate a good deal of Freudian thought without adopting his views on major mental illnesses or on sex and gender. As regards sexuality, Freud's contribution was his insistent (and brave) focus on the sexual repression of Victorian society and its continental equivalent; it may be unfair to expect someone reared in that setting to view sexuality in measured fashion.

Freud was much more on target, from our vantage point, when he turned away from the study of psychosis and sexuality to consider the working of the normal, or nearly normal, mind. Whether or not Freud makes sense of paranoia or of the paranoid younger sister, the concept he is trying to illustrate—projection—has proved durable and useful. By itself, and via its subsequent transformation into such ideas as transference and projective identification, it is an important element of a medical technology that most psychiatrists continue to value: psychotherapy. There are dangers inherent in relying on an analysis of projection, and Freud's letter to Fliess inadvertently exemplifies them: arbitrarily ascribing guilty desires to the victim, endorsing unverified historical accounts, attributing the therapist's thoughts to the patient, mistaking illness or temperament for defensiveness. But subsequent developments in theory and technique attempt to avoid these pitfalls. Examination of patients' projections remains a useful tool in the effort to help them make sense of their social interactions.

As members of the post-Freudian social world, we use the concept of projection daily. Open discussion of psychoanalytic theory may be less common than it was at mid-century, but routinely we still ask ourselves: Am I as my friend makes me out to be, or is it a matter of a particular sort of distortion—namely, projection—on the friend's part? Before jumping to a hasty conclusion, we examine our apprehensions to ascertain whether we have misleadingly projected a motivation onto a friend. In our efforts to understand others, we may be less bold or arbitrary than Freud in reading back from projection to the thought projected, but the concept of projection is an element in the commonsense perspective of our time.

Often it seems that Freud was best at understanding aspects of his own psychic makeup and expanding his results into conclusions about the normally troubled mind. Much of his writing looks like an attempt to justify or publicize these observations by forcing them onto accounts of treatments of the mentally ill. A more generous, but not entirely admiring, reading of the letter to Fliess would place it in this context. Freud understood that projection is a ubiquitous defense, but he erred in overgeneralizing its application. In the process, he showed himself to possess in goodly measure the personality traits long attributed to him: he is peremptory and egotistical, and he stretches facts on the procrustean bed of theory. Still, we remain in his debt.

Like the unconscious, projection existed before Freud. The *Oxford English Dictionary* gives an example from Emerson's 1838 oration "Literary Ethics": "The youth, intoxicated with his adulation of a hero, fails to see that it is only a projection of his soul which he admires." But it was Freud who allowed us to see a self-protective version of projection as a ubiquitous element in interpersonal interactions. In terms of the dichotomy posed by Lionel Trilling, it is Freud who taught us to demand that we be not just sincere but authentic—responsible for expressions of our unconscious life.[8] We can dismiss Freud only inauthentically, by ignoring how much he has given us and remains part of us. At the same time, much that is Freudian must be dismissed. Most four-year-olds have no trouble in the shoe store, and Freud's theories of sexual development are unlikely to help us understand those who do.

By referring to the ubiquity of Freud's thought, the way he permeates our culture (in the elegy, Auden called him "a whole climate of opinion"), I do not mean to take the part of those who would save Freud by discarding his claims as a scientist and locating his greatness in philosophy or literature. Martha Nussbaum, in *The Therapy of Desire*, demonstrates that much of Greek philosophy is concerned with the prescription of methods—largely methods of self-analysis—that will avert emotional perturbation.[9] Freud was that sort of philosopher, a successor to the Cynics, Stoics, and Epicureans, but today our word for that sort of philosopher, one who systematically examines the basis of affect, is "psychologist." If Freud's psychology proves false, what philosophy remains in his work? Freud's philosophy is trivial without his theory of mind. Besides, the evidence against Freud as a scientist could serve equally well as an accusation of philosophical bad faith. And what does it mean to praise Freud only as a writer? He is a celebrated stylist, to be sure, but are we to pass on him Auden's judgment of Yeats, Kipling, and Claudel—that despite his wrongheaded views, he should be pardoned for writing well?[10]

Freud is recategorized as a humanist because so many of his theories have been superseded within the sciences of mind. Child development has become a quasi-empirical discipline. Freud's admonitions to the contrary, psychotherapy has turned nonspecific, relying on empathy, reparenting, behavioral reprogramming, attention to maladaptive learning, and other nonanalytic approaches to the point where it seems dangerously close to the old "moral" cures. Even within psychoanalysis, the cutting-edge treatments—offshoots of the self psychology, object relations, attachment theory, or interpersonal schools—discard Freud's theory and technique.

But what remains of Freud is still psychology. We are all Freudians in our everyday thought, where we worry, to greater or lesser degree, about unconscious aggression, mother complexes, sexual repression, Freudian slips, and the like. Exactly how much of this century-old science—how much of this everyday thought—remains tenable is an open question. Despite generations of critique and revision, it is still hard to know what to make of the essence of Freudian theory, its structure and its language. Modern theorists are profoundly at odds over fundamental concepts like the dynamic unconscious. Certain notions—the defenses as elements of personality, staged development as an element of child psychology—have held up well, but it is hard to know whether they continue to be bolstered by a structure that can be called Freudian.

My own half-serious fantasy is a special "Freud project," one that would take each of the hundreds of Freud's concepts—developmental impasses, the expression of fantasy through symbolic behavior, the return of the repressed, projection—and ask, are we willing to own it? The auditor I have in mind would be sympathetic to Freudianism, or at least not hostile, but well versed in contemporary science, from cognitive psychology to neuropsychiatry, and in some harder-to-name discipline—call it sociology of popular thought. The standard to be applied would not be narrowly scientific but would extend to a consideration of which of the strictly unprovable notions that seem helpful we can still in good conscience entertain. As regards (for example) projection: Freud's provenance and justification of the concept aside, is projection, as a defense mechanism, an important aspect of the human psyche?

My fantasy about the results of this fantasized project is that, while broad swaths of the Freudian enterprise would prove to have no foundation, the inquiry would find a fair amount of "everyday" Freud intact. Freud's gift is the one he thought he brought: the introduction of mind to psychiatry. The courtship may have been conducted under false pretenses—paranoia is less tied to projected guilt than Freud posited. Like many who see clearly what others mistake or deny, Freud went too far—too far in ascribing aggressive sexual motives to the vulnerable, too far in linking suppressed thought to illness. But how much worse off we would be if he had not explored the role of unspeakable thoughts and feelings and the price paid for their repression. Surely Freud was right that examination of the emotional content of memory deserves a place in the medical enterprise and in our daily lives.

I suspect that my Freud project would leave us Freudians still: curious about the role of mind in health, the effect of experience on personality, the symbolism inherent in ostensibly trivial behavior. In important ways, we will continue to think as Freud led us to. As for Freud's character, my guess—despite the possibility of further disturbing evidence in the archives—is that we will come to be more forgiving and even, once again, admiring. Our list of Freud's flaws will change slightly. And then we will resume thanking him, as Auden did, for teaching "the unhappy Present to recite the Past like a poetry lesson," for reminding us "to be enthusiastic over the night," for opposing autocracy even if "some traces of the autocratic pose . . . still clung to his utterance and features."

Strange Hearts

ON THE PARADOXICAL LIAISON BETWEEN PSYCHOANALYSIS AND FEMINISM

Muriel Dimen

> Now, in a line of associations ambiguous words (or, as we
> may call them, "switch-words") act like points at a junction.
> If the points are switched across from the position in which
> they appear to lie in the dream, then we find ourselves on
> another set of rails; and along this second track run the
> thoughts which we are in search of but which still lie
> concealed behind the dream.[1]

PSYCHOANALYSIS MAKES A MAP, FEMINISTS MAKE WAVES

The sexual body, which, for good or ill, may rightly be judged a psychoanalytic creation, is also a map.[2] Consider the erogenous zones.
The terms "oral," "anal," "phallic," and so on designate sites of arousal
and chart stages of growth. At the same time they map ideas and allegiances. Body parts operate in psychoanalytic theory much as they do
in the unconscious—as "switch-words," to use Sigmund Freud's ver-
satile metaphor. Freud's anatomical map of a brave new sexual world
plots a passage that begins as though generic to Homo sapiens but
ends in masculinity. In a failure of nerve, it inscribes things female on
"a dark continent"[3] (a metaphor that buries in femininity the under-
problematized racism of psychoanalysis).[4] It then fantasizes about that
which, bedarkened, can no longer be seen:

> When at last the sexual act is permitted and the clitoris itself
> becomes excited, it still retains a function: the task, namely, of

transmitting excitation to the adjacent female sexual parts, just as—to use a simile—pine shavings can be kindled in order to set a log of harder wood on fire.[5]

In 1968, sixty-three years and three generations later, those were fighting words. The magnitude of the recent feminist revolt against Freudian tyranny over the female body can be measured by the fact that in 1990 this "strangely inappropriate identification of the cavity of the vagina with a burning log" could be called, with urbane sarcasm, "less than illuminating."[6] In and around 1970, however, when women were very, very angry (of course, we're still angry, but now some of us get to say so in publications like this), the vaginal orgasm, which topped the Freudian scale of maturity and mental health, was officially declared a myth.[7]

The feminism of that time saw in the psychoanalytic construction of the female body the pernicious machinery of patriarchal power. Freud's definition of the clitoris as nothing more than an instrument to be manipulated (literally) in order to get the vagina to work organized women's sexuality for men's pleasure: the penis, after all, wants the vagina, not the clitoris. The myth of the vaginal orgasm also served men's power: as a medical and political switch point, it "emerged out of the long historical repression of female sexuality in the interests of men's control over women's reproductive capacities."[8] Freudian psychoanalysis aimed at having women adapt to the oppressing and repressive bourgeois role of compliant and cheerful housewife and mother. Not only that; through a double bind of the sort theorized by Michel Foucault,[9] psychoanalysis secured a power base for itself: by debasing the clitoral orgasm, it aggravated the problem of frigidity that it then called upon itself to cure (not bad for business, as Kate Millett pointed out).[10] Strengthened by Masters and Johnson's empirical research claiming to demonstrate a unitary orgasm,[11] the second wave of feminism deposed Freud and (re)captured the clitoris.

How different from the first feminist response to Freud. Karen Horney, who began her campaign in the 1920s, was also angry—her sarcasm was equally urbane and no less biting—but her arguments were professional, not political.[12] Although she followed the sociologist Georg Simmel in noticing that psychoanalysis was part of a masculinist culture, she continued to work from within the clinical psychoanalytic fold. Not chiefly interested in the clitoris, Horney wanted to rescue the vagina from its developmentally secondary place; unlike the second-wave feminists, she did not question its orgasmic primacy. She wanted to show that penis envy is not a bedrock phenomenon, that femininity is as primary as masculinity.

Horney (and, in other ways, Ernest Jones and Melanie Klein)[13] took on Freud's theory of phallic monism: all children believe there is only one sex—male—until that catastrophic recognition of lack, traumatic in different ways for each sex, that only men have penises and women do not. Surviving the cataclysm of castration fear and anxiety is, in Freud's view, prerequisite to healthy, mature femininity and masculinity; furthermore, it underlies his theory of desire, neurosis, and human nature. Horney dissented, asserting: If boys are born boys, girls are born girls. The vagina's sensuality, at least equal to that of the clitoris, is demonstrably present from infancy onward. She concluded by arguing that *"behind the 'failure to discover' the vagina is a* [culturally motivated] *denial of its existence."*[14] Freud's response to this strong argument is tendentious, categorically stipulating the nonexistence of infantile vaginal sensations.[15] This preemptive strike not only foreclosed argument but required belief in the dogma of phallic monism for psychoanalytic legitimacy.[16]

Although Horney's intervention was evidently not the final answer—nor, as we shall see, does one yet exist—it was the first sign that the center of Freud's theory of sex, a red-hot manifesto for sexual liberation bound up by a blue-blooded scientific pedigree, doesn't quite hold. Psychoanalytic subversion contends, *tout court*, that humans desire. Psychoanalytic conformity insists they procreate. The classic psychoanalytic theory of sexuality is thus torn between these two masters, sex and reproduction, resulting in a conflict of loyalties whose contradictory effects are visited signally upon women. In the classic psychoanalytic story, libido is always masculine; women, insofar as they lust—and indeed they do in Freud's account—are male. Female desire is defined, and simultaneously nullified, by procreation, or, more precisely, by Freud's desire: sex as reproduction was Freud's royal road to authority. If the psychoanalytic theory of desire could be linked to the great chain of cause and effect running all the way back from biology and Darwin (one of his idols) to physics and Newton, it would be demonstrably true and could take its place in the noble roster of modern sciences. For Freud, anatomy, or, rather, biology, *was* destiny.[17]

There were two prizes in the battle between Freud and the feminists: one, overt, was female sexual subjectivity; the other, covert, was Freud's scientific standing. He sacrificed the first in order to win the second, a sacrifice symbolized by the instrumentalization of the clitoris on the psychoanalytic map.[18] Hence his perhaps guilty exasperation in asking Princess Marie Bonaparte, "What does a woman want?"[19] What his question disavowed, his affect acknowledged: Women do desire. They want sex. They need it. He knew it, and he dissociated what he knew.

Surely this dissociation of women's sexual desire registers the shock of feminism. Freud's theories of women as well as his asides on feminists can be diagnosed: they are littered with splitting and contempt, the defensive strategies characterizing the divided mind, variously termed hysterical, borderline, or dissociated, that splits the world into good and bad but cannot imagine anything in between. Think, for example, of Freud's famously weird reference to the "fact" of female castration that, if faithful to fantasy, nonetheless splits off the factuality of female anatomy and disavows his knowledge that women's genitalia are as intact as men's.[20] Recall his manipulative and condescending exemption of women analysts from femininity, which in his view always comes up short when compared with masculinity: the negative features of femininity did not, he said, apply to them, they were exceptions, "more masculine than feminine."[21] Remember his rage at the nameless lesbian, for whose unnecessary "treatment" he tries to account (she was "in no way neurotic") and whose ire he explains by jibing, "In fact, she was a feminist."[22] It is she whose gender he changes, in a mid-paragraph pronominal slip of the pen, from female to male.[23]

THREE'S COMPANY

One might say that Freud's dissociation of women's desire renders feminism a ghost come back to haunt psychoanalysis (and it is to tell you about this that I have sketched the fight between Freud and Horney, who serve here less as actual historic intellectuals than as switch points to intellectual history). Get rid of women as active desiring subjects, solve the "enigma of womanhood"[24] by equating femininity with passivity, and you get rid of feminism. It's that simple—and that complicated. Women's desire, and feminism, are not forgotten but disavowed; they are dissociated, not repressed. When we dissociate, we attempt to eliminate something that belongs to us by projecting it onto some other being, then feeling it was never part of us in the first place; but it returns to us in the guise of the Other, whom we hate with a debilitating passion.

All of which suggests that there was something for psychoanalysis to get rid of. Which there was. The early psychoanalytic world was, equally, a feminist one; the late nineteenth and early twentieth centuries were the temporal home of first-wave feminism. Horney may have been Freud's specific target,[25] but she was only one of many advocates of women's desire in the psychoanalytic orbit. The pseudonymous Anna O., Josef Breuer's patient who is said to have invented the "talking cure," was Bertha Pappenheim, a founder of German Jewish feminism.[26] Other feminist contemporaries adopted and revised varied portions of the psychoanalytic understanding of women's desire.[27] Later, luminaries in the arts, like H.D., sought out Freud and others for surcease of their psychic suffering.

I am proposing a dialectical view: psychoanalysis and feminism come in a package; they are, as Jessica Benjamin put it, the dialectical poles of a contradiction.[28] Psychoanalysis and feminism are causes (as both labeled themselves)[29] with much in common, like their "questioning of the moral status quo," and much to fight about, like their conceptions of femininity.[30] Their paradoxical liaison arises from their interimplicated evolutions. Each, of course, has its Enlightenment pioneers; for example, the Marquis de Puységur for psychoanalysis[31] and Mary Wollstonecraft for feminism. As full-blown movements, however, psychoanalysis and feminism are creatures of the fin de siècle. Embrangled, they not only constitute one another, they have never lived apart; to wit, the timing and context of Freud's antifeminist taunts "make it unclear whether it was he himself or feminists who first chose to make psychoanalysis a center of ideological struggle."[32] Just as psychoanalysis synthesizes and articulates in one convenient place the ruling ideas of patriarchy, thereby constituting both an attack on women and a means for feminism to deconstruct sexist ideology,[33] so feminism exerts a pressure on psychoanalytic thought.[34] Conversely, the predominance of female patients suggests a diagnosis of psychoanalysis as "itself a symptom of women."[35] Indeed, together psychoanalysis and feminism triangulate with social theory.

If psychoanalysis plots desire, it also records a changed and changing sexual landscape whose alterity alters it. The dark continent had already begun to explore herself by the time Freud declared her man's terra incognita. Exploration continued after him, now enhanced by a scientific imprimatur of desire that nevertheless required that women masquerade as good wife, dutiful daughter, or token woman.[36] What went around came around; two generations later, feminists addressed a different sexuality than Freud and Horney. Indeed, the second wave's focus on women's sexuality, departing from earlier bourgeois feminisms, is likely a legacy of psychoanalysis.[37] As Freud's first feminist critics pushed him to articulate his misrepresentation of women's sexuality, his assumption that women want/need sex reciprocally reconfigured erotic experience altogether, if only by speaking the hitherto taboo truth. Sex could be spoken about and women then had a public language in which to say that they knew something about their own pleasure that Freud had denied. If Horney gave them back the vagina, they could then reappropriate the clitoris; perhaps it's not too late to have both.

In principle, however, psychoanalysis and feminism were at a standoff until, in the late 1960s, a third term broke the polarized tension between them. Social theory, to put it broadly, or Marxism, to put it more evocatively, gave feminism what it needed to counter psychoanalytic misogyny: the idea that the Woman Question had a history and a future. Woman's place, her desire, even her erotic anatomy were contingent. So was man's. Historically constructed and socially contextualized, the battle between the sexes was a cultural, not a natural, phenomenon. More. It was a matter of power. Desire, and all the theories analyzing and regulating it, could be understood in political terms. Several truths emerged. Women were not just different from men but were also privately and publicly subordinated to them: their wages were inferior and their political clout minor; even women's needs, Susie Orbach charged, were deemed less legitimate than men's.[38] There were, too, profound differences among women—class, race, sexual preference, and so on. And these differences in turn correlated variously with socioeconomic privilege, family structure, gender role, and sexual possibility. All that psychoanalysis took for granted about the human sexual question suddenly became destabilized. The governing narrative of psychosexual development, the familial frame for subjectivity, the cultural arrangements for the heterosexualization of desire, could now be put into question.

Fortified with social theory but aware of its insufficiencies, feminists could turn to psychoanalysis for what they needed. Although social theory illumines the political dimension of sex and gender, it only flirts with the personal. Yet as feminists soon saw, "the personal is political" holds especially true for them insofar as women's lives are defined by the personal in a way that men's are not. Social theory unveils women's social role but does not unravel those interpersonal, personal, and intimate matters which it is women's cultural business to traffic with. Psychoanalysis takes up where social theory leaves off. Marxism, for example, leads right up to the bedroom door, to the hearth of family and psyche, where it stops. Thereupon psychoanalysis enters, bearing interpretations of women and desire, a theory and course of action in respect of the inner life, a construal of early object relations, and a way into the representational processes composing the symbolic systems of both psyche and society.

In this triangulation, feminist theory mediates social theory and psychoanalysis, completing a historical process. It continues a project, the "Marx-Freud synthesis," begun and then suspended in the 1920s and 1930s. The project uses psychoanalytic insights into interior life to understand, in order to alter, "the internalisation, effectivity and persistence of some of the most oppressive social norms."[39] The debate over psychoanalysis and politics[40] coincided with that over women,[41] but the two controversies were not to engage until nearly a half century later:

> It is rather as if the theoretical/clinical debate about female sexuality and the more explicitly Marxist debate about ideology and its forms were historically severed from each other— at least until [second-wave] feminism itself forged, or rather, demonstrated, the links.[42]

All influential feminist accounts of psychoanalysis, excepting Simone de Beauvoir's *Second Sex*,[43] emerge from this one historical and political moment: the women's liberation movement, where "the personal is political" also meant that the personal is theoretical, and that the theoretical requires validation by the personal.[44] Works by hostile critics, like Shulamith Firestone[45] and Kate Millett, and by admiring critics, like Gayle Rubin, and revisionists, like Juliet Mitchell, these, in the early 1970s, primed the psychoanalytic feminist effort to explain how "ideological processes are transformed, via individual subjects, into human actions and beliefs."[46] Between Rubin's work, which launched contemporary gender studies, and Mitchell's, which facilitated the Anglophone-feminist appropriation of Jacques Lacan's theory of sexed subjectivity, lies a field of tension holding the encounter between feminism and psychoanalysis.

ENTER FOUCAULT, LAUGHING

One might ask, however, which feminism? For that matter, which psychoanalysis? Perhaps each began with one impulse—psychoanalysis saw to the psyche; feminism, to women. As they traversed the twentieth century, however, the tides of change swept through them, and their internal uniformity dissolved into a montage of interests, theories, and constituencies. The meeting of different practices, like feminism, psychoanalysis, and social theory, produces new ideas, new allegiances and alliances, new enemies. Now there are many feminisms: white, black, lesbian, heterosexual, socialist, psychoanalytic, academic, grassroots, and so on. Likewise, as the psychoanalytic century has worn on, many psychoanalyses have materialized: (neo-)Freudian, object-relational, interpersonal, self-psychological, ego-psychological, Lacanian, Kleinian, and so on, as each splinter group schisms yet again.

So many voices, so little time. The noisy frontiers of psychosexual theory are a deconstructionist's delight but a rapporteur's nightmare. The report from the front must, then, be brief, a headline or two. For one thing, body parts no longer have quite the same place on the psychoanatomical map. In fact, they're hardly corporeal or sensate at all— take, for example, penis envy (not, of course, that anyone would want to). In psychoanalytic thought, the penis was once a biological organ that little boys had and little girls wanted. Many objects, especially cigars, symbolized it. Not anymore. Now Freud's penis has become Jacques Lacan's phallus, which stands for (a pun that is *always* intended) what all want and none can have: to be the object of mother's desire, an impossible state of grace and power accorded not even to father—it's your mother, not his own, who desires him, after all. However, that Lacan claims this law of desire as the true account of human culture is, as I will shortly suggest, a misleading bit of politics.

For now, the next headline: Never fear, mother is here. A near absence in the Freudian corpus and still a wordless void in Lacan's cosmology—from which Lacanian loyalist Julia Kristeva, and neo-Freudians Janine Chasseguet-Smirgel and Joyce McDougall, are trying to rescue her—mother elsewhere receives the mark of psychoanalytic distinction, a symbol of her own.[47] Thanks to Klein,[48] the breast now rivals the phallus. Klein and, perhaps more dramatically and certainly more accessibly, D. W. Winnicott—both synonymous with object relations theory—have created a new primal scene: one's first trauma is not the *sight* of father screwing mother but the *feeling* that the good breast has turned sour—a mother absent or too present, actively bad or just so plain wonderful that all you can do is hate her for the unbearably intense love she inspires.[49]

Phallus and breast, however, are incommensurate. Even if mother has joined father at the head of the psychoanalytic table—or, rather, at a separate table, since Lacanian and object-relational theories do not really translate—different is not the same as equal. This inequality is not quite a matter of paternal power. Men's unconscious awe of maternal power may indeed underlie, as Dorothy Dinnerstein contends, the near-universal degradation of the feminine, perhaps triggering their often deathlike grip on public power and control. Femininity, moreover, is not passive (as Freud recognized in a famous footnote)[50] but active, even, as Adrienne Harris writes, aggressive, sometimes similarly to men but also, as Carol Gilligan and Jean Baker Miller propound, differently.[51]

Still, femininity remains, here as everywhere, the marked category. That psychoanalytic gender (explicated by Irene Fast and Ethel Person)[52] corresponds to gender injustice remains a knotty theoretical and, among clinicians, professional problem. Male and female belong to a "system of difference"[53] whose hierarchical privileging of masculinity has unconscious correlates that, Virginia Goldner explains,[54] require not only decoding (a task furthered by academic psychoanalytic feminism) but healing. By promising to lead us to sexual health, developmental accounts of how girls grow up to become what boys are not, and vice versa, serve also as moral recommendations. Analysts, educators, and parents need Benjamin's object-relational interpretation of penis envy: the sense of inadequacy girls feel in the absence of paternal recognition has its partner in the repudiation of femininity that, as Nancy Chodorow shows us, engenders the conventional construction of masculinity and the "oedipal asymmetries and heterosexual knots" of marital intimacy.[55]

Description, however, is often also prescription. Psychoanalytic and feminist theories slip between registers, between what is and what ought to be: you may find yourself talking about one when you meant to be talking about the other. Many have noticed the political face of knowledge, not least Foucault in his answer to Karl Marx. Domination, he explains, depends not only on material might. People imprison themselves with a little help from their friends in Freud's three "impossible professions": education, government, and psychoanalysis.[56] Domination is produced by a spiral of power, knowledge, and pleasure[57] that, in reaching out to hearts and minds, binds them up to ensure the functioning of the modern state.

The challenge is to remember the political while retaining the psychical. Barring one not-insignificant problem, one could agree with Jacqueline Rose's elegant phrasing of the problem:

> The difficulty is to pull psychoanalysis in the direction of both these insights—towards a recognition of the fully social constitution of identity and norms, and then back again to that point of tension between ego and unconscious where they are endlessly remodeled and endlessly break.[58]

The problem is power: the social construction of desire is also political, an aspect that psychoanalysis resolutely denies as a threat to its own institutional power. Psychoanalysis entertains only two legitimate bases for speech: the biological and the psychical. In other words, it excludes the sociopolitical, which nevertheless sneaks back into discourse in the service of the normative or, effectively the same thing, the universal.

In suggesting a relation between power structures and the unconscious, Lacanian thought seems to meet this challenge. For Lacan, building his argument on structural linguistics, sex is a place in, and a matter of, language, but language is itself a matter of law and culture.[59] To be (psychically) sexed is to speak, to become a person, and to enter culture, all in the same terms. Judith Butler puts it this way:

> Whereas [in object-relations theory] gender appears to be a cultural determination that a pre-existing subject acquires, sexual difference [in Lacanian theory] appears to constitute the matrix that gives rise to the subject itself.[60]

Subjectivity is primally and multiply split, its coherence founded in a linguistic fiction, a single sex: one is either male or female. Alternative sexual inclinations endure, unforgotten and unremembered, perceptible only in "the gaps, silences, absences in speech"[61] which therapists attend so closely to for clues to pain. Or they remain in the abject spaces of culture where cultural critics and queer theorists like Butler locate a marginalized and dissociated homosexuality that haunts mainstream heterosexuality with the melancholy of its loss.[62]

In spite of this, Lacanian theory defaults on its promise. It indicates the discontinuities, prohibitions, and losses of sex. Yet its main pointer is the phallus—an obdurately male symbol that eclipses female desire. True, the theory of the phallus as the (appropriately named) master signifier of desire, sanity, meaning, and culture describes how patriarchy works awfully well,[63] or, at least, how it represents itself as working.[64] However, no one has yet adequately explained why the phallus has to be the human key symbol.[65] We must agree with Elizabeth Grosz: "The relation between the penis and the phallus is not arbitrary but is clearly socially and politically motivated."[66] The phallus is not a universal but rather the ideology, the theory and practice, of patriarchy.[67]

The final headline from the front is this: If mother is here, can women's desire be far behind? The breast is a switch point to mother's desire, yet not women's. And the phallus, I suppose, switches us to infinity. Lacanian theory, so subtle about desire's fluidity, uncertainty, and intractability, is remarkably positivist about women's subjectivity. Female desire's unspeakability may indicate its own social erasure.[68] To represent that effacement by a falsely universal symbol is, however, to prescribe the practice of misogyny as timeless, fixed. Nor is object-relational gender theory free of prescriptivity; narratives of gender identity and development cannot help but (re)present the normative structures they mean to deconstruct. Yet at the same time, theories of gender as social construction index the historical multiplicity of women's desire, revealing it as the contradictory thing it is—present here and absent there, flaring here and doused there, its ambiguity, difficulty, and elusiveness the alternate truth of all, of anyone's desire.[69]

ENCOUNTERING PARADOX: STRANGE HEARTS

I want to suggest the trope and habit of paradox.[70] Consider Teresa Brennan's paradoxical resolution of the false choice between object relations and Lacanian feminisms: "Sexual difference is not only the result of socialization but its condition."[71] To put this another way, psychoanalysis and feminism share what Naomi Scheman terms the core modern epistemological problem of identifying and then bridging gaps, such as those between mind and body, masculine and feminine, psyche and society, and so on.[72] Resolving dualism means not splitting in the first place. It means the maintaining of possibility: the mobile, dynamic space between binaries yields resolutions that in turn give rise to new complexity.

It's like having to choose between vagina and clitoris. Why bother when we can have both? With the psychoanatomical map redrawn, our train of thought shifts tracks. Like bodies of thought and intellectual/political movements, sexual bodies are neither singular nor dual; they are multiple, and require paradoxical thinking. We can agree with Valerie Traub's critique without giving up the body:

> The elevation of the clitoris (or labia) as the sine qua non of "lesbian" sexuality overvalues not only the genitals as a source of pleasure but the power of bodily metonymy to represent that pleasure.[73]

The problem, and solution, is that no single organ represents woman's desire (much less anyone else's). There really is no queen to consort with King Phallus, whose sovereignty produces the resistance inevitably triggered by domination. Feminist/women's refusal to be either same or Other, the spirit inspiring Luce Irigaray,[74] transforms sexual splitting into paradox. Dissension in the feminist ranks matches the multiplicity of women's desire, a cacophony exceeding the body's symbolic capacity.

Women don't want only the genitals; they, we, want whatever is erotic—you name it. Perhaps Lacan's mysterious and sometimes mystifying *jouissance* is nothing more than this mundane multiformity of sex, its "excess over . . . the bare choreographies of procreation"[75] symbolized not only by the distinction of clitoris from vagina but also by their concrete possibilities: women can, want, and do have both clitoral and vaginal orgasms, maybe not the same woman, maybe not at the same time, maybe not each time, and maybe alternately or simultaneously with other climaxes like those of the "G-spot,"[76] anus, or . . . who knows?[77]

Like orgasm, psychoanalysis and feminism are open questions, uncertainties waiting to cohere, only to fall apart and then begin again. Their relationship neither does nor should resemble a harmonious marriage or any kind of primal scene whatsoever. No, family therapy is not indicated. Rather, nonmonogamy is the treatment of choice; think of their ménage à trois with Marxian, Saussurean, and Foucauldian social theory. Their relations should always be tense, the radicalism of each bestowed by their promiscuity (feminist intercourse with social reality, psychoanalytic congress with psychic reality), answering the other's conformist and dominating tendencies.

The uncertainty at feminism's heart is the tension between its two main goals, one ameliorative, the other revolutionary. On the one hand, feminism aims to better the lives women lead; hence the women's liberation movement. On the other, feminism aims to radically reconfigure what we *mean* by "woman"; hence feminist postmodernism. On the face of it, these goals are not new to anyone. However, if you look closely, you find that they contradict one another. Feminism tries to empower women so that they can create the lives they want, but it also simultaneously puts their very desires into question, for it asks whether there are wants women have not yet begun, or dared, to imagine. Like any progressive social movement, feminism tries to improve on what already exists while at the same time undermining the status quo. In so doing, it generates a tension, a paradox, between the desire and need to better women's lives and the wish and necessity to redefine them.

The heart of psychoanalysis is equally strange. Indeed, it is this strangeness, the initial, revolutionary shock of psychoanalytic theory, that Lacan's impossible language is meant to memorialize. Lacan wants to combat the ameliorating pull of clinical practice toward rationalizing the weirdness, "undecidability," and difficulty of the psychic interior.[78] The theory of the unconscious, so at odds with daily life and ordinary speech, remains the most radical of Freud's contributions (even though the idea of it had long preceded him).[79] For it is here, in the once known and then repressed, or, as some analysts are thinking these days, in the never known and dissociated,[80] that exists what cannot be thought. In the tension between conscious and unconscious lies the potential for psychic integration, for, paradoxically, personal change and meaning. The psychoanalytic session is a chance to say the unspeakable and think the unthinkable, to imagine what does not yet exist, "to seek [not] plenitude or completion in the other [but] recognition for parts of the self that have been rendered illegitimate" or have not yet emerged.[81] It's not much fun: psychoanalysis offers individuals what feminism and other varieties of political action offer collectivities—the subversive opportunity of digging up the ground beneath your feet. But like feminism, it's got possibilities.

The Other Road

FREUD AS NEUROLOGIST

Oliver Sacks

It is making severe demands on the unity of the personality to try and make me identify myself with the author of the paper on the spinal ganglia of the petromyzon. Nevertheless I must be he, and I think I was happier about that discovery than about others since.

Sigmund Freud to Karl Abraham,
September 21, 1924

EVERYONE KNOWS Freud as the father of psychoanalysis, but most people know little about the twenty years (1876–96) when he was primarily a neurologist and anatomist; Freud himself rarely referred to them in later life. Yet his "other," neurological life was the precursor to his psychoanalytic one, and perhaps an essential key to it.

An early and enduring passion for Darwin (along with Goethe's *Ode to Nature*), Freud tells us in his *Autobiography*, made him decide to become a medical student; and already, in his first year at university, he was attending courses on "Biology and Darwinism," as well as lectures by the physiologist Ernst Brücke. Two years later, eager to do some real, hands-on research, Freud asked Brücke if he could work in his laboratory. Though, as Freud was later to write, he already felt that the human brain and mind might be the ultimate subject of his explorations, he was intensely curious, after reading Darwin, about the early forms and origins of nervous systems and wished to get a sense of their slow evolution first.

Brücke suggested that Freud look at the nervous system of a very primitive fish—*Petromyzon*, the lamprey—and in particular at the curious "Reissner" cells clustered about the spinal cord. These cells had attracted attention since Brücke's own student days forty years before, but their nature and function had never been understood. Freud was able to detect the precursors of these cells in the singular larval form of the lamprey, and to show they were homologous with the posterior spinal ganglia cells of higher fish—a significant discovery. (This larva of *Petromyzon* is so different from the mature form that it was long considered to be a separate genus, *Ammocoetes*.) He then turned to studying an invertebrate nervous system, that of the crayfish. Although at that time the nerve elements of invertebrate nervous systems were considered to be radically different from those of vertebrate ones, Freud was able to show that they were, in fact, morphologically identical, and therefore that it was not the cellular elements which differed in primitive and advanced animals but their *organization*. Thus there emerged, even in Freud's earliest researches, a sense of a Darwinian evolution whereby, using the most conservative means (i.e., the same basic anatomic cellular elements), more and more complex nervous systems could be built.*

It was natural that in the early 1880s—he now had his medical degree—Freud should move on to clinical neurology; but it was equally crucial to him that he continue his anatomical work, too, looking at human nervous systems, and this he did in the laboratory of the neuroanatomist and psychiatrist Theodor Meynert.† For Meynert (as for Paul Emile Flechsig, and other neuroanatomists at the time) such a conjunction did not seem at all strange. There was assumed to be a simple, almost mechanical relation of mind and brain, both in health

---

*It was generally felt at this time that the nervous system was a synctium, a continuous mass of nerve tissue, and it was not until the late 1880s and 1890s, through the efforts of Ramón y Cajal and Waldeyer, that the existence of discrete nerve cells—neurons—was appreciated. Freud, however, came very close to discovering this himself in his early studies. That he did not make his thoughts fully explicit at the time, and gain any of the fame that went to Cajal and Waldeyer, was a later source of mortification to him.

†Freud published a number of neuroanatomical studies while in Meynert's lab, focusing especially on the tracts and connections of the brain stem. He often called these anatomical studies his "real" scientific work, and he subsequently considered writing a general text on cerebral anatomy, but the book was never finished, and only a very condensed version of it was ever published, in Villaret's *Handbuch*.

and disease; thus Meynert's 1884 magnum opus, entitled *Psychiatry*, bore the subtitle *A Clinical Treatise on Diseases of the Fore-Brain*.

Although phrenology itself had fallen into disrepute, the localizationist impulse had been given new life in 1861, when the French neurologist Paul Broca was able to demonstrate that a highly specific loss of function—of expressive language, a so-called expressive aphasia—followed damage to a particular part of the brain (the third frontal convolution) on the left side. Other correlations were quick in coming, and by the mid-1880s something akin to the phrenological dream seemed to be approaching realization, with "centers" being described for expressive language, receptive language, color perception, writing, and many other specific capabilities. Meynert reveled in this localizationist atmosphere—indeed he himself, after showing that the auditory nerves projected to a specific area of the cerebral cortex (the *Klang-feld*, or sound field), postulated that damage to this was present in all cases of sensory aphasia.

But Freud, it was evident, was disquieted at this theory of localization, and, at a deeper level, profoundly dissatisfied, too, for he was coming to feel that all localizationism had a mechanical quality, treating the brain and nervous system as a sort of ingenious but idiotic machine, with a one-to-one correlation between elementary components and functions, denying it organization or evolution or history.

During this period (1882–85), he spent time on the wards of the Vienna General Hospital, and it was here that he honed his skills as a clinical observer and neurologist. His heightened skill and narrative powers, his sense of the importance of a detailed case history, are evident in the clinicopathological papers he wrote at the time: of a boy who died from a cerebral hemorrhage associated with scurvy, an eighteen-year-old baker's apprentice with acute multiple neuritis, and a thirty-six-year-old man with a rare spinal condition—syringomyelia—who had lost pain and temperature sense, but not the sense of touch (a dissociation caused by the very circumscribed destruction within the spinal cord).

In 1886, after spending four months with the great neurologist Jean Martin Charcot in Paris, Freud returned to Vienna to set up his own neurological practice. It is not entirely easy to reconstruct—from Freud's letters or from the vast numbers of studies and biographies about him—exactly what "neurological life" consisted of for him. He saw patients in his consulting room at 19 Berggasse, presumably a mixed bag of patients, as might come to any neurologist then, or now: some with everyday neurological disorders—strokes, tremors, neuropathies, seizures, migraines; and others with functional disorders—hysterias, obsessive-compulsive conditions, and neuroses of various sorts.

He also worked at the Institute for Children's Diseases, where he held a neurological clinic several times a week. (His clinical experience here led to the books for which he became best known to his contemporaries—his three monographs on the infantile cerebral paralyses of children. These were greatly respected among the neurologists of his time, and are still, on occasion, referred to even now.)

As he continued with his neurological practice, Freud's curiosity, his imagination, his theorizing powers, were on the rise, demanding more complex intellectual tasks and challenges. His earlier neurological investigations, during his years at the General Hospital, had been of a very skillful but conventional type, but now, as he pondered the much more complex question of the aphasias, he became convinced that a different view of the brain was needed. A more dynamic vision of the brain was taking hold of him.

IT WOULD be of great interest to know exactly how and when Freud discovered the work of the English neurologist Hughlings Jackson, who, very quietly, stubbornly, persistently, was developing an evolutionary view of the nervous system, unmoved by the localizationist frenzy all around him. Jackson, twenty years Freud's senior, had been moved to an evolutionary view of nature with the publication of Darwin's *Origin of Species* and by Herbert Spencer's evolutionary philosophy. In the early 1870s Jackson proposed a hierarchic view of the nervous system, picturing how it might have evolved from the most primitive reflex levels, up through a series of higher and higher levels, to those of consciousness and voluntary action. In disease, Jackson conceived, this sequence was reversed, so that a dis-evolution or dissolution or regression occurred, and with this a "release" of primitive functions normally held in check by higher ones.

Although Jackson's views had first arisen in reference to certain epileptic seizures (we still speak of these as "Jacksonian" seizures today), they were then applied to a variety of neurological diseases, as well as to dreams, deliria, and insanities; and in 1879 Jackson applied them to the problem of aphasia, which had long fascinated those neurologists interested in higher cognitive function.

In his own 1891 monograph *On Aphasia*, a dozen years later, Freud repeatedly acknowledged his debt to Jackson. He considered in great detail many of the special phenomena which may be seen in aphasias: the loss of new languages while the mother tongue is preserved, the preservation of the most commonly used words and associations, the retention of series of words (days of the week, etc.) more than single ones, the paraphasias or verbal substitutions that might occur. Above all, he was intrigued by the stereotyped, seemingly meaningless phrases that are sometimes the sole residue of speech, and which may be, as Jackson had remarked, the last utterance of the patient before his stroke. For Freud, as for Jackson, this represented the traumatic "fixation" (and thereafter the helpless repetition) of a proposition or an idea, a notion that was to assume a crucial importance in his theory of the neuroses.

Further, Freud observed that many symptoms of aphasia seemed to share associations of a more psychological rather than physiological sort. Thus verbal errors in aphasias might arise from verbal associations, with words of similar sound or similar meanings tending to be substituted for the correct word. Sometimes the substitution was of a more complex nature, and was not comprehensible as a homonym or homophone, but arose from some particular association that had been forged in the individual's past. (Here there was an intimation or premonition of Freud's later views, as set out in *The Psychopathology of Everyday Life*, of paraphasias and parapraxes as *interpretable*, as historically and personally meaningful.) Thus, he emphasized, we must look not so much to the anatomy or physiology of the brain as to the nature of words and their associations (formal or personal), to the universes of language and psychology, the universe of *meaning*, if we wish to understand paraphasias.

His study of aphasia convinced Freud that the complex manifestations of aphasia were incompatible with any simplistic notion of word images lodged in the cells of a "center":

Under the influence of Meynert's teachings the theory has been evolved that the speech apparatus consists of distinct cortical centers; their cells are supposed to contain the word images (word concepts or word impressions); these centers are said to be separated by functionless cortical territory, and linked to each other by the association tracts. One may first of all raise the question as to whether such an assumption is at all correct, and even permissible. I do not believe it to be. (*On Aphasia*, p. 54)

Instead of centers—static depots of images—Freud wrote, one must think of "cortical fields," large areas of cortex endowed with a variety of functions, some facilitating, some inhibiting each other. One could not make sense of the phenomena of aphasia, he continued, unless one thought in such dynamic, Jacksonian terms. Such systems, moreover, were not all at the same "level." Jackson had suggested a vertically structured organization in the brain, with repeated representations or embodiments of function at many hierarchic levels—thus when higher-level, propositional speech has become impossible, there might still be the "regressions" characteristic of aphasia, the (sometimes explosive) emergence of primitive, emotional speech. Freud was the first to bring this Jacksonian notion of regression into neurology, and the first to import it into psychiatry; one feels, indeed, that Freud's use of the concept of regression in *On Aphasia* paved the way to his much more extensive and powerful use of it in psychiatry. (One wonders what Hughlings Jackson might have thought of this vast and surprising expansion of his idea, but though he lived until 1911, we do not know whether he had ever heard of Freud.)*

---

*If a strange silence or blindness attended Hughlings Jackson's work (his *Selected Writings* were only published in book form in 1931–32), a similar neglect attended Freud's book on aphasia. More or less ignored on publication, *On Aphasia* remained virtually unknown and unavailable for many years—even Henry Head's great monograph on aphasia, published in 1926, makes no reference to it—and was only translated into English in 1953. Freud himself spoke of *On Aphasia* as "a respectable flop" and contrasted this with the reception of his more conventional book on the cerebral paralyses of infancy:

> There is something comic about the incongruity between one's own and other people's estimation of one's work. Look at my book on the diplegias, which I knocked together almost casually, with a minimum of interest and effort. It has been a huge success. . . . But for the really good things, like the "Aphasia," the "Obsessional Ideas," which threatens to appear shortly, and the coming aetiology and theory of the neuroses, I can expect no more than a respectable flop.

Freud indeed went beyond Jackson when he implied that there were no autonomous, isolable centers or functions in the brain but, rather, *systems* for achieving cognitive goals—systems that have many components, and which can be created or greatly modified by the experiences of the individual. Thus, given that literacy was not innate, it was not useful, he felt, to think of a "center" for writing (as his friend and former colleague Sigmund Exner had postulated); one had, rather, to think of a system, or systems, being constructed in the brain as the person learns (this was a striking anticipation of the notion of "functional systems," developed by A. R. Luria, the founder of neuropsychology, fifty years later).

In addition to these empirical and evolutionary considerations, Freud laid great emphasis on epistemological considerations—the confusion of categories, as he saw it, the promiscuous mixing of physical and mental:

> The relationship between the chain of physiological events in the nervous system and the mental processes is probably not one of cause and effect. The former do not cease when the latter set in . . . but, from a certain moment, a mental phenomenon corresponds to each part of the chain, or to several parts. The psychic is, therefore, a process parallel to the physiological, "a dependent concomitant." (*On Aphasia*, p. 55)

Freud here endorsed and elaborated Jackson's views: "I do not trouble myself about the mode of connection between mind and matter," Jackson had written. "It is enough to assume a parallelism." Psychological processes have their own laws, principles, autonomies, coherences; and these must be examined independently, irrespective of whatever physiological processes may be going on in parallel. Jackson's epistemology of parallelism or concomitance gave Freud an enormous freedom to pay attention to the phenomena in unprecedented detail, to theorize, to seek a purely psychological understanding without any premature need to correlate them with physiological processes (though he never doubted that such concomitant processes must exist).

As Freud's views evolved in relation to aphasia, moving from a "center" or "lesion" way of thinking toward a dynamic view of the brain, there was a parallel movement in his views on hysteria. Charcot was convinced (and had convinced Freud at first) that although no anatomical lesions could be demonstrated in patients with *hysterical* paralyses, there must nonetheless be a "physiological lesion" (an *état dynamique*) located in the same part of the brain where, in an established *neurological* paralysis, an anatomical lesion (an *état statique*) would be found. Thus, Charcot conceived, hysterical paralyses were physiologically identical with organic ones; and hysteria was to be seen, essentially, as a neurological problem, a special reactivity peculiar to certain pathologically sensitive individuals or "neuropaths."

To Freud, still saturated in anatomical and neurological thinking and very much under Charcot's spell, this seemed entirely acceptable. It was extremely difficult for him to "de-neurologize" his thinking, even in this new realm where so much was mysterious. But within a year he had become less certain. The whole neurological profession was in conflict over the question of whether hypnosis was physical or mental. In 1889 Freud paid a visit to Charcot's contemporary, Hippolyte Bernheim, in Nancy—Bernheim had proposed a psychological origin for hypnosis, and believed that its results could be explained in terms of ideas or suggestion alone—and this seems to have influenced him deeply. He had begun to move away from Charcot's notion of a circumscribed (if physiological) lesion in hysterical paralysis toward a vaguer, but more complex, sense of physiological changes distributed among several different parts of the nervous system, a vision which paralleled the emerging insights of *On Aphasia*.

Charcot had suggested to Freud that he try to clarify the controversy by making a comparative examination of organic and hysterical paralyses.* This Freud was well equipped to do, for when he returned to Vienna and set up his private practice, he started to see a number of patients with hysterical paralyses, and, of course, many patients with organic paralyses, too, and to attempt to elucidate their mechanisms for himself.

*The same problem was also suggested to Joseph Babinski, another young neurologist attending Charcot's clinics (and later to become one of the most famous neurologists in France). While Babinski agreed with Freud on the distinction between organic paralyses and hysterical ones, he later came to consider, when examining injured soldiers in World War I, that there was "a third realm": paralyses, anesthesias, and other neurological problems based neither on localized anatomical lesions nor on "ideas," but on broad "fields" of synaptic inhibition in the spinal cord and elsewhere. Babinski spoke here of a "*syndrome physiopathique*." Such syndromes, which may follow gross physical trauma or surgical procedures, have puzzled neurologists since Silas Weir Mitchell first described them in the Civil War, for they may incapacitate diffuse areas of the body which have neither specific innervation nor affective significance.

By 1893 he had made a complete break with all organic explanations of hysteria:

> The lesion in hysterical paralyses must be completely independent of the nervous system, since in its paralyses and other manifestations hysteria behaves as though anatomy did not exist or as though it had no knowledge of it.

This was the moment of crossover, of transit, when (in a sense) Freud would give up neurology, and notions of a neurological or physiological basis for psychiatric states, and turn to looking at these states exclusively in their own terms. He was to make one final, highly theoretical attempt to delineate the neural basis of mental states in his *Project for a Scientific Psychology*, and he never gave up the notion that there must ultimately be a biological "bedrock" to all psychological conditions and theories. But for practical purposes he felt he could, and must, put these aside for a time.

THOUGH FREUD turned increasingly to his psychiatric work in the late 1880s and 1890s, he continued to write occasional shorter papers on his neurological work. In 1888 he published the first description of hemianopsia in children, and in 1895 a paper on an unusual compression neuropathy (meralgia paresthetica), a condition he himself suffered from, and which he had observed in several patients under his care. Freud also suffered from classical migraine and saw many patients with this in his neurological practice. At one point he apparently considered writing a short book on this subject, too, but, in the event, did no more than make a summary of ten "Established Points" which he sent to his friend Wilhelm Fliess in April 1895. There is a strongly physiological, quantitative tone in this summary, "an economics of nerve-force," which hinted at the extraordinary outburst of thought and writing which was to occur later in the year.

It is curious and intriguing that even with figures like Freud, who published so much, the most suggestive and prescient ideas may appear only in the course of their private letters and journals. No period in Freud's life was more productive of such ideas than the "secret" years in the mid-1890s, when the thoughts he was incubating in himself were shared with no one except Fliess. Late in 1895 Freud

launched on an ambitious attempt to bring together all his psychological observations and insights and ground them in a plausible physiology. At this point his letters to Fliess are exuberant, almost ecstatic:

> One evening last week when I was hard at work . . . the barri-
> ers were suddenly lifted, the veil drawn aside, and I had a clear
> vision from the details of the neuroses to the conditions that
> make consciousness possible. Everything seemed to connect
> up, the whole worked well together, and one had the impres-
> sion that the Thing was now really a machine and would soon
> go by itself. . . . Naturally I don't know how to contain myself
> for pleasure. (October 20, 1895)

But this vision in which everything seemed to connect up, this
vision of a complete working model of the brain and mind which presented itself to Freud with an almost revelatory lucidity, is not at all
easy to grasp now (and indeed Freud himself was to write, only a few
months later, "I no longer understand the state of mind in which I
hatched out the 'Psychology' ").*

There has been intensive discussion about this *Project for a Scientific
Psychology*, as it is now named (Freud's working title had been "A Psychology for Neurologists"). The *Project* makes very difficult reading,
partly because of the intrinsic difficulty and originality of many of its
concepts; partly because Freud uses outmoded and sometimes idiosyncratic terms that we have to translate into more familiar ones; partly
because it was written at furious speed in a sort of shorthand; and partly
because it may never have been intended for anyone's eyes but his own.

And yet the *Project* does bring together, or attempts to bring
together, the domains of memory, attention, consciousness, perception, wishes, dreams, sexuality, defense, repression, and primary and
secondary thought processes (as he called them) into a single coherent
vision of the mind, and to ground all of these processes in a basic physiological framework, constituted by different systems of neurons, their
interactions and modifiable "contact barriers," and free and bound
states of neural excitation.

---

*Freud never reclaimed his manuscript from Fliess, and it was presumed lost until
the 1950s, when it was finally found and published—although what was found was
only a fragment of the many drafts Freud wrote in late 1895.

Though the language of the *Project* is inevitably that of the 1890s, a number of its notions retain (or have assumed) striking relevance to many current ideas in neuroscience—and this has caused it to be reexamined by Karl Pribram and Merton Gill, among others. Pribram and Gill, indeed, call the *Project* "a Rosetta Stone" for those who wish to make connections between neurology and psychology. Many of the ideas Freud advanced in the *Project*, moreover, can now be examined experimentally in ways that would have been impossible at the time they were formulated.

The nature of memory occupied Freud from first to last. Aphasia he saw as a sort of forgetting, and he had observed in his notes that an early symptom in migraine was often the forgetting of proper names. He saw a pathology of memory as central in hysteria ("Hysterics suffer mainly from reminiscences"), and in the *Project* he attempted to explicate the physiological basis of memory at many levels. One physiological prerequisite for memory, he postulated, was a system of "contact barriers" between certain neurons—his so-called psi system (this was a decade before Sir Charles Scott Sherrington gave synapses their name). Freud's contact barriers were capable of selective facilitation or inhibition, thus allowing permanent neuronal changes that corresponded to the acquisition of new information and new memories—a theory of learning basically similar to that which Donald Hebb was to propose in the 1940s, and which is now supported by experimental findings.

At a higher level, Freud regarded memory and motive as inseparable. Recollection could have no force, no meaning, unless it was allied with motive. The two had always to be coupled together, and in the *Project*, as Pribram and Gill emphasize, "both memory and motive are psi processes based on selective facilitation . . . memories [being] the retrospective aspect of these facilitations; motives the prospective aspects."*

Thus remembering, for Freud, though it required such local neuronal traces (of the sort we now call "long-term potentiation"), went far beyond them, and was essentially a dynamic, transforming, reorga-

---

*The inseparability of memory and motive, Freud pointed out, opened the possibility of understanding certain *illusions* of memory based on intentionality: the illusion that one has written to a person, for instance, when one has not but intended to; or that one has run the bath when one has merely intended to do so. We do not have such illusions unless there has been a preceding intention.

nizing process throughout the course of life. Nothing was more central to the formation of identity than the power of memory; nothing more guaranteed one's continuity as an individual. But memories shift, and no one was more sensitive than Freud to the reconstructive potential of memory, to the fact that memories are continually worked over and revised, and that their essence, indeed, *is* recategorization.

Arnold Modell has taken up this point with regard to both the therapeutic potential of psychoanalysis and, more generally, the formation of a private self. He quotes a letter Freud wrote to Fliess in December 1896, in which he uses the term *Nachträglichkeit*, which Modell feels is most accurately rendered as "retranscription."

> As you know [Freud wrote] I am working on the assumption that our psychic mechanism has come into being by a process of stratification, the material present in the form of memory traces being subjected from time to time to a *rearrangement* in accordance with fresh circumstances—a *retranscription*. Thus . . . memory is present not once but several times over . . . the successive registrations representing the psychic achievement of successive epochs of life. . . . I explain the peculiarities of the psychoneuroses by supposing that this translation has not taken place in the case of some of the material.

The potential for therapy, for change, therefore, lies in the capacity to exhume such "fixated" material into the present so that it can be subjected to the creative process of retranscription, allowing the stalled individual to grow and change once again.

Such remodelings are not only crucial, Modell feels, in the therapeutic process but are a constant part of human life both for day-to-day "updating" (an updating that those with amnesia cannot do) and for the major (and sometimes cataclysmic) transformations, the "revaluations of all values" (as Nietzsche would say) which are necessary for the evolution of a unique private self.

THAT MEMORY does construct and reconstruct, endlessly, was a central conclusion of the experimental studies carried out by Frederic Bartlett in the 1930s. Bartlett showed in these, very clearly (and sometimes very entertainingly), how with retelling—either to others or to oneself—a story, the memory of a story, or of a picture, is continually changed. There was never, Bartlett felt, a simple mechanical reproduction in memory; it was always an individual and imaginative reconstruction. He wrote:

> Remembering is not the re-excitation of innumerable fixed, lifeless and fragmentary traces. It is an imaginative reconstruction, or construction, built out of the relation of our attitude towards a whole active mass of organized past reactions or experience, and to a little outstanding detail which commonly appears in image or in language form. It is thus hardly ever really exact, even in the most rudimentary cases of rote recapitulation, and it is not at all important that it should be so.

In the last third of the twentieth century, the whole tenor of neurology and neuroscience has itself been moving toward such a dynamic and constructional view of the brain, a sense that even at the most elementary levels—as, for example, in the "filling in" of a blind spot or scotoma, or the seeing of a visual illusion, as both Richard Gregory and V. S. Ramachandran have demonstrated—the brain constructs a plausible hypothesis or pattern or scene. Gerald Edelman, above all—drawing on the data of current neuroanatomy and neurophysiology, of embryology and evolutionary biology, of clinical and experimental work, and of synthetic neural modeling—has been creating a most detailed neurobiological model of the mind. In this model, the brain's central role is precisely that of constructing categories—first perceptual, then conceptual—and of an ascending process, a "bootstrapping," where through repeated recategorization at higher and higher levels, consciousness is finally achieved. Thus, for Edelman, every perception is a creation and every memory is a re-creation or recategorization.*

---

*There are, of course, innumerable areas in neuroscience and neurobiology besides that of memory where Freud's influence, direct or indirect, has been profound. There are marked analogies between psychoanalysis and neuropsychology, as Mark Solms and Michael Saling discuss in their 1986 paper "On Psychoanalysis and Neuroscience: Freud's Attitude to the Localizationist Tradition." And A. R. Luria was fascinated by Freud's work as a very young man, and wrote to him in 1922 regarding the new Psychoanalytic Society that he had founded in Kazan. Luria was thrilled, he wrote in his autobiography, *The Making of Mind*, to receive a courteous reply from the great man, addressing him as "Mr. President" and giving him permission to translate some of his works into Russian.

Such categories depend on the "values" of the organism, those biases or dispositions (partly innate, partly learned) which, for Freud, were characterized as "drives," "instincts," and "affects." Thus "retranscription" becomes the model for the brain/mind's most fundamental activity. The attunement here between Freud's views and Edelman's is striking—here, at least, one has the sense that psychoanalysis and neurobiology can be fully at home with one another, congruent and mutually supportive. And it may be that in this equation of *Nachträglichkeit* with "recategorization" we see a hint of how the two seemingly disparate universes—the universes of human meaning and of natural science—may come together.

Ernest Jones spoke of Freud as "the Darwin of the mind," and Edelman, in his latest book on neural Darwinism, dedicates it to the memory of Darwin and Freud. And this is not "just" the Freud of psychoanalysis but the Freud who spent his first twenty adult years as a neuroanatomist, a clinical neurologist, and a neurotheorist—and laid the foundations upon which psychoanalysis could arise.

NOTES

Quotations from *The Standard Edition of the Complete Psychological Works of Sigmund Freud*, ed. and trans. James Strachey (London: Hogarth Press and Institute of Psycho-Analysis, 1953–74), are cited using the abbreviation *SE*.

" 'Nothing About the Totem Meal!': On Freud's Notes," by Ilse Grubrich-Simitis

1. For a more detailed account of the results of my research, cf. Ilse Grubrich-Simitis, *Zurück zu Freuds Texten* (1993; English-language edition: *Back to Freud's Texts*, 1996).

2. Cf. Paul Roazen and Bluma Swerdloff, *Heresy: Sandor Rado and the Psychoanalytic Movement* (1995), 44–45.

3. *The Complete Letters of Sigmund Freud to Wilhelm Fliess, 1887–1904*, ed. and trans. Jeffrey Moussaieff Masson (1985), 278.

4. Ibid., 181.

5. Sigmund Freud, "Recommendations to Physicians Practising Psycho-Analysis," in *SE* 12:113.

6. Josef Breuer and Sigmund Freud, "On the Psychical Mechanism of Hysterical Phenomena: Preliminary Communication," in *SE* 2:3–17.

7. Josef Breuer and Sigmund Freud, *Studies on Hysteria*, in *SE* 2.

8. *The Complete Letters of Sigmund Freud to Wilhelm Fliess, 1887–1904*, 342.

9. My emphasis.

10. Sigmund Freud, *The Interpretation of Dreams*, in *SE* 4:297 n. 1.

11. Ibid., 232.

12. Sigmund Freud, *Totem and Taboo*, in *SE* 13:141.

13. Quoted in Sigmund Freud, *A Phylogenetic Fantasy: Overview of the Transference Neuroses*, ed. Ilse Grubrich-Simitis (1987), 83.

14. Sigmund Freud, "The Disposition to Obsessional Neurosis," in *SE* 12:320.

"Freud's World of Work," by Patrick J. Mahony

1. Freud, "Instincts and Their Vicissitudes," in *SE* 18:67–143, 122.

2. Freud, *The Interpretation of Dreams*, in *SE* 4–5, 567; cf. Mahony, "Freud: Man at Work."

3. Freud, *Civilization and Its Discontents*, in *SE* 21:49–148, 80fn.

4. Freud, "Recommendations to Physicians Practising Psycho-Analysis," in *SE* 12:109–20, 199; cf. "Leistungs- und Genussfähigkeit," in *Gesammelte Werke* 8:385.

5. Freud, letter of March 1, 1896, in *The Complete Letters of Sigmund Freud to Wilhelm Fliess: 1887–1904*, ed. and trans. Jeffrey Moussaieff Masson (Cambridge: Harvard University Press, 1985), 75.

6. Ibid., 254.

7. Ibid., 344.

8. Ibid., 356.

9. Ibid., 365–66.

10. Freud, letter of February 8, 1920, in *The Complete Correspondence of Sigmund Freud and Ernest Jones, 1908–1939*, ed. R. A. Paskauskas (Cambridge: Harvard University Press, 1993), 368.

11. Freud, letter of January 27, 1920, in *Psychoanalysis and Faith: The Letters of Sigmund Freud and Oskar Pfister*, ed. H. Meng and E. Federn (London: Hogarth Press, 1963), 75.

12. Letter of March 6, 1910, ibid., 35.

13. Freud, letter of February 2, 1886, in *Letters of Sigmund Freud, 1873–1939*, ed. E. Freud (London: Hogarth Press, 1961), 215–16.

14. Nietzsche explained in his preface to *Ecce Homo*: "Error is cowardice. Every conquest, all progress in knowledge, is the result of courage, of hardness towards one's self, of cleanliness towards one's self."

15. Freud, *Group Psychology and the Analysis of the Ego*, in *SE* 23:209–53, 117.

16. The essay "Nature" is reprinted in Wittels, *Freud and His Time* (New York: Horace Liverwright Press, 1931), 31–34.

17. Nunberg and Federn, *Minutes of the Vienna Psychoanalytic Society*, vol. 2 (New York: International Universities Press, 1967), 348.

18. Freud, "On the History of the Psycho-Analytic Movement," in *SE* 18:67–143, 15.

19. Mahony, *Freud as a Writer*, rev. 2d ed. (New Haven, Conn.: Yale University Press, 1987).

20. Freud, *Cocaine Papers*, ed. R. Byck (New York: New American Library, 1974), 60.

21. Jones, *The Life and Work of Sigmund Freud* (New York: Basic Books, 1953–1957), 309, 385.

22. Letters of December 2, 1919, and March 16, 1926, located in the Library of Congress.

23. Letter of February 13, 1916, to Abraham, cited in Jones, *Life and Work*, 189.

24. Freud, *Project for a Scientific Psychology*, in *SE* 1:283–398, 370.

25. Freud, letter of May 25, 1895, *Complete Letters of Sigmund Freud to Wilhelm Fliess, 1887–1904*, 129.

26. Howard Gruber, *Darwin on Man*, 2d ed. (Chicago: University of Chicago Press, 1982).

27. Anzieu, *L'Auto-analyse de Freud et la découverte de la psychanalyse* (Paris: Presses Universitaires de France, 1975).

28. Mahony, "Psychoanalysis—the Writing Cure," in *One Year of Psychoanalysis*, ed. A. Haynal and E. Falseder (Geneva: Cahiers Psychiatriques, 1994), 101–19.

29. Letter of August 8, 1921, located in the Library of Congress; her letter of August 4, 1921, is also pertinent.

30. Freud, letter of July 3, 1912, in *A Psychoanalytic Dialogue: The Letters of Sigmund Freud and Karl Abraham, 1907–1926*, ed. H. Abraham and E. Freud (London: Hogarth Press, 1965), 120. See also Mahony, *Freud as a Writer*, chapter 7.

31. The excerpt I have translated is in letter 143 of St. Augustine's *Omnia Opera*, vol. 8 (Paris: Gaume, 1836).

32. Mahony, *Psychoanalysis and Discourse* (London: Methuen & Tavistock, 1986); *Freud as a Writer; On Defining Freud's Discourse* (New Haven, Conn.: Yale University Press, 1989).

33. Freud, *Beyond the Pleasure Principle*, 60.

34. Mahony, *Freud and the Rat Man* (New Haven, Conn.: Yale University Press, 1986); "Freud's Cases: Are They Valuable Today?," in *International Journal of Psychoanalysis* 74 (1993): 1027–35; *Les Hurlements de l'homme aux loupes*, rev. 2d ed. (Paris: Presses Universitaires de France, 1995); *Freud's Dora: A Psychoanalytical, Historical, and Textual Study* (New Haven, Conn.: Yale University Press, 1997).

35. Mahony, *Freud's Dora*, chapter 6.

"Sigmund Freud's Notes on Faces and Men: National Portrait Gallery, September 13, 1908," by Michael Molnar

1. From the holograph in the Freud Museum archive, London. This document in the original German, with annotations, is to be published in *Sigmund Freud's Reisebriefe* (provisional title), ed. Christfried Tögel and Michael Molnar (German publication pending).

2. *Cooks Traveller's Gazette* 57 (September 1908): 19.

3. *Five Lectures on Psycho-Analysis*, in *SE* 11:16. The final phrase quoted is italicized in the original.

4. Freud to Freud family (*"Meine Lieben"*), September 5 and 12, 1908 [ms. copies in Freud Museum].

5. "This nephew, and this younger brother [Julius] have determined, then, what is neurotic, but also what is intense, in all my friendships" (Freud to Wilhelm Fliess, October 3, 1897, in *The Complete Letters of Sigmund Freud to Wilhelm Fliess, 1887–1904*, ed. and trans. Jeffrey Moussaieff Masson [Harvard University Press, 1985]). This letter refers to John as still living in Manchester in 1897. In fact, John disappeared twice from Freud's life. The first disappearance was part of the traumatic breakup of the primal Freudian horde in 1859, when the extended family split up and the first idyllic phase of Freud's life, in the country town of Freiberg, came to an end. The half-brothers and their side of the family, including John, emigrated to Manchester, while a nuclear family consisting of his parents, him, and his younger sister Anna left by train for Breslau, then Leipzig, and finally Vienna. The self-analysis trawled up such memories of the train journeys as gaslights at a station like souls in hell and the image of his beautiful young mother naked—in effect, the myth of paradise lost and the fall from grace, and also the root of a later neurotic fear of trains and journeys in conflict with his strong urge to travel.

6. The letter is reproduced in *Sigmund Freud: His Life in Pictures and Words*, ed. Ernst Freud, Lucie Freud, and Ilse Grubrich-Simitis; trans. Christine Trollope (1978; Norton, 1985), pl. 12. The concept of sublimation features in " 'Civilized' Sexual Morality and Modern Nervous Illness" (1908; in *SE* 9:181) as the basis of civilization, for it is the means by which disruptive sexual drives are diverted and tamed. It is defined as follows: "This capacity to exchange its originally sexual aim for another one, which is no longer sexual but which is psychically related to the first aim, is called the capacity for *sublimation*" (ibid., 187).

7. "The Aetiology of Hysteria" (1896), in *SE* 3:203.

8. Freud gave the source of this fanciful derivation of Shakespeare from Jacques-Pierre as "a very erudite old gentleman, Prof. Gentilli, who now lives in Nervi" (see Sigmund Freud to Ernest Jones, October 31, 1909, in *The Complete Correspondence of Sigmund Freud and Ernest Jones 1908–1939*, ed. R. Andrew Paskauskas [Harvard University Press, Belknap Press, 1993]).

9. Freud's racial preconceptions were made explicit in a letter to Jung on July 18, 1908, where he wrote: "I find the racial mixture in our group most interesting; he [Jones] is a Celt and consequently not quite accessible to us, the Teuton and the Mediterranean man" (see *The Freud/Jung Letters*, ed. William McGuire; trans. Ralph Manheim and R. F. C. Hull [Hogarth Press and Routledge, 1974]). Jones says that Freud commented on the shape of his head at their first meeting in Salzburg in April 1908 (Ernest Jones, *The Life and Work of Sigmund Freud* [Basic Books, 1953–1957], 2:47). Jones explains this interest in craniology as follows: "That was in the days when physical anthropologists tended to confound nations with primitive races and to make far-reaching inferences from skull measurements" (ibid., 3:460).

10. Freud to Lytton Strachey, December 25, 1928, in *Sigmund Freud: Briefe, 1873–1939*, ed. Ernst and Lucie Freud (Fischer, 1960). This letter does not appear in the English edition of the selected letters.

11. *SE* 7:238–39.

12. In the triumvirate of heroic artists, Freud was referring to Edward Bulwer-Lytton (1803–1873), the novelist. But the painting of him by Henry William Pickersgill does not match Freud's description of it as heroic. That would certainly fit the G. F. Watts portrait of the novelist's namesake, Edward Bulwer-Lytton (1831–1891), viceroy of India. Freud appears to have conflated the novelist and the viceroy.

A full documentation of the portraits can be found in *National Portrait Gallery: Complete Illustrated Catalogue, 1856–1979*, comp. K. K. Yung; ed. Mary Pettman (National Portrait Gallery, 1981). An impression of the gallery at the turn of the century is recorded in a pamphlet by Sir Joshua Fitch, M.A., LL.D., "The National Portrait Gallery," reprinted from the *Educational Record*, June 1907. I would like to thank Jonathan Franklin and Emma Floyd of the National Portrait Gallery's Heinz Archive and Library for their kind assistance.

13. Freud to Eduard Silberstein, September 9, 1875, in *The Letters of Sigmund Freud to Eduard Silberstein, 1871–1881*, ed. Walter Boehlich; trans. Arnold J. Pomerans (Harvard University Press, 1990). Freud's earlier ambition was not just research but also exploration. At that time Darwin was still alive in Down House; Freud knew of the voyage of the *Beagle*, and that might have fired his initial ambition. In 1875 he even acquired a newly published collection of essays called *Anleitung zu wissenschaftlichen Beobachtungen auf Reisen*, edited by G. Neumayer, containing advice for budding explorer/scientists as to what instruments they required and the best modes of collecting and recording data. Freud's switch to applied medical research was not an exclusion of his former ambition but rather a sublimation of it, for the explorer (*Forschungsreisender*) simply mutated into a research scientist (*Forscher*) exploring new therapy. My thanks to Dr. C. Tögel for the reference to Neumayer.

14. Jones 1:195.

15. Freud to Lytton Strachey, December 25, 1928.

16. See notes for July 17 and 19, 1938, in *The Diary of Sigmund Freud, 1929–1939*, ed. and trans. Michael Molnar (Scribner, 1992).

"*Portrait of a Dream Reader,*" *by John Forrester*

1. A considerably extended version of this paper appears in John Forrester, *Dispatches from the Freud Wars: Psychoanalysis and Its Passions* (Cambridge: Harvard University Press, 1997).

2. Freud, "Preface to the Third (Revised) English Edition of *The Interpretation of Dreams*" (1932), in *SE* 4:32.

3. For a representative spread, see Ernest Jones, *Sigmund Freud: Life and Work* (London: Hogarth Press, 1953–57), vol. 1; Richard Wollheim, *Freud* (London: Fontana, 1970); Clark Glymour, "The Theory of Your Dreams," in R. S. Cohen and L. Laudan, eds., *Physics, Philosophy and Psychoanalysis: Essays in Honor of Adolf Grünbaum* (Dordrecht, Boston, and Lancaster, Eng.: Reidel, 1983), 57–71; Frederick Crews, *Skeptical Engagements* (New York and Oxford: Oxford University Press, 1986); K. Frieden, *Freud's Dream of Interpretation* (Albany: State University of New York Press, 1990); Patricia Kitcher, *Freud's Dream: A Complete Interdisciplinary Science of the Mind* (Cambridge: MIT Press, 1992).

4. *SE* 4:xxvi (preface to 2d edition of 1909), translation modified.

5. Jacques Derrida, *The Post Card: From Socrates to Freud and Beyond*, trans. Alan Bass (Chicago: University of Chicago Press, 1987), 305, translation modified. This is not the first time I have considered the question that Derrida so penetratingly asks; see my "Who Is in Analysis with Whom? Freud, Lacan, Derrida," in John Forrester, *The Seductions of Psychoanalysis: Freud, Lacan and Derrida* (Cambridge: Cambridge University Press, 1990), esp. 233ff.

6. For detailed and illuminating explorations of the record of Freud's self-analysis and its relation to the development of his theories in the 1890s and beyond, see Didier Anzieu, *L'Auto-analyse de Freud et la découverte de la psychanalyse* (Paris: Presses Universitaires de France, 1975), translated as *Freud's Self-analysis* by Peter Graham (London: Hogarth Press and Institute of Psycho-Analysis, 1986); further detailed information concerning Freud's dreams has been explored by Alexander Grinstein in his books *Sigmund Freud's Dreams*, 2d ed. (New York: International Universities Press, 1980), *Freud's Rules of Dream Interpretation* (New York: International Universities Press, 1983), and *Freud at the Crossroads* (Madison, Conn.: International Universities Press, 1990).

7. Thomas S. Kuhn, *The Structure of Scientific Revolutions* (Chicago: University of Chicago Press, 1962); for Kuhn's replacement of the term "paradigm" by "exemplar," see the second edition of 1969 and also idem, "Second Thoughts on Paradigms," in *The Essential Tension* (Chicago: University of Chicago Press, 1977), 318–19.

8. *SE* 4:103; Anzieu (*Freud's Self-analysis*, 578) also focuses on Freud's writing as crucial, but from a psychological rather than an intersubjective standpoint.

9. *The Complete Letters of Sigmund Freud to Wilhelm Fliess, 1887–1904*, ed. and trans. Jeffrey Moussaieff Masson (Cambridge: Harvard University Press, 1984) (hereafter abbreviated as *FF*), February 23, 1898, 300.

10. *FF*, December 22, 1897, 289. Anzieu (*Freud's Self-analysis*, 465) notes that this is the first use of the word "censorship" in the correspondence with Fliess.

11. *FF*, May 18, 1898, 313.

12. Ibid., June 20, 1898, 317.

13. Ibid., June 9, 1898, 315.

14. *SE* 4:xxiii–xxiv.

15. Ibid., 104–5.

16. Ibid., 105–6: "Nun muss ich aber den Leser bitten, für eine ganze Weile meine Interessen zu den seinigen zu machen und sich mit mir in die kleinsten Einzelheiten meines Lebens zu versenken, denn solche Übertragungen fordert gebieterisch das Interesse für die versteckte Bedeutung der Träume" (*Die Traumdetung*, Studienausgabe Edition [Frankfurt: Fischer, 1969–75], 2:125).

17. I use the pronoun "he" to refer to the "reader" of *The Interpretation of Dreams* throughout, partly following the masculine gender of the German word *der Leser*, whose fortunes I will be following, and partly to avoid the clumsiness of the phrase "he or she."

18. See Alexander Welsh, *Freud's Wishful Dream Book* (Princeton, N.J.: Princeton University Press, 1994), 30–32.

19. *FF*, August 6, 1899, 365.

20. The literature reexamining this dream is substantial; much of it is drawn upon in Lisa Appignanesi and John Forrester, *Freud's Women* (New York: Basic Books, 1992), chap. 4, "The Dream of Psychoanalysis," 117–45; see in particular Erik H. Erikson, "The Dream Specimen of Psychoanalysis," *Journal of the American Psychoanalytical Association* 2 (1954): 5–56; Frank R. Hartman, "A Reappraisal of the Emma Episode and the Specimen Dream," *Journal of the American Psychoanalytic Association* 31 (1983): 555–85; Robert Langs, "Freud's Irma Dream and the Origins of Psychoanalysis," *Psychoanalytic Review* 71 (1984): 591–617; Carl Schorske, "Politics and Patricide in Freud's *Interpretation of Dreams*," in idem, *Fin-de-siècle Vienna: Politics and Culture* (New York: Knopf, 1980); Max Schur, "Some Additional 'Day Residues' of the Specimen Dream of Psychoanalysis," in *Psychoanalysis: A General Psychology: Essays in Honor of Heinz Hartmann*, ed. Rudolph M. Loewenstein, Lottie M. Newman, Max Schur, and Albert J. Solnit (New York: International Universities Press, 1966), 45–85.

21. *SE* 4:122.

22. Ibid., 121.

23. Welsh, *Dream Theory*, 35

24. *SE* 4:134.

25. Ibid., 135.

26. *FF*, June 12, 1900, 417.

27. *SE* 4:142.

28. Paul Ricoeur, *Freud and Philosophy: An Essay on Interpretation*, trans. Denis Savage (New Haven, Conn.: Yale University Press, 1970), 7.

29. *SE* 4:142.

30. It is not possible for me here to explore extensively the analogy between political struggle and the inner psychic world of Freud's theories; the connection between politics and psyche has been explored by Schorske (see note 20 above) and by William McGrath in his excellent *Freud's Discovery of Psychoanalysis: The Politics of Hysteria* (Ithaca, N.Y., and London: Cornell University Press, 1986); see also the discussion in Welsh, *Freud's Wishful Dream Book*, 8off.

31. *SE* 4:297n. Note in passing Freud's challenge to the reader when he modestly acquits himself of the charge of being a funny man in waking reality. If a reader finds his book singularly lacking in wit or charm, he will reluctantly have to agree with his argument that the ingenuity of dreams is not *his* responsibility; if the reader is, in fact, charmed and amused by the book, it is less likely that he will really hold Freud's ingenious wit against him. Nonetheless, a considerable number of the charges leveled

against Freud by skeptics of dream interpretation and psychoanalysis in general do have this form: they consist in finding Freud too clever for the good of his own claims concerning the meaning of dreams. I may have occasion to consider this argument toward the end of this paper.

32. Ibid., 5:523.

33. Ibid., 4:146.

34. Ibid.

35. Ibid., 151.

36. Ibid., 151–52.

37. Adolf Grünbaum is only the most recent in a long line to have been taken in by this particular dream in his logical refutation of Freud's use of it to corral skeptics onto his side; see Grünbaum, "Two New Major Difficulties for Freud's Theory of Dreams," in idem, *Validation in the Clinical Theory of Psychoanalysis* (Madison, Conn.: International Universities Press, 1993), 357–84.

38. *SE* 4:157–58 (incorporating part of a footnote added in 1911).

39. See my "Contracting the Disease of Love: Authority and Freedom in the Origins of Psychoanalysis," in Forrester, *Seductions of Psychoanalysis*, 30–47.

40. Freud, *Introductory Lectures on Psycho-Analysis*, in *SE* 15:214.

41. On the rise of statistical thinking, see Alain Desrosières, *La Politique des grands nombres: Histoire de la raison statistique* (Paris: La Découverte, 1993); Ian Hacking, *The Emergence of Probability* (Cambridge: Cambridge University Press, 1975) and *The Taming of Chance* (Cambridge: Cambridge University Press, 1990); Theodore M. Porter, *The Rise of Statistical Thinking, 1820–1900* (Princeton, N.J.: Princeton University Press, 1986); Stephen M. Stigler, *The History of Statistics: The Measurement of Uncertainty Before 1900* (Cambridge: Harvard University Press, Belknap Press, 1986).

42. *SE* 4:xxv (preface to 2d edition of 1909).

43. "Prefatory Note to a Paper by E. Pickworth Farrow" (1926), in *SE* 20:280.

44. For the theory of obligatory passage points, see Bruno Latour, *Science in Action* (Milton Keynes, Eng.: Open University Press, 1987).

45. Jacques Derrida, "Freud and the Scene of Writing" (1965), *Yale French Studies* 48 (1972): 74–117.

"Having and Being: The Evolution of Freud's Oedipus Theory as a Moral Fable," by John E. Toews

1. *The Complete Letters of Sigmund Freud to Wilhelm Fliess, 1887–1904*, ed. and trans. Jeffrey Moussaieff Masson (Cambridge: Harvard University Press, Belknap Press, 1985), 272 (hereafter cited as *Freud/Fliess*).

2. *Totem and Taboo* (1913), in *SE* 13:156.

3. Ernest Jones, *The Life and Work of Sigmund Freud*, 3 vols. (New York: Basic Books, 1953–57), 2:14.

4. Freud, *The Interpretation of Dreams* (1900), in *SE* 14:262–63.

5. Ibid.

6. Freud, "The Aetiology of Hysteria" (1896), in *SE* 3:203, 206–7.

7. *Freud/Fliess*, 264.

8. "Zur Geschichte der psychoanalystische Bewegung," in Sigmund Freud, *Gesammelte Werke*, 19 vols. (London, 1940–87), 10:55.

9. *Freud/Fliess*, 265.

10. "Notes upon a Case of Obsessional Neuroses" (1909), in Sigmund Freud, *Collected Papers*, 5 vols., ed. and trans. Alix and James Strachey (New York: Basic Books, 1959), 3:345fn.

11. *Introductory Lectures on Psycho-Analysis* (1916–17), in *SE* 16:333.

12. *Interpretation of Dreams*, 4:217.

13. "From the History of an Infantile Neurosis" (1918), in *Collected Papers*, 3:547.

14. *The Ego and the Id* (1923), in *SE* 19:36–37.

15. Ibid., 37.

16. *New Introductory Lectures on Psycho-Analysis* (1933), in *SE* 22:118.

17. "The Passing of the Oedipus Complex" (1924), in *Collected Papers*, 2:274.

18. "Some Psychical Consequences of the Anatomical Distinction Between the Sexes" (1925), in *SE* 19:256.

19. "Female Sexuality" (1931), in *SE* 21:229.

20. "Some Psychical Consequences," 19:257–58.

"Oedipus Politicus: Freud's Paradigm of Social Relations," by José Brunner

1. I am grateful to Arnona Zahavi for her comments. This essay provides a revised—in some aspects more condensed, in others more elaborate—treatment of some of the themes that I have discussed in part 4 of my *Freud and the Politics of Psychoanalysis* (Oxford: Blackwell, 1995).

2. Freud, *Group Psychology and the Analysis of the Ego*, in *SE* 18:101 n. 1.

3. Freud, *Civilization and Its Discontents*, in *SE* 21:112.

4. Ibid., 122.

5. Ibid., 111.

6. Freud, *Group Psychology*, 18:91.

7. Ibid., 92.

8. Ibid., 102.

9. *The Complete Letters of Sigmund Freud to Wilhelm Fliess, 1887–1904*, ed. and trans. Jeffrey Moussaieff Masson (Cambridge: Harvard University Press: 1985), 272.

10. See John Forrester, *Language and the Origins of Psychoanalysis* (London: Macmillan, 1980), 90–96.

11. Freud, *An Outline of Psycho-Analysis*, in *SE* 23:192–93.

12. Freud, *Five Lectures on Psycho-Analysis*, in *SE* 11:47; "A Special Type of Choice of Object Made by Men," in *SE* 11:171.

13. Freud, *Three Essays on the Theory of Sexuality*, in *SE* 7:226n.

14. See Bennet Simon and Rachel Blass, "The Development and Vicissitudes of Freud's Ideas on the Oedipus Complex," in Jerome Neu, ed., *The Cambridge Companion to Freud* (Cambridge: Cambridge University Press, 1991), 161–74.

15. Freud, *Civilization and Its Discontents*, 21:66–67.

16. Freud, *The Ego and the Id*, in *SE* 19:27.

17. Freud, *Group Psychology*, 18:105.

18. Freud, "On Narcissism: An Introduction," in *SE* 14:90.

19. Freud, *The Interpretation of Dreams*, in *SE* 4:258; see Joseph Sandler, "The Background of Safety," *International Journal of Psycho-Analysis* 41 (1960): 352–56.

20. Freud, *Inhibitions, Symptoms, and Anxiety*, in *SE* 20:155.

21. Freud, *Three Essays*, 7:150.

22. Freud, "Family Romances," in *SE* 9:237.

23. Freud, "The Dissolution of the Oedipus Complex," in *SE* 19:176.

24. Freud, *Three Essays*, 7:199 n. 1.

25. Freud, "The Infantile Genital Organization," in *SE* 19:145 (original emphasis).
26. Freud, *Introductory Lectures on Psycho-Analysis*, in *SE* 15:206.
27. Freud, "Dissolution of the Oedipus Complex," 19:176.
28. Freud, *New Introductory Lectures on Psycho-Analysis*, in *SE* 22:129.
29. Freud, *Outline*, 23:194.
30. Freud, "The Taboo of Virginity," in *SE* 11:205.
31. Freud, *Three Essays*, 7:226 n. 1.
32. Freud, "Family Romances," 9:237.
33. Freud, "Dissolution of the Oedipus Complex," 19:176.
34. Freud, *Civilization and Its Discontents*, 21:129.
35. Freud, *Ego and the Id*, 19:34 (original emphasis).
36. Freud, "Thoughts for the Times of War and Death," in *SE* 14:282.
37. Freud, *Group Psychology*, 18:105.
38. Jean Laplanche, *Life and Death in Psychoanalysis* (Baltimore: Johns Hopkins University Press, 1976), 45.
39. Freud, *Totem and Taboo*, 13:142.
40. Ibid., 148.
41. Ibid., 143.
42. Ibid., 144.
43. Freud, *Moses and Monotheism*, in *SE* 23:101.
44. Ibid., 109.
45. Freud, *The Future of an Illusion*, in *SE* 21:8.

"*From Suggestion to Insight, from Hypnosis
to Psychoanalysis,*" *by Harold P. Blum*

1. Sigmund Freud, *Introductory Lectures on Psycho-Analysis*, in *SE* 15 and 16:462.
2. Harold P. Blum, "The Curative and Creative Aspects of Insight," *Journal of the American Psychoanalytic Association* (suppl.) 27 (1979): 41–69.
3. Freud, "A Case of Successful Treatment by Hypnotism" (1893), in *SE* 1:119.
4. Quoted in ibid.
5. Quoted in ibid., 63.
6. Ernest Jones, *The Life and Work of Sigmund Freud*, vol. 1 (Basic Books, 1953).
7. Freud, "Successful Treatment by Hypnotism," 1:286.
8. Freud, *An Autobiographical Study*, in *SE* 20:27.
9. Josef Breuer and Sigmund Freud, *Studies on Hysteria*, in *SE* 2.
10. Quoted in ibid.
11. Jones, *Life and Work*; Peter Gay, *Freud: A Life for Our Time* (Norton, 1988).
12. Freud, *Group Psychology and the Analysis of the Ego*, in *SE* 18:76.
13. Quoted in ibid., 35.

"*Freud's 'Dora' Case: The Crucible of the Psychoanalytic Concept
of Transference,*" *by Hannah S. Decker*

1. Josef Breuer and Sigmund Freud, *Studies on Hysteria* (1893–95), in *SE* 2:160–61.
2. For the complete story of Dora, her family, and her relationship to Freud, see my *Freud, Dora, and Vienna 1900* (Free Press, 1991).
3. Chapter 1 of *Freud, Dora, and Vienna 1900* discusses nineteenth-century electrotherapy and hydrotherapy in some detail.

4. Sigmund Freud, "Fragment of an Analysis of a Case of Hysteria," in *SE* 7:57–58, 61–62.

5. Ibid., 98.

6. Ibid., 34.

7. Breuer and Freud, *Studies on Hysteria*, 2:301–4.

8. Freud, *The Interpretation of Dreams* (1900), in *SE* 4:200, 5:562n.; *The Psychopathology of Everyday Life* (1901), in *SE* 6:172.

9. Freud's letter to Fliess, April 16, 1900, in *The Complete Letters of Sigmund Freud to Wilhelm Fliess, 1887–1904*, ed. and trans. Jeffrey Moussaieff Masson (Harvard University Press, Belknap Press, 1985), 409.

10. Freud, "Fragment," 7:118.

11. Ibid.

12. Hyman Muslin and Merton Gill, "Transference in the Dora Case," *Journal of the American Psychoanalytic Association* 26 (1978): 322.

13. Freud, "Fragment," 7:70 n. 2.

14. Ibid., 118.

15. Ibid., 73–74.

16. Ibid., 22.

17. Ibid., 120.

18. See chapter 2 and pages 199–205 in *Freud, Dora, and Vienna 1900*.

19. Ernest Jones, *The Life and Work of Sigmund Freud* (Basic Books, 1955), 2:257.

"*Freud's Reception in the United States,*" by Edith Kurzweil

1. According to Nathan G. Hale (*Freud and the Americans*, 1971), "This moral system tried to coerce a recalcitrant and hostile actuality" (p. 25) and was congruent with business success, a fierce passion for upward mobility, and the acquisition of wealth. But continence, religious purity, devotion to hard work, and the possibility of married celibacy were inducing "mental problems."

2. Ibid., 165.

3. David M. Levy, in *New Fields in Psychiatry* (1947), notes that child guidance had been nonexistent until 1920, when the Institute for Juvenile Research was founded, following the ideas of Adolf Meyer, Alfred Binet, and Freud; that there they learned about recidivism; and that by 1932 there were 674 clinics providing services to juveniles.

4. *The Question of Lay Analysis* (1926), in *SE* 20:179–258.

5. Nathan G. Hale, ed., *James Jackson Putnam and Psychoanalysis* (Cambridge: Harvard University Press, 1971), 86.

6. Ibid., 89.

7. Isador H. Coriat, *What Is Psychoanalysis?* (New York: Moffat, 1919).

8. Hale, *James Jackson Putnam*, 397.

9. For details, see Edith Kurzweil, *The Freudians: A Comparative Perspective* (1989); and idem, "USA," in *A Guide to Psychoanalysis Throughout the World*, ed. P. Kutter (Hillsdale, N.J.: Analytic Press, 1995), 186–234.

10. Sanford Gifford (1977), in *Encyclopedia of Behavioral Sciences*, ed. B. B. Wolman, 374–84.

11. Otto Rank, *Art and the Artist* (1907; New York: Tudor, 1932).

12. H. Hartmann, E. Kris, and R. M. Loewenstein, "Comments on the Formation of Psychic Structure," *Psychoanalytic Study of the Child* 2 (1946): 11–38.

"Psychoanalysis: The American Experience," by Robert Coles

1. From tape-recorded interview conducted in Erik H. Erikson's Widener Library study, Harvard University, October, 9, 1968.

2. Anna Freud, *Difficulties in the Path of Psychoanalysis: A Confrontation of Past with Present Viewpoints* (International Universities Press, 1969), 20.

3. From tape-recorded interview conducted in Dr. Bibring's Cambridge home, April 15, 1960.

4. From tape-recorded interview conducted at Yale University, March 1970.

5. Anna Freud, *Normality and Pathology in Children* (International Universities Press, 1965).

6. Allen Wheelis, *The Quest for Identity* (Norton, 1958).

7. Sara Lawrence Lightfoot, *Balm in Gilead* (Addison-Wesley, 1988).

"Freud, Film, and Culture," by E. Ann Kaplan

1. Krin Gabbard and Glen O. Gabbard, *Psychiatry and the Cinema* (University of Chicago Press, 1987).

2. Interestingly, the image of mental illness in this film sparked debate among psychiatrists in the *New York Times*. Specifically mentioned in one letter to the editor was the "misinformation" regarding electroconvulsive therapy, which the writer, Dr. Rosenberg, claimed is "among the most effective treatments known to medicine," and the film's excessive stress on parental influence in the development of mental illness. Rosenberg joked that "the cinematic David seems to have a severe case of 'movie madness' . . ." ("*Shine* Depicts False View of Mental Illness," *New York Times*, March 15, 1997). A response argued that family environment often indeed plays a large part in mental illness, and that the film therefore had not overstressed this. As we can see, cinema is viewed as impacting on people's ideas of mental illness.

3. See Janet Walker's 1993 volume *Couching Resistance: Women, Film and Psychoanalytic Psychiatry* (University of Minnesota Press).

4. See Christian Metz, *The Imaginary Signifier: Psychoanalysis and Cinema* (Indiana University Press, 1981).

5. See E. Ann Kaplan, ed. *Psychoanalysis and Cinema* (Routledge, 1990).

6. See Mary Ann Doane, *The Desire to Desire* (Indiana University Press, 1987); Laura Mulvey, *Visual and Other Pleasures* (Indiana University Press, 1989); E. Ann Kaplan, *Motherhood and Representation* (Routledge, 1992).

7. See Juliet Mitchell, *Psychoanalysis and Feminism* (Penguin, 1975); Sara Kofman, *The Enigma of Woman* (Cornell University Press, 1985); Teresa de Lauretis, *The Practice of Love* (Indiana University Press, 1994).

8. See Freud, "The Psychogenesis of a Case of Homosexuality in a Woman" (1920), in *Sexuality and the Psychology of Love* (Collier, 1963).

9. See de Lauretis, *Practice of Love*.

10. See E. Ann Kaplan, "The Couch Affair: Gender and the Transference in Hollywood Film," in *American Imago* 50 (Winter 1993): 481–514.

11. Several film and cultural scholars have commented on American and European imperialism: viz., Mary Ann Doane, "Dark Continents: Epistemologies of Racial and Sexual Difference in Psychoanalysis and the Cinema," in idem, ed., *Femmes Fatales* (Routledge, 1991), 209–48; Edward Said, *Culture and Imperialism* (Knopf, 1992); Ella Shohat and Robert Stam, *Unthinking Eurocentrism* (Routledge, 1995).

12. See Susan Handelman, *The Slayers of Moses* (Routledge, 1990).

13. Although many studio heads were Jewish, they were also (and perhaps especially) anxious to promote an assimilationist set of values, partly by continuing to allow prevailing anti-Semitism to be expressed in film. See research by Patricia Erens and Lester Friedman in Lester Friedman, ed., *Unspeakable Images: Ethnicity and the American Cinema* (Urbana: University of Illinois Press, 1991).

14. Anthony Barthelemy discusses Renaissance attitudes toward blacks in his *Black Face, Maligned Race* (Louisiana State University Press, 1987).

15. See, for instance, Christopher Lane, ed., "The Psychoanalysis of Race," *Discourse* (special issue) 19 (Winter 1997).

16. Krin and Glen O. Gabbard have described such films in their *Psychiatry and the Cinema*.

17. Freud, *Jokes and Their Relation to the Unconscious*, in *SE*.

18. See Kaplan, "Couch Affair."

"The Freud Controversy: What Is at Issue?," by Frank Cioffi

1. L. L. Whyte, *The Unconscious Before Freud* (Tavistock Publications, 1962), 177.

2. Frederick Crews, *The Memory Wars: Freud's Legacy in Dispute* (New York Review of Books, 1995), 8.

3. Peter Medawar, *New York Review of Books*, January 23, 1975.

4. "On the History of the Psycho-Analytic Movement," in *SE* 14:23–24.

5. Charles Brenner, "Classical Psychoanalysis," in *International Encyclopedia of the Social Sciences*.

6. I have lost my source for this.

7. Ludwig Wittgenstein, *Lectures and Conversations on Psychology* (Oxford: Blackwell, 1966), 24.

8. E. Kris, *The Origins of Psychoanalysis* (New York: Basic Books, 1954), 78.

9. *SE* 1:51.

10. Richard Wollheim, *Freud* (Fontana, 1991), 33.

11. "Is Freudian Psychoanalytic Theory Pseudo-scientific by Karl Popper's Criterion of Demarcation?," *American Philosophical Quarterly* 16, no. 2 (April 1979).

12. Robert Woodworth, *Science* (1913): 930.

13. *SE* 3:205.

14. Ibid., 19:116.

15. Paul Meehl, "Some Methodological Reflections on the Difficulties of Psychoanalytic Research," *Minnesota Studies in the Philosophy of Science* (1970): 407.

16. Ernest Jones, *Papers on Psycho-Analysis* (Beacon, 1927), 414; see also Oberndorf, *A History of Psychoanalysis in America* (Harper Torchbooks, 1964), 123.

17. See "Why Psychoanalysis Is a Testimonial Science," in Frank Cioffi, *Freud and the Question of Pseudo-Science* (Open Court, 1998).

18. Janet Malcolm, *The Impossible Profession* (Picador, 1982), 35.

19. Han Israël and Morton Schatzman, "The Seduction Theory," *History of Psychiatry* 4 (1993): 23–59. See also Allen Esterson, "Jeffrey Masson and Freud's Seduction Theory: A New Fable Based on Old Myths," *History of the Human Sciences*, February 1998; Frank Cioffi, "Was Freud a Liar?" and "From Freud's 'Scientific Fairy Tale' to Masson's Politically Correct One," in *Freud and the Question of Pseudo-Science*.

20. *Betrayers of the Truth* (Touchstone, 1982).

21. *Contemporary Psychology* 33, no. 5 (1988).

22. *SE* 23:191.

23. Ibid., 21:184.

"*A Century of Psychoanalysis: Critical Retrospect
and Prospect,*" by Adolf Grünbaum

1. *SE* 3:151 (1896).

2. For further details, see Adolf Grünbaum, *The Foundations of Psychoanalysis: A Philosophical Critique* (University of California Press, 1984). There are German, Italian, Japanese, French and Hungarian translations. See also idem, "Is Freud's Theory Well-Founded?," *Behavioral and Brain Sciences* 9 (1986): 266–81; idem, *Validation in the Clinical Theory of Psychoanalysis: A Study in the Philosophy of Psychoanalysis* (International Universities Press, 1993); and idem, "One Hundred Years of Psychoanalytic Theory and Therapy: Retrospect and Prospect," in *Mindscapes: Philosophy, Science, and the Mind*, ed. Martin Carrier and Peter Machamer (University of Pittsburgh Press and University of Konstanz Press, 1997), 340–43.

3. Marcel Zentner, *Die Flucht ins Vergessen: Die Anfänge der Psychoanalyse Freuds bei Schopenhauer* (Wissenschaftliche Buchgessellschaft, 1995), 248.

4. *SE* 14:15–16 (1914).

5. Morris Eagle, "The Psychoanalytic and the Cognitive Unconscious," in *Theories of the Unconscious and Theories of the Self*, ed. R. Stern (Analytic Press, 1987), 155–89.

6. *SE* 5:566–67 (1900).

7. Morris Eagle, "The Dynamics of Theory Change in Psychoanalysis," in *Philosophical Problems of the Internal and External Worlds: Essays on the Philosophy of Adolf Grünbaum*, ed. J. Earman et al. (University of Pittsburgh Press and University of Konstanz Press, 1993), chap. 15, 374–76.

8. Eagle, "Dynamics of Theory Change," 161–65.

9. Howard Shevrin et al., "Event-Related Potential Indicators of the Dynamic Unconscious," *Consciousness and Cognition* 1 (1992): 340–41.

10. Eagle, "Psychoanalytic and Cognitive Unconscious," 166–86.

11. E.g., Michael Basch, "Psychoanalysis, Science and Epistemology," *Bulletin of the Institute for Psychoanalysis* (Chicago) 4, no. 2 (1994): 1.

12. Thomas Nagel, "Freud's Permanent Revolution," *New York Review of Books*, May 12, 1994, 34–38.

13. Adolf Grünbaum, letter to the editor, *New York Review of Books*, August 11, 1994, 54–55. Contra Thomas Nagel's "Freud's Permanent Revolution."

14. Henri Ellenberger, *The Discovery of the Unconscious* (Basic Books, 1970), 547–49.

15. *SE* 6:239 (1901).

16. Ibid., 15:47 (1916).

17. Ibid., 14:16 (1914).

18. Ibid., 20:45 (1925); 16:301 (1917).

19. Helmut Thomä and Horst Kächele, *Psychoanalytic Practice*, vol. 1 (Springer Verlag, 1987), 107–11.

20. *SE* 6:144 (1901).

21. Ibid., 6:147 (1901).

22. Ibid., 15:76–77 (1916).

23. Ibid., 5:528 (1900); Grünbaum, *Validation in the Clinical Theory of Psychoanalysis*, 24–26.

24. Grünbaum, "One Hundred Years of Psychoanalytic Theory and Therapy," 340–43.

25. *SE* 2:6–7 (1893).

26. Ibid., 20:27 (1925); 23:216–253 (1937).

27. Ibid., 2:34–35 (1895).

28. Henri Ellenberger, "The Story of Anna O.: A Critical Review with New Data," *Journal of the History of the Behavioral Sciences* 8 (1972): 267–79; and Mikkel Borch-Jacobsen, *Remembering Anna O.: 100 Years of Psychoanalytic Mystification* (Routledge, 1996).

29. See Adolf Grünbaum, "The Placebo Concept in Medicine and Psychiatry," in *Non-Specific Aspects of Treatment*, ed. M. Shepherd and N. Sartorius; published for the World Health Organization (Hans Huber Verlag, 1989), 7–38.

30. H. Bachrach et al., "On the Efficacy of Psychoanalysis," *Journal of the American Psychoanalytic Association* 39 (1991): 871–916; S. Vaughan and S. Roose, "The Analytic Process: Clinical and Research Definitions," *International Journal of Psycho-Analysis* 76 (1995): 343–56.

31. *SE* 4:100–101 (1900).

32. Ibid., 20:44 (1925).

33. Ibid., 5:546, 548–49, 552–54, 567–68, 583–84 (1900).

34. Ibid., 20:44 (1925).

35. Ibid., 4:234; 5:680 (1900).

36. Grünbaum, *Foundations of Psychoanalysis*, chap. 5.

37. Adolf Grünbaum, "A New Critique of Freud's 1895 Neurobiological Dream Theory" (forthcoming).

38. *SE* 4:134–35 (1900); 20:44 (1925).

39. Ibid., 5:553 (1900); 20:44 (1925).

40. Ibid., 20:45 (1925).

41. Clark Glymour, "The Theory of Your Dreams," in *Physics, Philosophy, and Psychoanalysis: Essays in Honor of Adolf Grünbaum*, ed. Robert Cohen and Larry Laudan (Reidel, 1983), 57–71.

42. *SE* 20:44 (1925).

43. Shakespeare, *Hamlet*, act 1, sc. 5.

44. Paul Ricoeur, *Freud and Philosophy* (Yale University Press, 1970), 358.

45. Barbara von Eckardt, "Adolf Grünbaum and Psychoanalytic Epistemology," in *Beyond Freud: A Study of Modern Psychoanalytic Theorists*, ed. J. Reppen (Analytic Press, 1985), 356–64.

46. Grünbaum, *Foundations of Psychoanalysis*, 1–94; idem, " 'Meaning' Connections and Causal Connections in the Human Sciences: The Poverty of Hermeneutic Philosophy," *Journal of the American Psychoanalytic Association* 38, no. 3 (1990): 559–77; and idem, *Validation in the Clinical Theory of Psychoanalysis*, chap. 4.

47. Anthony Storr, "Human Understanding and Scientific Validation," in Open Peer Commentary, *Behavioral & Brain Sciences* 9, no. 2 (June 1986): 260.

48. Grünbaum, *Foundations of Psychoanalysis*, chap. 7.

49. Eagle, "Dynamics of Theory Change," 373–408.

50. Ibid., 374.

51. Ibid., 388.

52. Ibid., 404.

53. André Green, "Against Lacanism," *Journal of European Psychoanalysis* 2 (1995/1996): 169–85.

54. Jacob Arlow and Charles Brenner, "The Future of Psychoanalysis," *Psychoanalytic Quarterly* 57 (1988): 13.

55. Paul E. Meehl, "Commentary: Psychoanalysis as Science," *Journal of the American Psychoanalytic Association* 43, no. 4 (1995): 1021.

56. Grünbaum, " 'Meaning' Connections and Causal Connections in the Human Sciences"; and idem, *Validation in the Clinical Theory of Psychoanalysis*, chap. 4.

57. Philip Holzman, "Hilgard on Psychoanalysis as Science," *Psychological Science* 5, no. 4 (July 1994): 190.

58. Private communication.

"Freud: Current Projections," by Peter D. Kramer

1. An account of that analysis and those years appears in Peter D. Kramer, *Moments of Engagement* (New York: Norton, 1989; Penguin, 1994).

2. Lavinia Edmunds, "His Master's Choice," *John Hopkins Magazine*, April 1988, 40–49.

3. W. H. Auden, "In Memory of Sigmund Freud," in *Collected Poems* (New York: Vintage, 1991), 273–76.

4. Freud, "Extracts from the Fliess Papers; Draft H: Paranoia," in *SE* 1:206–12. I discuss this case in a different context in Peter D. Kramer, *Should You Leave?* (New York: Scribner, 1997).

5. Freud, "Extracts," 1:207–8.

6. Freud, "Further Remarks on the Neuro-Psychoses of Defence, III: Analysis of a Case of Chronic Paranoia," in *SE* 3:174–85. Again, Freud ignores the possibility that this "affair between children" acted as an external trauma; he likewise has no impulse to entertain doubts about his patient's recollection.

7. Freud, "Psycho-Analytic Notes on an Autobiographical Account of a Case of Paranoia (Dementia Paranoides)," in *SE* 12:1–82. See also, for example, Z. Lothane, *In Defense of Schreber: Soul Murder and Psychiatry* (Hillsdale, N.J.: Analytic Press, 1992).

8. Lionel Trilling, *Sincerity and Authenticity* (Cambridge: Harvard University Press, 1972).

9. Martha Nussbaum, *The Therapy of Desire* (Princeton, N.J.: Princeton University Press, 1994).

10. Auden, "In Memory of W. B. Yeats," in *Collected Poems*, 247–49.

"Strange Hearts: On the Paradoxical Liaison Between Psychoanalysis and Feminism," by Muriel Dimen

1. Sigmund Freud, "Fragment of an Analysis of a Case of Hysteria" (1905), in *SE* 7:7–124, 65 n. 1.

2. My thanks to Adrienne Harris, Natalie Kampen, Michael Roth, and Sue Shapiro, who helped much in this essay's formation, but who are in no way responsible for its shortcomings.

3. In a letter of 1928, Freud told Ernest Jones that he found the adult woman's sexual life "something of 'a dark continent' " (Peter Gay, *Freud: A Life for Our Time* [Norton, 1988], 501).

4. There have been several recent attempts to remedy this lacuna: Elizabeth Abel, "Race, Class, and Psychoanalysis? Opening Questions," in *Conflicts in Feminism*, ed. Marianne Hirsch and Evelyn Fox Keller (Routledge, 1990); Mary Anne Doane,

Femmes Fatales: Feminism, Film Theory, Psychoanalysis (Routledge, 1991); Sander L. Gilman, *Freud, Race, and Gender* (Princeton University Press, 1993); Claudia Tate, "Psychoanalysis as Enemy and Ally of African Americans," *Journal for the Psychoanalysis of Culture and Society* 1(1996): 53–62; Jean Walton, "Re-placing Race in (White) Psychoanalytic Discourse: Founding Narratives of Feminism," *Critical Inquiry* 21 (1995): 775–804.

5. Freud, *Three Essays on the Theory of Sexuality* (1905), in *SE* 7:135–248, 221.

6. Thomas Laqueur, *Making Sex* (Harvard University Press, 1990), 235.

7. Anne Koedt, "The Myth of the Vaginal Orgasm," in *Radical Feminism*, ed. Anne Koedt, Ellen Levin, and Anita Rapone (Quadrangle, 1970), 198–207.

8. Lynne Segal, *Straight Sex* (Virago, 1994), 36.

9. Michel Foucault, *The History of Sexuality*, vol. 1, trans. R. Hurley (1976; Vintage, 1980).

10. Kate Millet, *Sexual Politics* (New York: Doubleday, 1970).

11. William H. Masters and Virginia Johnson, *Human Sexual Response* (Boston: Little, Brown, 1966).

12. Karen Horney, "On the Genesis of the Castration Complex in Women," in *Feminine Psychology*, ed. Harold Kelman (Norton, 1967), 37–53; "The Flight from Womanhood," 54–70; "The Denial of the Vagina," 147–61.

13. Ernest Jones, "Early Development of Female Sexuality, in *Papers on Psycho-Analysis* (Beacon, 1927), 438–51; Melanie Klein, "Early Stages of the Oedipus Conflict," *International Journal of Psycho-Analysis* 9 (1928): 167–80.

14. Horney, "Denial of the Vagina," 160 (original italics).

15. Freud, "On Femininity" (1933), in *New Introductory Lectures on Psycho-Analysis*, in *SE* 22:112–34, 118; *An Outline of Psycho-Analysis*, in *SE* 23:141–208, 154 n. 2.

16. Zenia Fliegel, "Women's Development in Analytic Theory: Six Decades of Controversy," in *Psychoanalysis and Women: Contemporary Reappraisals*, ed. Judith L. Alpert (Analytic Press, 1986), 3–32.

17. As is by now well known, the famous equation of anatomy with destiny refers not to gender and character but to the sexual inhibition caused by the fact that "*inter urinas et faeces nascimur* [we are born between urine and feces]," as Freud observed in *Civilization and Its Discontents* (1930), in *SE* 21:106 n. 3.

18. That this strategy failed is another story, which time lacks to tell, of contemporary psychoanalysis and feminism.

19. Freud in a letter to Marie Bonaparte, quoted in Ernest Jones, *The Life and Work of Sigmund Freud* (Basic Books, 1953), 2:421.

20. Freud, "Female Sexuality" (1931), in *SE* 21:221–45, 229. That this slip can be interpreted, however dubiously, as representing the content of the child's psyche does not explain what would then become Freud's failure to distinguish his point of view from the child's.

21. Freud, "On Femininity," 22:112–24, 116–17.

22. Freud, "The Psychogenesis of a Case of Homosexuality in a Woman," in *SE* 18:145–72, 158 n. 2.

23. Ibid., 150–51. See Adrienne Harris's incisive assessment of this case, "Gender as Contradiction," *Psychoanalytic Dialogues: A Journal of Relational Perspectives* 1 (1991): 197–224, for an interpretation of this slip.

24. Freud, "On Femininity"; Sarah Kofman, *The Enigma of Woman*, trans. Catherine Porter (Cornell University Press, 1985).

25. According to Fliegel, "Women's Development," 7ff., Freud targeted Horney in "Some Psychical Consequences of the Anatomical Distinction Between the Sexes" (1925), in *SE* 19:241–59, and in "On Femininity."

26. Ann Jackowitz, "Anna O./Bertha Pappenheim and Me," in *Between Women*, ed. Carol Ascher, Louise DeSalvo, and Sara Ruddick (Beacon, 1984), 253–310.

27. See Harriet Anderson, "Psychoanalysis and Feminism: An Ambivalent Alliance; Viennese Feminist Responses to Freud, 1900–30," in *Psychoanalysis in Its Cultural Context; Austrian Studies III*, ed. Edward Timms and Ritchie Robertson (Edinburgh University Press, 1992), 81–94.

28. Jessica Benjamin, "The Primal Leap of Psychoanalysis, from Body to Speech," in *Shadow of the Other* (Routledge, 1998), 3.

29. Sally Alexander, "Feminist History," in *Feminism and Psychoanalysis: A Critical Dictionary*, ed. Elizabeth Wright (Blackwell, 1992), 108–13, 109.

30. Anderson, "Psychoanalysis and Feminism," 73.

31. Henri F. Ellenberger, *The Discovery of the Unconscious: The History and Evolution of Dynamic Psychiatry* (Basic Books, 1970), 70ff.

32. Nancy Chodorow, *Feminism and Psychoanalytic Theory* (Yale University Press, 1989), 175.

33. Gayle Rubin, "The Traffic in Women: Notes Toward the Political Economy of Sex," in *Toward an Anthropology of Women*, ed. Rayna Rapp Reiter (Monthly Review Press, 1975), 157–210.

34. In an appendix to her important *Psychoanalysis and Feminism: Freud, Reich, Lang and Women* (New York: Pantheon, 1974), Juliet Mitchell observes the contemporaneity of psychoanalysis and feminism in Freud's Vienna. Instead of seeing them as mutually influential, however, she depicts the latter as reacting to the former.

35. John Forrester, "Freud's Female Patients/Female Analysts," in *Feminism and Psychoanalysis*, 134–39, 134.

36. Joan Rivière, "Womanliness as a Masquerade," *International Journal of Psycho-Analysis* 10 (1929): 303–13.

37. Rosalind Delmar, "What Is Feminism?," in *What Is Feminism?*, ed. Juliet Mitchell and Ann Oakley (Pantheon, 1986), 8–33, 27.

38. Susie Orbach, *Fat Is a Feminist Issue* (Berkley, 1978), 3–23.

39. Jacqueline Rose, *Sexuality in the Field of Vision* (Verso, 1986), 6, 8. Having independently proposed that feminism is the legatee of the Marx-Freud project, I was pleased to come upon Jacqueline Rose's elegant conceptualization, which documents and complements my own perspective.

40. Freud's quarrel with the Marxist psychoanalyst Wilhelm Reich may perhaps here stand as switch word to this debate.

41. This coincidence is not surprising in a time of cultural and political ferment when, in fact, many second-generation analysts were receiving their intellectual formation. Not only Sándor Ferenczi and Otto Fenichel but such figures as Edith Jacobson, George Gero, and Annie Reich were steeped in left-wing politics. While some, like Wilhelm Reich and Erich Fromm, kept striving for synthesis, others abandoned their politics, a yielding impelled more by their Holocaust-driven escape to an anti-Communist United States (with its medicalized and anti-intellectual psychoanalysis) than by the inherent incompatibility of two cherished and imaginative conceptions of human potential. See Russell Jacoby, *The Repression of Psychoanalysis: Otto Fenichel and the Political Freudians* (University of Chicago Press, 1983).

42. Rose, *Sexuality in the Field of Vision*, 8.

43. Simone de Beauvoir, *The Second Sex*, trans. H. M. Parshley (1949; Vintage, 1974).

44. Chodorow, *Feminism and Psychoanalytic Theory*, 213. If a single work could be said to represent this moment, it is Gayle Rubin's "Traffic in Women," in which Karl Marx, Sigmund Freud, Claude Lévi-Strauss, and Jacques Lacan are each hoist on their own petards in the service of both illuminating and calling for a new theory of what she then called the "sex/gender" system. Situating sexuality between psyche and politics requires, on the other hand, a theory, a psychoanalytic explanation of how ideology is psychically transformed into behavior and personal conviction. Contemporaneously, Juliet Mitchell contends that this theory is at hand: Jacques Lacan would provide the means to route Marx through Freud so that women's subordination might be explained. Later, in "Thinking Sex: Notes for a Radical Theory of the Politics of Sexuality," in *Pleasure and Danger: Exploring Female Sexuality*, ed. Carole S. Vance (Routledge, 1984), 267–319, Rubin redivides sex from gender, arguing for distinct if mutually implicated theories of each.

45. Shulamith Firestone, *The Dialectic of Sex* (New York: Morrow, 1970).

46. Rose, *Sexuality in the Field of Vision*, 7.

47. Julia Kristeva, *Tales of Love*, trans. L. S. Roudiez (Columbia University Press, 1983); Janine Chasseguet-Smirgel, *Sexuality and Mind* (New York University Press, 1986); Joyce McDougall, *The Many Faces of Eros* (Norton, 1995).

48. Klein, granting Freud's wish, excavated the "Minoan-Mycenean" stratum beneath the Oedipal floor, finding there even more primal origins for civilization's discontents than Freud had imagined, an argument that Dinnerstein took up a generation later. See Freud, "Female Sexuality," 21:226; Melanie Klein, "The Oedipus Complex in the Light of Early Anxieties"; Dorothy Dinnerstein, *The Mermaid and the Minotaur* (Harper, 1976).

49. D. W. Winnicott, *Through Paediatrics to Psycho-Analysis* (Basic Books, 1975).

50. Freud, *Civilization and Its Discontents*, 21:105 n. 3.

51. Adrienne Harris, "Bringing Artemis to Life: A Plea for Militance and Aggression in Feminist Peace Politics," in *Rocking the Ship of State*, ed. Adrienne Harris and Ynestra King (Westview Press, 1989), 93–114; Carol Gilligan, *In a Different Voice* (Harvard University Press, 1982); Jean Baker Miller, *Toward a New Psychology of Women* (Beacon, 1976).

52. Irene Fast, *Gender Identity: A Differentiation Model* (Analytic Press, 1984); Ethel Person, "Sexuality as the Mainstay of Identity," *Signs* 5 (1980): 605–30.

53. Jessica Benjamin, "Discussion of Jordan's 'The Relational Self: A New Perspective for Understanding Women's Development,'" *Contemporary Psychotherapy Review* 7 (1992): 82–96, 90.

54. Virginia Goldner, "Toward a Critical Relational Theory of Gender," *Psychoanalytic Dialogues* 1 (1991): 249–72.

55. Jessica Benjamin, *The Bonds of Love* (Pantheon, 1988); Nancy Chodorow, *The Reproduction of Mothering* (University of California Press, 1978).

56. Freud comes up with this classic phrase in "Preface to Aichhorn's *Wayward Youth*" (1925), in *SE* 19:272–75. Foucault, in *History of Sexuality*, theorizes the political and discursive condition for this impossibility. Barbara Ehrenreich, in *Fear of Falling* (Pantheon, 1989), traces the impossible professions' historical roots and socioeconomic structure.

57. This is a pleasure that we may fairly call sadomasochistic.

58. Rose, *Sexuality in the Field of Vision*, 7.

59. As developed by Ferdinand de Saussure and Roman Jakobson, whose work together led to Claude Lévi-Strauss's mid-century structuralism.

60. Judith Butler, "Gender," in *Feminism and Psychoanalysis*, 140–45, 140. "Gender" is a term that Freud never did use and that Lacanian feminists refuse; see Juliet Mitchell, "Commentary on 'Deconstructing Difference: Gender, Splitting, and Transitional Space' by Muriel Dimen," *Psychoanalytic Dialogues* 2 (1991): 353–58.

61. Alexander, "Feminist History," 109.

62. Judith Butler, "Melancholy Gender/Refused Identification," *Psychoanalytic Dialogues* 5 (1995): 165–80.

63. Rose claims this putative veridicality as Lacan's chief virtue for feminism in "Introduction II," in *Feminine Sexuality: Jacques Lacan and l'école freudienne*, ed. Juliet Mitchell and Jacqueline Rose (Pantheon, 1982), 27–58.

64. Malcolm Bowie, *Lacan* (Harvard University Press, 1990), 130.

65. A "key" symbol is an element of meaning (which would include what Lacanians call the "signifier") that, in an ethnographic perspective, simultaneously expresses and creates a culture's central ideas, describes and prescribes its values and behavior. See Sherry Ortner, "On Key Symbols," *American Anthropologist* 75 (1973): 1338–46.

66. Grosz, in "Phallus: Feminist Implications," in *Feminism and Psychoanalysis*, 320–23, precedes this remark by insisting that "feminists cannot afford to ignore the a priori privileging of the masculine within [Lacan's] account, nor can they too readily accept Lacan's claim that the phallus is a signifier like any other" (p. 322). Jane Flax makes a similar argument in *Thinking Fragments: Psychoanalysis, Feminism, and Post-Modernism in the Contemporary West* (University of California Press, 1990). Using somewhat bizarre imagery to heighten the strangeness of her target, she says: "Lacan's claims that the phallus exists purely upon a symbolic plane, that it does not signify penis, and that any relationship between signifier and signified is arbitrary are disingenuous. Would we be persuaded by Lacan if he claims that the mother lacks, say, 'a mouse' or that her desire for the child is to be the 'waxpaper'?" (p. 322).

67. Not only does Lacan shore up Freud's patriarchy, he strengthens it by eliminating the biological determinism clouding Freud's account. The phallus is not the penis, or so he insists. Rose paraphrases: "The importance of the phallus is that its status in the development of human sexuality is something which nature cannot account for" (*Feminine Sexuality*, 40).

68. "Only the concept of a subjectivity at odds with itself gives back to women the right to an impasse at the point of sexual identity, with no nostalgia whatsoever for its possible or future integration into a norm" (Rose, *Sexuality in the Field of Vision*, 15).

69. The inconstancy of desire might well be symbolized by what Bowie, an eagle-eyed but sympathetic interpreter of Lacan, calls "the everyday uncertainties that beset the male member." He wonders why Lacan does not see that the penis's unpredictability "make[s] it into a dialectician par excellence, a nexus of signifying opportunities, a fine example, in all of its modes, of the Freudian *fort/da*" (*Lacan*, 125).

70. The notion of paradox, recently so well deployed by Winnicott and those he has influenced, reveals how unexpectedly polarizing not only Lacan's but Foucault's thought can occasionally be. David Harvey, in *The Condition of Postmodernity* (Blackwell, 1989), reminded me of the Marxist theory of "internal relations" elaborated by Bertell Ollman, *Alienation: Marx's Conception of Man in Capitalist Society*, 2d ed. (Cam-

bridge University Press, 1976), which suggests a way of thinking paradoxically in Marxist terms.

71. Teresa Brennan, "Introduction," in idem, ed., *Between Feminism and Psychoanalysis* (Routledge, 1989), 1–24, 8.

72. Naomi Scheman, *Engenderings* (Routledge, 1993), 3.

73. Valerie Traub, "The Psychomorphology of the Clitoris," *GLQ* 2 (1995): 100.

74. Luce Irigaray, *This Sex Which Is Not One*, trans. C. Porter with C. Burke (Cornell University Press, 1985).

75. Eve Kosofsky Sedgewick, *Epistemology of the Closet* (University of California Press, 1990), 29.

76. Beverly Whipple and B. R. Komisaruk, "The G-spot, Orgasm and Female Ejaculation: Are They Related?," in *Proceedings: First International Conference on Orgasm*, ed. P. Kohari (VRP Publishers, 1991), 27–237.

77. Daniel Odier, a master of Tantra, speaks of "orgasms in the eyeballs" in *Tantric Quest*, trans. Jody Gladding (Inner Traditions, 1997), 156.

78. Bowie, *Lacan*, 196; Rose, *Sexuality in the Field of Vision*, 15.

79. Ellenberger, *Discovery of the Unconscious*, passim.

80. For example, see Philip Bromberg, " 'Speak! That I May See You': Some Reflections on Dissociation, Reality, and Psychoanalytic Listening," *Psychoanalytic Dialogues* 4 (1994): 517–48. See also Jody Messler Davies and Mary Gail Frawley, "Dissociative Processes and Transference-Countertransference Paradigms in the Psychoanalytically Oriented Treatment of Adult Survivors of Childhood Sexual Abuse," *Psychoanalytic Dialogues* 2 (1992): 5–36.

81. Lynne Layton, "Reply to Judith Butler," *Gender and Psychoanalysis* 2 (1997): 521–24, 523.

SELECTED BIBLIOGRAPHY

Abel, Elizabeth. "Race, Class, and Psychoanalysis? Opening Questions." In *Conflicts in Feminism*, edited by Marianne Hirsch and Evelyn Fox Keller, 184–204. New York: Routledge, 1990.

Abraham, Karl. "A Short Study of the Development of the Libido, Viewed in the Light of Mental Disorders." 1924. In *Selected Papers on Psycho-Analysis*, edited by Ernest Jones, 184–204. New York: Brunner/Mazel, 1927.

Alexander, Sally. "Feminist History." In *Feminism and Psychoanalysis: A Critical Dictionary*, edited by Elizabeth Wright, 108–13. Oxford: Blackwell, 1992.

Anderson, Harriet. "Psychoanalysis and Feminism: An Ambivalent Alliance; Viennese Feminist Responses to Freud, 1900–30." In *Psychoanalysis in Its Cultural Context; Austrian Studies III*, edited by Edward Timms and Ritchie Robertson, 81–94. Edinburgh: Edinburgh University Press, 1992.

Anthony, J., and T. Benedek. *Parenthood, Its Psychology and Psychopathology*. Boston: Little, Brown, 1970.

Anzieu, D. *L'Auto-analyse de Freud et la découverte de la psychanalyse*. Paris: Presses Universitaires de France, 1975.

Appignanesi, Lisa, and John Forrester. *Freud's Women*. New York: Basic Books, 1992.

Augustine, Saint. *Omnia Opera*. Vol. 8. Paris: Gaume, 1836.

Barthelemy, Anthony. *Black Face, Maligned Race: The Representation of Blacks in English Drama from Shakespeare to Southerne*. Baton Rouge: Louisiana State University Press, 1987.

Beauvoir, Simone de. *The Second Sex*. Translated by H. M. Parshley. New York: Vintage, 1974.

Benjamin, Jessica. *The Bonds of Love*. New York: Pantheon, 1988.

———. "Discussion of Jordan's 'The Relational Self: A New Perspective for Understanding Women's Development.' " In *Contemporary Psychotherapy Review* 7 (1992): 82–96.

———. *Shadow of the Other*. New York: Routledge, 1998.

Blum, H. P. "The Curative and Creative Aspects of Insight." In *Journal of the American Psychoanalytic Association* (supp.) 27 (1979): 41–69.

———. "The Maternal Ego Ideal and the Regulation of Maternal Qualities." In *The Course of Life*, vol. 3, *Adulthood and the Aging Process*, edited by George Pollock and Stanley Greenspan, 91–114. Washington, D.C.: National Institute of Mental Health, 1981.

Bowie, Malcolm. *Lacan*. Cambridge: Harvard University Press, 1991.

Brennan, Teresa, ed. *Between Feminism and Psychoanalysis*. New York: Routledge, 1989.

Breuer, Josef, and Sigmund Freud. *Studies on Hysteria*. In *SE 2*, 1895.

Bromberg, Philip. " 'Speak! That I May See You': Some Reflections on Dissociation, Reality, and Psychoanalytic Listening." In *Psychoanalytic Dialogues* 4 (1994): 517–48.

Butler, Judith. "Gender." In *Feminism and Psychoanalysis: A Critical Dictionary*, edited by Elizabeth Wright, 140–45. Oxford: Blackwell, 1992.

———. "Melancholy Gender/Refused Identification." In *Psychoanalytic Dialogues* 5 (1995): 165–80.

Chasseguet-Smirgel, Janine. *Sexuality and Mind*. New York: New York University Press, 1986.

Chodorow, Nancy. *The Reproduction of Mothering*. Berkeley: University of California Press, 1978.

———. *Feminism and Psychoanalytic Theory*. New Haven, Conn.: Yale University Press, 1989.

Cioffi, Frank. *Freud and the Question of Pseudo-Science*. Chicago: Open Court, 1998.

———. *Wittgenstein on Freud and Frazer*. New York: Cambridge University Press, 1998.

Crews, Frederick. *Skeptical Engagements*. New York: Oxford University Press, 1986.

———. *The Memory Wars: Freud's Legacy in Dispute*. New York: *New York Review of Books*, 1995.

———, ed. *Unauthorized Freud: Scholars Confront a Legend*. New York: Viking Penguin, 1998.

Dalbiez, Roland. *The Method and Doctrine of Freud*. London: Longman, 1941.

Davies, Jody Messler, and Mary Gail Frawley. "Dissociative Processes and Transference-Countertransference Paradigms in the Psychoanalytically Oriented Treatment of Adult Survivors of Childhood Sexual Abuse." In *Psychoanalytic Dialogues* 2 (1992): 5–36.

Decker, Hannah S. *Freud, Dora, and Vienna 1900*. New York: Free Press, 1991.

de Lauretis, Teresa. *The Practice of Love: Lesbian Desire and Perverse Sexuality*. Bloomington: Indiana University Press, 1994.

Delmar, Rosalind. "What Is Feminism?" In *What Is Feminism?*, edited by Juliet Mitchell and Anne Oakley, 8–33. New York: Pantheon, 1986.

Dimen, Muriel. *Surviving Sexual Contradictions*. New York: Macmillan, 1986.

———. "Power, Sexuality, and Intimacy." In *Gender/Body/Knowledge: Feminist Reconstructions of Being and Knowing*, edited by Alison M. Jaggar and Susan Bordo, 34–51. New Brunswick, N.J.: Rutgers University Press, 1989.

Dinnerstein, Dorothy. *The Mermaid and the Minotaur*. New York: Harper & Row, 1976.

Doane, Mary Ann. *The Desire to Desire: The Woman's Film of the 1940s*. Bloomington: Indiana University Press, 1987.

———. "Dark Continents: Epistemologies of Racial and Sexual Difference in Psychoanalysis and the Cinema." In *Femmes Fatales*, edited by Mary Ann Doane, 209–48. New York: Routledge, 1991.

Earman, J., et al., eds. *Philosophical Problems of the External and Internal Worlds: Essays on the Philosophy of Adolf Grünbaum*. University of Pittsburgh Press and University of Konstanz Press, 1993.

Edelman, Gerald M. *Bright Air, Brilliant Fire: On the Matter of the Mind*. New York: Basic Books, 1992.

Ehrenreich, Barbara. *Fear of Falling*. New York: Pantheon, 1989.

Ellenberger, Henri F. *The Discovery of the Unconscious: The History and Evolution of Dynamic Psychiatry.* New York: Basic Books, 1970.

Esterson, Allen. *Seductive Mirage.* Chicago: Open Court, 1993.

Farrell, Brian. *The Standing of Psychoanalysis.* New York: Oxford University Press, 1981.

Fast, Irene. *Gender Identity: A Differentiation Model.* Hillsdale, N.J.: Analytic Press, 1984.

Firestone, Shulamith. *The Dialectic of Sex.* New York: Morrow, 1970.

Flax, Jane. *Thinking Fragments: Psychoanalysis, Feminism, and Post-Modernism in the Contemporary West.* Berkeley: University of California Press, 1990.

Fliegel, Zenia. "Women's Development in Analytic Theory: Six Decades of Controversy." In *Psychoanalysis and Women: Contemporary Reappraisals,* edited by Judith L. Alpert, 3–32. Hillsdale, N.J.: Analytic Press, 1986.

Forrester, John. *Language and the Origins of Psychoanalysis.* New York: Columbia University Press, 1980.

———. "Freud's Female Patients/Female Analysts." In *Feminism and Psychoanalysis: A Critical Dictionary,* edited by Elizabeth Wright, 134–39. Oxford: Blackwell, 1992.

———. *Dispatches from the Freud Wars: Psychoanalysis and Its Passions.* Cambridge: Harvard University Press, 1997.

———. *The Seductions of Psychoanalysis: Freud, Lacan and Derrida.* New York: Cambridge University Press, 1991.

Foucault, Michel. *The History of Sexuality.* Vol. 1. Translated by R. Hurley. New York: Vintage Books, 1980.

Freud, Sigmund. *The Standard Edition of the Complete Psychological Works of Sigmund Freud,* edited and translated by James Strachey. 24 vols. London: Hogarth Press and Institute of Psycho-Analysis, 1953–74.

———. *Gesammelte Werke.* Frankfurt: Fischer, 1945.

———. *Letters of Sigmund Freud, 1873–1939.* Edited by E. Freud. London: Hogarth Press, 1961.

———. *The Complete Letters of Sigmund Freud to Wilhelm Fliess, 1887–1904.* Edited and translated by Jeffrey Moussaieff Masson. Cambridge: Harvard University Press, Belknap Press, 1987.

———. *A Phylogenetic Fantasy: Overview of the Transference Neuroses.* Edited and with an essay by Ilse Grubrich-Simitis. Cambridge: Harvard University Press, Belknap Press, 1987.

———. *Psychoanalysis and Faith: The Letters of Sigmund Freud and Oskar Pfister.* Edited by H. Meng and E. Federn. London: Hogarth Press, 1963.

———. *A Psychoanalytic Dialogue: The Letters of Sigmund Freud and Karl Abraham, 1907–1926.* Edited by H. Abraham and E. Freud. London: Hogarth Press, 1965.

———. *Cocaine Papers.* Edited by R. Byck. New York: New American Library, 1974.

———. *The Letters of Sigmund Freud to Eduard Silberstein, 1871–1881.* Edited by W. Boelich. Cambridge: Harvard University Press, 1993.

———. *The Complete Correspondence of Sigmund Freud and Ernest Jones, 1908–1939.* Edited by R. A. Paskauskas. Cambridge: Harvard University Press, 1993.

———. *The Correspondence of Sigmund Freud and Sándor Ferenczi.* Edited by E. Brabant, E. Falzeder, and A. Haynal. Cambridge: Harvard University Press, 1994.

———. "The Psychogenesis of a Case of Homosexuality in a Woman." In *Sexuality and the Psychology of Love,* edited by Philip Rieff. New York: Collier, 1963.

———. "Creative Writers and Daydreaming" and "Family Romances." In *Sexuality and the Psychology of Love*, edited by Philip Rieff. New York: Collier, 1963.

———. *On Aphasia*. Translated by E. Stengel. London, Imago Press, 1953.

Gabbard, Krin, and Glen O. Gabbard. *Psychiatry and the Cinema*. Chicago: University of Chicago Press, 1987.

Gay, Peter. *Freud: A Life for Our Time*. New York: Norton, 1988.

Geiger, Lazarus. *Der Ursprung der Sprache*. Stuttgart: Cotta'sche Buchhandlung, 1869.

Gellner, Ernest. *The Psychoanalytic Movement*. London: Paladin, 1985.

Gilligan, Carol. *In a Different Voice*. Cambridge: Harvard University Press, 1982.

Gilman, Sander L. *Freud, Race, and Gender*. Princeton, N.J.: Princeton University Press, 1993.

Goldner, Virginia. "Toward a Critical Relational Theory of Gender." In *Psychoanalytic Dialogues* 1 (1991): 249–72.

Granoff, Wladimir. *Filiations*. Paris: Editions de Minuit, 1975.

Grosz, Elizabeth. "Phallus: Feminist Implications." In *Feminism and Psychoanalysis: A Critical Dictionary*, edited by Elizabeth Wright, 320–23. Oxford: Blackwell, 1992.

Gruber, H. *Darwin on Man*. 2d ed. Chicago: University of Chicago Press, 1982.

Grubrich-Simitis, Ilse. *Zurück zu Freuds Texten: Stumme Dokumente sprechen machen*. Frankfurt am Main: S. Fischer, 1993. (English language edition: *Back to Freud's Texts: Making Silent Documents Speak*. Translated by Philip Slotkin. New Haven, Conn.: Yale University Press, 1996).

Grünbaum, Adolf. *The Foundations of Psychoanalysis*. Berkeley: University of California Press, 1984.

———. "Is Freud's Theory Well-Founded?" In *Behavioral and Brain Sciences* 9 (1986): 266–81.

———. *Validation in the Clinical Theory of Psychoanalysis: A Study in the Philosophy of Psychoanalysis*. Madison, Conn.: International Universities Press, 1993.

———. "One Hundred Years of Psychoanalytic Theory and Therapy: Retrospect and Prospect." In *Mindscapes: Philosophy, Science, and the Mind*, edited by Martin Carrier and Peter Machamer, 340–43. University of Pittsburgh Press and University of Konstanz Press, 1997.

Handelman, Susan. *The Slayers of Moses: The Emergence of Rabbinic Interpretation*. Albany: State University of New York Press, 1982.

Harris, Adrienne. "Bringing Artemis to Life: A Plea for Militance and Aggression in Feminist Peace Politics." In *Rocking the Ship of State*, edited by Adrienne Harris and Ynestra King, 93–114. Boulder, Colo.: Westview Press, 1989.

———. "Gender as Contradiction." In *Psychoanalytic Dialogues* 1 (1991): 197–224.

Horney, Karen. "On the Genesis of the Castration Complex in Women." 1924. In *Feminine Psychology*, edited by Harold Kelman, 37–53. New York: Norton, 1967.

———. "The Flight from Womanhood." 1926. In Horney, *Feminine Psychology*, 54–70.

———. "The Denial of the Vagina." 1933. In Horney, *Feminine Psychology*, 147–61.

Irigaray, Luce. *This Sex Which Is Not One*. Translated by Catherine Porter with Carolyn Burke. Ithaca, N.Y.: Cornell University Press, 1985.

Jackowitz, Anne. "Anna O./Bertha Pappenheim and Me." In *Between Women*, edited by Carol Ascher, Louise DeSalvo, and Sara Ruddick, 253–310. Boston: Beacon, 1984.

Jackson, John Hughlings. *Selected Writings, 1931–1932*. Edited by James Taylor, Gordon Holmes, and F.M.R. Walshe. 2 vols. Nijmegen, Netherlands: Arts & Boeve, 1996.

Jacoby, Russell. *The Repression of Psychoanalysis: Otto Fenichel and the Political Freudians.* Chicago: University of Chicago Press, 1983.

Jelliffe, Smith Ely. "Sigmund Freud as a Neurologist." In *Journal of Nervous and Mental Diseases* 85 (1937): 696–97.

Jones, Ernest. "Early Development of Female Sexuality." In *Papers on Psycho-Analysis*, 438–51. Boston: Beacon, 1927.

———. *The Life and Work of Sigmund Freud.* 3 vols. New York: Basic Books, 1953–57.

Kaplan, E. Ann, ed. *Psychoanalysis and Cinema.* New York: Routledge, 1990.

———. *Motherhood and Representation: The Mother in Popular Culture and Melodrama.* New York: Routledge, 1992.

———. "The Couch Affair: Gender and the Transference in Hollywood Film." In *American Imago* 50 (Winter 1993): 481–514.

———. *Looking for the Other: Feminism, Film and the Imperial Gaze.* New York: Routledge, 1997.

Kernberg, Otto. *Love Relations: Pathology and Normality.* New Haven, Conn.: Yale University Press, 1995.

Klein, Melanie. "Early Stages of the Oedipus Conflict." In *International Journal of Psycho-Analysis* 9 (1928): 167–80.

Koedt, Anne. "The Myth of the Vaginal Orgasm." 1968. In *Radical Feminism*, edited by Anne Koedt, Ellen Levin, and Anita Rapone, 198–20. New York: Quadrangle Books, 1970.

Kofman, Sarah. *The Enigma of Woman: Women in Freud's Writings.* Translated by Catherine Porter. Ithaca, N.Y.: Cornell University Press, 1985.

Kovel, Joel. *White Racism: A Psychohistory.* New York: Pantheon, 1970.

Kramer, Peter D. *Moments of Engagement: Intimate Psychotherapy in a Technological Age.* New York: W. W. Norton, 1989.

———. *Listening to Prozac.* New York: Viking, 1993.

———. *Should You Leave?* New York: Scribners, 1997.

Kristeva, Julia. *Tales of Love.* Translated by L. S. Roudiez. New York: Columbia University Press, 1983.

Kurzweil, Edith. *Freudians and Feminists.* Boulder, Colo.: Westview Press, 1995.

———. *The Freudians: A Comparative Perspective.* New Brunswick, N.J.: Transaction Publishers, 1996.

Lacan, Jacques. *Feminine Sexuality.* Edited by Juliet Mitchell and Jacqueline Rose; translated by Jacqueline Rose. New York: Norton, 1982.

Lane, Christopher, ed. "The Psychoanalysis of Race." In *Discourse: Theoretical Studies in Media and Culture* (special issue) 19 (Winter 1997).

Laqueur, Thomas. *Making Sex.* Cambridge: Harvard University Press, 1990.

Le Bon, G. *The Crowd: A Study of the Popular Mind.* London, 1920. (Originally published as *Psychologie des foules*, 1895.)

Luria, A. R. *Psychoanalysis in Light of the Principal Tendencies in Contemporary Psychology.* In Russian. Moscow: Kazan, 1922.

———. *The Making of Mind: A Personal Account of Soviet Psychology.* Edited by Michael and Sheila Cole. Cambridge: Harvard University Press, 1990.

Macmillan, Malcolm. *Freud Evaluated.* Cambridge, Mass.: MIT Press, 1997.

Mahony, P. J. *Freud and the Rat Man.* New Haven, Conn.: Yale University Press, 1986.

———. *Psychoanalysis and Discourse.* London: Methuen and Tavistock, 1986.

———. *Freud as a Writer.* Rev. 2d ed. New Haven, Conn.: Yale University Press, 1987.

————. *On Defining Freud's Discourse*. New Haven, Conn.: Yale University Press, 1989.

————. "Freud's Cases: Are They Valuable Today?" In *International Journal of Psycho-Analysis* 74: 1027–35, 1993.

————. "Psychoanalysis—the Writing Cure." In *One Year of Psychoanalysis*, edited by A. Haynal and E. Falzeder, 101–19. Geneva: Cahiers Psychiatriques, 1994.

————. *Les hurlements de l'homme aux loups*. Rev. 2d ed. Paris: Presses Universitaires de France, 1995.

————. "Freud: Man at Work." In *Work and Its Inhibitions: Psychoanalytic Essays*, edited by C. Socarides and S. Kramer. Madison, Conn.: International Universities Press, 1996.

————. *Freud's Dora: A Psychoanalytical, Historical, and Textual Study*. New Haven, Conn.: Yale University Press, 1997.

Masson, Jeffrey Moussaieff. *Final Analysis: The Making and Unmaking of a Psychoanalyst*. New York: Addison-Wesley, 1990.

————. *Against Therapy*. Monroe, Maine: Common Courage Press, 1994.

Masters, William H., and Virginia Johnson. *Human Sexual Response*. Boston: Little, Brown, 1966.

McDougall, Joyce. *The Many Faces of Eros*. New York: Norton, 1995.

Metz, Christian. *The Imaginary Signifier: Psychoanalysis and the Cinema*. Translated by Celia Britton et al. Bloomington: Indiana University Press, 1981.

Millett, Kate. *Sexual Politics: A Surprising Examination of Society's Most Arbitrary Folly*. New York: Doubleday, 1970.

Mitchell, Juliet. *Psychoanalysis and Feminism: Freud, Reich, Lang and Women*. New York: Pantheon, 1974.

————. "Commentary on 'Deconstructing Difference: Gender, Splitting, and Transitional Space,' by Muriel Dimen." In *Psychoanalytic Dialogues* 1 (1991): 353–58.

Modell, Arnold. *Other Times, Other Realities: Towards a Theory of Psychoanalytic Treatment*. Cambridge: Harvard University Press, 1990.

————. *The Private Self*. Cambridge: Harvard University Press, 1993.

Nietzsche, F. *The Philosophy of Nietzsche*. New York: Modern Library, 1954.

Nunberg, H., and E. Federn, eds. *Minutes of the Vienna Psychoanalytic Society*. Vol. 2. New York: International Universities Press, 1967.

Orbach, Susie. *Fat Is a Feminist Issue*. New York: Berkley, 1978.

Ortner, Sherry. "On Key Symbols." In *American Anthropologist* 75 (1973):1338–46.

Person, Ethel. "Sexuality as the Mainstay of Identity." In *Signs* 5 (1980): 605–30.

Pribram, Karl H., and Merton M. Gill. *Freud's "Project" Reassessed*. New York: Basic Books, 1976.

Ricoeur, Paul. *Freud and Philosophy*. New Haven, Conn.: Yale University Press, 1970.

Rieff, Philip. *Freud: The Mind of the Moralist*. New York: Viking, 1959.

————. *The Triumph of the Therapeutic*. London: Chatto & Windus, 1966.

Rivière, Joan. "Womanliness as a Masquerade." In *International Journal of Psycho-Analysis* 10 (1929): 303–13.

Roazen, Paul, and Bluma Swerdloff. *Heresy: Sandor Rado and the Psychoanalytic Movement*. Northvale, N.J.: Jason Aronson, 1995.

Robinson, Paul. *Three Critics of Freud*. Berkeley: University of California Press, 1995.

Rose, Jacqueline. *Sexuality in the Field of Vision*. London: Verso, 1986.

Roth, Michael S. *Psycho-Analysis as History: Negation and Freedom in Freud*. Ithaca, N.Y.: Cornell University Press, 1995.

Roth, Michael S. "Freud's Use and Abuse of the Past." In *The Ironist's Cage: Memory, Trauma and the Construction of History*. New York: Columbia University Press, 1995.

Rubin, Gayle. "The Traffic in Women: Notes Toward the Political Economy of Sex." In *Toward an Anthropology of Women*, edited by Rayna Rapp Reiter, 157–210. New York: Monthly Review Press, 1975.

———. "Thinking Sex: Notes for a Radical Theory of the Politics of Sexuality." In *Pleasure and Danger: Exploring Female Sexuality*, edited by Carole S. Vance, 267–319. New York: Routledge, 1984.

Said, Edward. *Culture and Imperialism*. New York: Knopf, 1992.

Scheman, Naomi. *Engenderings*. New York: Routledge, 1993.

Schor, Naomi. "Female Paranoia: The Case for Psychoanalytic Feminist Criticism." In *Yale French Studies* 62 (1981): 204–19.

Schorske, Carl E. *Fin de Siècle Vienna: Politics and Culture*. New York: Knopf, 1981.

Sedgewick, Eve Kosofsky. *Epistemology of the Closet*. Berkeley: University of California Press, 1990.

Segal, Lynne. *Straight Sex: The Politics of Pleasure*. London: Virago, 1994.

Shohat, Ella, and Robert Stam. *Unthinking Eurocentrism*. New York: Routledge, 1995.

Solms, Mark, and Michael Saling. "On Psychoanalysis and Neuroscience: Freud's Attitude to the Localizationist Tradition." In *International Journal of Psycho-Analysis* 67 (1986): 397–415.

Sulloway, Frank J. *Freud, Biologist of the Mind: Beyond the Psychoanalytic Legend*. Cambridge: Harvard University Press, 1992.

Tate, Claudia. "Psychoanalysis as Enemy and Ally of African Americans." In *Journal for the Psychoanalysis of Culture and Society* 1 (1996): 53–62.

Traub, Valerie. "The Psychomorphology of the Clitoris." In *GLQ* 2 (1995): 81–114.

Waelder, Robert. *Basic Theory of Psychoanalysis*. New York: International Universities Press, 1960.

Walker, Janet. *Couching Resistance: Women, Film and Psychoanalytic Psychiatry*. Minneapolis: University of Minnesota Press, 1993.

Walton, Jean. "Re-placing Race in (White) Psychoanalytic Discourse: Founding Narratives of Feminism." In *Critical Inquiry* 21 (1995): 775–804.

Webster, Richard. *Why Freud Was Wrong*. New York: HarperCollins, 1995.

Whipple, Beverly, and B. R. Komisaruk. "The G-spot, Orgasm and Female Ejaculation: Are They Related?" In *Proceedings: First International Conference on Orgasm*, edited by P. Kohari, 27–237. Bombay, India: VRP Publishers, 1991.

Wilcocks, Robert. *Sigmund Freud and the Rhetoric of Deceit*. London: Rowan & Littlefield, 1994.

Wittels, F. *Freud and His Time*. New York: Horace Liverwright, 1931.

Wollheim, Richard. *Sigmund Freud*. New York: Cambridge University Press, 1989.

Wright, Elizabeth, ed. *Feminism and Psychoanalysis: A Critical Dictionary*. Oxford: Blackwell, 1992.

Young, Lola. *Fear of the Dark: 'Race,' Gender and Sexuality in Cinema*. New York: Routledge, 1995.

ACKNOWLEDGMENTS

There was no shortage of advice offered to me as I put together this collection, and I want to acknowledge those who had a real impact, even if the result was not always what was intended. In the early stages of preparation, Frederick Crews and Peter Swales made useful suggestions, as did Inge Scholz-Strasser and Lydia Marinelli. Carl Schorske has been a generous adviser throughout the planning process. Ralph Eubanks and Iris Newsom of the Publishing Office of the Library of Congress helped turn the idea for this book into a concrete reality. The careful, intelligent work of Cheryl Regan and Irene Chambers, both of the Interpretive Programs Office of the Library of Congress, was fundamental to planning the exhibition and this companion volume. Their perseverance and creativity have been crucial.

I began this project during a sabbatical as a Getty Scholar at the Getty Research Institute for the History of Art and the Humanities. I am finishing it as the Associate Director of this institute. The Getty has been a hospitable place for research and discussion, and I am grateful for the assistance I have received, especially from Elizabeth Garrett, for this book. My wife, Kari Weil, has been more than supportive during the conflicts that surrounded the creation of this book and the exhibition. Her intelligent and reasoned perspective was almost as valuable as her care and attention.

This book is dedicated to my children.

M.S.R.

CONTRIBUTORS

HAROLD P. BLUM, M.D., is the director of the Sigmund Freud Archives, a clinical professor of psychiatry at New York University, a past editor in chief of the *Journal of the American Psychoanalytic Association*, and the author of *Reconstruction in Psychoanalysis: Childhood Revisited and Recreated*.

JOSÉ BRUNNER is Senior Lecturer at the Buchmann Faculty of Law and the Cohn Institute of the History and Philosophy of Science and Ideas at Tel Aviv University and the author of publications on the history and politics of psychoanalysis and contemporary political theory. His *Freud and the Politics of Psychoanalysis* was published by Blackwell, in Oxford, in 1995.

FRANK CIOFFI is Senior Research Fellow in Philosophy at the University of Kent at Canterbury. He is the author of *Freud and the Question of Pseudo-science* and *Wittgenstein on Freud and Frazer*.

ROBERT COLES, a child psychiatrist at Harvard Medical School, is the author of numerous books, including *The Spiritual Life of Children* and *The Moral Intelligence of Children*, as well as biographies of Anna Freud and Erik Erikson.

HANNAH S. DECKER is a professor of history at the University of Houston, an adjunct professor of medical history in the Department of Psychiatry at Baylor College of Medicine in Houston, and Adjunct Faculty, Houston-Galveston Psychoanalytic Institute. A leading authority on the life and times of Freud, she has written *Freud in Germany: Revolution and Reaction in Science* and *Freud, Dora, and Vienna 1900*.

MURIEL DIMEN is a psychoanalyst, a clinical professor of psychology in the Postdoctoral Program in Psychotherapy and Psychoanalysis at New York University, the author of *Surviving Sexual Contradictions*, the coeditor of *Gender in Psychoanalytic Space*, and a fellow of the New York Institute for the Humanities at New York University. She has served on the editorial boards for *Psychoanalytic Dialogues* and *Studies in Gender and Sexuality*.

JOHN FORRESTER, Reader in the Department of History and Philosophy of Science at Cambridge University, is the coauthor of *Freud's Women* and the author of *Language and the Origins of Psychoanalysis*, *The Seductions of Psychoanalysis*, *Dispatches from the Freud Wars*, and *Truth Games, Lies, Money, and Psychoanalysis*.

PETER GAY, Sterling Professor of History Emeritus at Yale University, is a Freud biographer and a prolific historian whose works include the seminal study *Freud: A Life for Our Time, Freud for Historians, Reading Freud,* and the five-volume history *The Bourgeois Experience: Victoria to Freud.*

ILSE GRUBRICH-SIMITIS is a psychoanalyst and an editor of Freud texts, including the important *Sigmund Freud: His Life in Pictures and Words* (with coeditors Ernst and Lucie Freud) and *A Phylogenetic Fantasy: Overview of the Transference Neuroses.* She is the author of the recent studies *Back to Freud's Texts* and *Early Freud and Late Freud.*

ADOLF GRÜNBAUM, Andrew Mellon Professor of Philosophy of Science, research professor of psychiatry, and chairman of the Center for Philosophy of Science at the University of Pittsburgh, is the author of twelve books, including *Philosophical Problems of Space and Time, The Foundations of Psychoanalysis: A Philosophical Critique,* and *Validation in the Clinical Theory of Psychoanalysis: A Study in the Philosophy of Psychoanalysis.* His offices include the presidency of the American Philosophical Association (Eastern Division) and of the Philosophy of Science Association, Fellow of the American Academy of Arts and Sciences and of the American Association for the Advancement of Science, and Laureate of the International Academy of Humanism.

E. ANN KAPLAN is a professor of English and Comparative Studies at the State University of New York at Stony Brook and the director of the Humanities Institute. She has written and lectured internationally on women in film, postmodernism, psychoanalysis, feminist theory, music television, and cultural studies. Her many books include *Women in Film: Both Sides of the Camera, Psychoanalysis and Cinema, Motherhood and Representation: The Mother in Popular Culture and Melodrama,* and *Looking for the Other: Feminism, Film and the Imperial Gaze.*

PETER D. KRAMER practices psychiatry in Providence, Rhode Island, where he is a clinical professor of psychiatry at Brown University. He is the author of *Should You Leave?, Moments of Engagement,* and the international best-seller *Listening to Prozac.* His essays have appeared in the *New York Times Book Review,* the *New York Times Magazine,* the *Washington Post Book World,* the *Times Literary Supplement* (London), and elsewhere.

EDITH KURZWEIL is the editor of *Partisan Review* and University Professor at Adelphi University. She is the author of, among other books, *The Age of Structuralism: Lévi-Strauss to Foucault, The Freudians: A Comparative Perspective,* and *Freudians and Feminists.*

PATRICK J. MAHONY is a professor emeritus of the Université de Montréal, a supervising and training analyst at the Canadian Institute of Psychoanalysis, and a fellow of the Royal Society of Canada. The recipient of a number of international prizes and distinctions, he is the author of many volumes and articles on Freud's work, including *Freud as a Writer, Freud and the Rat Man,* and *Freud's Dora: A Psychoanalytic, Historical, and Textual Study.*

MICHAEL MOLNAR is the research director of the Freud Museum in London, the final home of the Freud family. He has translated and edited Freud's *Kürzeste Chronik*—published as *The Diary of Sigmund Freud, 1929–1939*—and contributed to *Reading Freud's Reading*, edited by Sander L. Gilman.

MICHAEL S. ROTH is Associate Director of the Getty Research Institute for the History of Art and the Humanities. He is the author of *The Ironist's Cage: Memory, Trauma, and the Construction of History, Psycho-Analysis as History: Negation and Freedom in Freud,* and *Knowing and History: Appropriations of Hegel in Twentieth-Century France.* His edited volumes include *History and . . . : Histories Within the Human Sciences* and *Rediscovering History: Culture, Politics, and the Psyche.*

OLIVER SACKS was born in London and educated in London, Oxford, and California. He is a professor of neurology at the Albert Einstein College of Medicine in New York City and the author of seven books, including the best-sellers *Awakenings, The Man Who Mistook His Wife for a Hat,* and *An Anthropologist on Mars.* He lives on City Island in New York, where he swims and raises cycads and ferns.

ART SPIEGELMAN, a freelance artist and comic illustrator, is the founder of Raw Books and Graphics (with Françoise Mouly), the creator of *Maus* and *Maus II,* and a frequent contributor to *The New Yorker* magazine.

JOHN E. TOEWS, a professor of history and the director of the Program in Comparative History of Ideas at the University of Washington, is the author of *Hegelianism: The Path Toward Dialectical Humanism* and numerous articles on the history of psychoanalysis and the theory and practice of historical writing.

INDEX

PERMISSIONS ACKNOWLEDGMENTS

Grateful acknowledgment is made to the following for permission to reprint previously published material:

Basic Books and The Hogarth Press: Excerpts from *The Interpretation of Dreams* by Sigmund Freud. Rights outside the United States for *The Standard Edition of the Complete Psychological Works of Sigmund Freud*, translated and edited by James Strachey, administered by The Hogarth Press, an imprint of Random House UK Limited, London. Reprinted by permission of Basic Books, a subsidiary of Perseus Books LLC, and The Hogarth Press, the Sigmund Freud Copyrights, and The Institute of Psycho-Analysis.

Harvard University Press: Excerpts from *The Complete Letters of Sigmund Freud to Wilhelm Fliess, 1887–1904*, translated and edited by Jeffrey Moussaieff Masson (Cambridge, Mass.: Harvard University Press), copyright © 1985 by Sigmund Freud Copyrights Ltd. and copyright © 1985 by J. M. Masson for translation and editorial matter. Reprinted by permission of Harvard University Press.

W. W. Norton & Company, Inc., and The Hogarth Press: Excerpts from *Civilization and Its Discontents* by Sigmund Freud, translated by James Strachey, translation copyright © 1961 by James Strachey, copyright renewed 1989 by Alix Strachey. Rights outside the United States for *The Standard Edition of the Complete Psychological Works of Sigmund Freud*, translated and edited by James Strachey, administered by The Hogarth Press, an imprint of Random House UK Limited, London. Reprinted by permission of W. W. Norton & Company, Inc., and The Hogarth Press, the Sigmund Freud Copyrights, and The Institute of Psycho-Analysis.

A NOTE ON THE TYPE

This book was set in Janson, a typeface long thought to have
been made by the Dutchman Anton Janson, who was a
practicing typefounder in Leipzig during the years 1668 to
1687. However, it has been conclusively demonstrated that
these types are actually the work of Nicholas Kis (1650–1702),
a Hungarian, who most probably learned his trade from the
master Dutch typefounder Dirk Voskens. The type is an
excellent example of the influential and sturdy Dutch types
that prevailed in England up to the time William Caslon
(1692–1766) developed his own incomparable designs
from them.

Composed by North Market Street Graphics,
Lancaster, Pennsylvania
Printed and bound by Quebecor Printing,
Martinsburg, West Virginia
Designed by Virginia Tan